In a Grand and Awful Time

In a

Grand and Awful Time

Essays from the Librarian's Desk on
Twentieth Century Man and His Books

By

William Hugh Carlson

Illustrated by

Nelson Sandgren

Corvallis:

OREGON STATE UNIVERSITY PRESS

Z665
.C25
C11

© 1967 Oregon State University Press
Library of Congress Catalog Number: 67-16715
Printed in the United States of America

DEDICATED to an Oregon State alumna who has attained
best sellerdom as a novelist, who once wrote:

"... *remembering Oregon State, my dear teachers, the beloved
Library (where only on all the campus I was completely happy), and
how the Memorial Union Building looks on a green evening through
blue rain, with the lights just coming on.*"

AN INTRODUCTION

THE ESSAYS here presented are grounded in "Cover Sheet Commentaries" with which, for a period of twenty years, I prefaced the monthly *New Booklist* of the Oregon State University Library. I have been encouraged by a substantial file of appreciative comment which came to me over the years from readers on the Oregon State campus, and to a considerable extent from friends and colleagues throughout the library profession, including a few abroad, to offer these reflections, updated and edited, in book form.

From simple beginnings, concerned chiefly with the details of managing and developing the library, the monthly commentaries expanded, little by little, to range the entire gamut of the affairs, deeds, misdeeds, hopes and aspirations, the noble ideals, the evil schemings, and the tremendous intellectual achievements of the creature Homo Sapiens. Man's rise, from the first simple life forms of the primeval deep of his planet to dominate it all, this has furnished rich food for reflection.

In one way or another these commentaries are always book connected or library connected. This is eminently appropriate, I have maintained in various ways, because it has been through Man's unique skill and persevering habit of evolving sounds and symbols to record his ideas and experiences, of using them to express himself in staggering profusion, and of carefully organizing the written expressions in repositories, large and small, that he has attained dominance of planet Earth and all the creatures on it.

There are no profundities presented here, no startling or new theories, no glib or easy solutions. Neither is there any idolatry or bowing down before the Book in its individual manifestations. The concern is rather with the total graphic record which Man has created, in all its complexities and varied forms, books, journals, maps, films, newspapers from the earliest surviving examples to the present. There is throughout a considerable awe and amazement, perhaps somewhat naive but shared, nevertheless, by many hardened librarians of the day, about the sheer and rapidly increasing magnitude of the record. The acute problems of housing, organization, and management which the massive quantitative increase has brought, these pervade the essays as they also do and must the thoughts, the plans, and the activities of all knowledgeable and conscientious librarians of these mid-century years.

The amazement about both the quantity and complexity of Man's writings can be typified by one of possibly the only two lines ever written by Carl Sandburg in Swedish. In a poem celebrating the mysteries and beauty of modern Stockholm as seen from the air, Sandburg says this view would surely have had the old time kings saying in wonderment, "Vad i hela min tid!" This is a phrase of astonishment and disbelief which literally translated is "What in all my time!" The connotation is better expressed in English by "Never in all my born days!" What has happened and is happening to, in, and because of our libraries, gives a sense of astonishment validity, I believe, for many of us.

The essays are based on the belief that the written record is basic, that only through it and because of it has Man been able to reach his high intellectual and technological achievements. It follows then that those who have the responsibility for organizing and managing the record and for making it available for use, hopefully conveniently and easily, are vitally important people, more important than is generally recognized. This belief too is evident in the essays, more often by implication than in direct comment.

The twenty years during which the essays were written have been a fantastic time of technological and scientific break-through. It has been given to my generation as to no other to witness and to be a part of the increasingly rapid fruition of Man's never ceasing propensity to wonder, to think, to search and to probe, to seek to know, to understand, and to manipulate and control an often harsh environment for his convenience. How slowly from the viewpoint of an individual life it all proceeded, amidst prejudices and conflict! But how rapidly, how very rapidly, in terms of Man's relatively brief time on his planet!

Harrassment, cruelty, ridicule, and sometimes death, these were too often the lot of those breaking or seeking to break out of the traditions and mores and religious concepts evolved throughout the ages. Little by little, almost imperceptibly at first, the first faint tides of increasing understanding did lap at and begin to gradually submerge the shorelines of Man's ignorance and prejudices. Ignorance and prejudice are still prevalent, of course, abundantly so. They are however yielding steadily, and in some areas they are in full retreat before reason, logic, and proven facts. Only because of the graphic record preserving all the attainments which have gone before has this been possible. These are some of the things the essays seek to accentuate.

It has been my privilege to edit these essays while in residence in the community in Sweden from which my parents emigrated to America more than eight decades ago. It is my hope that this environment of different ways, people, and attitudes, plus visits to selected European libraries which preceded the editing, has brought increased detachment to preparing the essays for publication.

My chief hope in offering these reflections in book form is that they will help to place and keep in perspective the evolution *in,* as well as *of* libraries, and their contributions to this turbulent century of fruition. Historical awareness and the deeper meanings of the struggles of our current society and culture to keep the graphic records of its evolution under control and manageable; these too are objectives sought.

If in addition these essays should be found to be pleasant and occasionally provocative reading, as I have been told by various readers over the years, I shall indeed be happy. Did I not feel that at least some of these attributes and qualities are present, I would not have the temerity to add yet another book to the millions upon millions flowing from the presses to the shelves of libraries everywhere. Diffidently then, but hopefully, I invite all so inclined to the following pages.

WM. H. CARLSON

Rockneby, Sweden
August 15, 1965

TABLE OF CONTENTS

Part I
THE BOOK: ITS RICH AND VARIED MANIFESTATIONS AND INFLUENCES

Emily Dickinson, in her delightfully inimitable way, wrote of her "precious mouldering pleasure" in meeting a book "in just the dress his Century wore." The grouping of essays about books in this first part, their influences, the making of them, and the reactions they call forth typifies the bookish dress that this, our magnificent and troubled century, wears. It could indeed not be otherwise.

There is much in the "dress" of our times that is great, very great indeed. In the mastery of his physical world Man has exceeded the wildest dreams of earlier times and even the earlier years of the century. In the mastery of himself and of living with his fellowman the failures have, in many ways, been dismal, very dismal. It seems fitting, therefore, that this book should begin with the following essay.

In a Grand and Awful Time

"WE ARE LIVING, we are dwelling, in a grand and awful time." So goes a church hymn written by Arthur C. Coxe in 1840. It is appropriate, as our free-wheeling society and civilization moves toward the two thousandth year since the birth of Christ and somewhere around the six-thousandth since man has been leaving consciously dated tracks, to reflect on this smoothly flowing thought.

It is probable that most generations, possibly all of them, have seen much that was awful in the life about them, in the trials and the difficulties that faced them and in the all too frequent instances of greed, selfishness, lust, and Man's inhumanity to Man, which have been with us ever since Eve bit the apple. Perhaps Mr. Coxe, in 1840, was looking at and reflecting on the horrible facts of men held in bondage as chattel goods and sold and bartered, just as are cattle, on the open market. Possibly he foresaw the cataclysmic struggle, so ominously then on the horizon, which would be needed to free the dark and captive peoples of our land.

There was, however, much that was grand too in the society and the times in which Mr. Coxe brought his hymn into being. A raw and rich continent lay waiting. Industrious, ambitious, and intrepid men and women came flocking from elsewhere, to measure themselves against it. From the oppressed and the poverty stricken of other nations they came, working, planning, striving, suffering, often incredibly, in the hopes of a better and a fairer life than they had known. Some too weak or too timid perished in the fray but for the majority achievement and realization came, sometimes unevenly, frequently ruthlessly. Before them the wilderness and the forests gave way, slowly undoubtedly from their viewpoint, but with unbelievable, almost instantaneous quickness on the historical measuring sticks of this Earth. Yes, there was much that was grand, excitingly grand, in this favored land of ours when Mr. Coxe put his hymn to paper.

What of this mid-century time which finds us well on the way

to the rounding out of yet another century on God's eternal clock. The generations now active on the stage have certainly perpetrated and been a part of much that is awful. In the memories of most of us there is the great and awful second World War. In the memories of many of us there is also the first World War, memories of the mismanagement and the brutalities, the fear and greed, the military strutting and posturing that followed it, and that led surely and inevitably to that second and greater holocaust. The awfulest parts of this period, and of the war that inevitably followed, were the concentration camps of a great but misled nation, and their grisly accompaniment of gas chambers and soap factories and the retrieving of gold from the teeth of humans done to death in quantity. Surely nothing in the history of mankind has been more inhumane, more brutish, more awful than this.

But even amidst all of this there was much that was grand, because if wars reflect the worst emotions and instincts of men there is often, among those who do the fighting and the killing, much, very much, that is grand. On every battlefield men have fought and bled and given up their lives for their friends in arms, and even for treasured pets. With fighting and dying all around they have stood sometimes entranced by the song of a bird, or to marvel at the beauty of a tree, or to note and wonder at how the poppies grow. In nobility of the soul such as this lies the hope, a grand and glorious hope, of the human race.

WILLIAM HUGH CARLSON   13

Incredible and grand, but with overtones and undertones of awfulness have been the tremendous scientific advances of these later years, none of which could have happened without the writings accumulated, treasured, and organized in the libraries of the world. Atomic bombs, hydrogen bombs, guided missiles, supersonic jet planes, sputniks, moon shots, and journeys of man-made objects to photograph Mars and to send back word of the very Sun itself —these achievements have followed, one upon the other, in a veritable crescendo. It has become fashionable, understandably so, to view all this with alarm and to wonder if Man can control all the things his active and probing mind has created. Over all hangs an awful question mark, the "Bomb." Will it be loosed for evil by another madman, or can it be harnessed for good?

There has been grandeur certainly in the medical advances of these recent years. Contrast the relative security of all of us now, and of the babies arriving in unprecendented numbers, with the ravages of pestilence and disease faced by people in earlier times, such as, for instance, the great plagues of the fifteenth century, when people died, million upon million. As late as 1907, 1,300,000 people perished in a plague in India in that single year. The slower and less spectacular deaths by disease throughout the ages have indeed, in the aggregate, been more awful than our modern wars. In spite of our fighting and

killing and of the threat of the bomb, Man, because of his medical conquests, lives in these present years, even in the less privileged lands, better fed, in more security, and in greater comfort than has ever before been true in the history of this Planet. This is so because he has for centuries written down and preserved his ideas, his thoughts, and his findings.

In spite of all his technological know-how and his tremendous material progress, Man has yet to learn how to live with

himself, to control his avarice and greed, his efforts to impose ideologies and philosophies on his fellow man and his ruthless passion for power. In the early years after the first great holocaust and blood letting in my personal memory, a poet, Siegfried Sassoon, caught the ominous implications of the ancient, enduring, and ruthless quest for power in lines fittingly applicable to this warring century in which the awful and the grand are locked in struggle for ascendancy:

At the Cenotaph

"*I saw the Prince of Darkness, with his Staff,*
Standing bare-headed by the Cenotaph:
Unostentatious and respectful, there
he stood, and offered up the following prayer.
    '*Make them forget, O Lord, what this memorial*
        means; their discredited ideas revive;
    Breed new beliefs that War is purgatorial
        Proof of the pride and power of being alive;
    Men's biologic urge to readjust
        The map of (Earth,) Lord of Hosts, increase;
    Lift up their hearts in large destructive lust;
        And crown their heads with blind vindictive Peace.'
The Prince of Darkness to the Cenotaph
bowed. As he walked away I heard him laugh."

SIEGFRIED SASSOON

Reflections on a Rooftop

*The key that may open the
door to the solution of
modern day problems.*

ON AN EARLY OCTOBER afternoon
and evening of 1952, I sat for
four hours on the roof of Dearborn Hall of Oregon State University, listening and watching as
a participant in a military scare,
Operation Skywatch, for an
enemy who was not there. With
only an ear cocked for the power-
filled roar of the giants of the air,
I was free to think and to relax.
Sitting there in the golden beauty
of an afternoon that a whole
glorious summer and autumn had
not matched, the always appreciated beauty of the Willamette
Valley came home to me with
poignant force.

To the east, rising dimly into
the autumnal haze, but substantial and real, were the high Cas-
cades, with Mt. Jefferson barely
visible. To the north lay McDonald Forest, golden in the slanting
sun, and to the west Marys Peak
and the lesser hills patiently
waiting, in the infinity of days, to
once again mask the sun from
the land. In perfect unison, as
the sun rimmed the hills in golden beauty and sank away, came
the moon, pale and enormous,
shouldering over the eastern
mountains with a speed that
made the spinning of our orb
almost feelable.

To my listening ears came only
sounds of peace and happiness,
the shrieks and the laughter of
children happily at play, the continuous hum of cars busily scurrying homeward, the noises of a
few local birdmen soaring easily
aloft in the waning light, sure
and confident of the single motor
and the frail wings that did their
bidding. And then came the
twinkling lights of home and
fireside, taking the place, at the
touch of a finger, of the departing sun.

All was peace and beauty, and
yet here I sat, as did citizens at
that precise moment all about
our great land, waiting and
watching for an enemy who, said
those who were supposed to
know, was poised, ready, and
unpredictable. Through the
length and breadth of our nation, east and west, north and
south, on the high mountains and
in the valleys, on the sparsely
peopled tablelands of the Rockies, amidst the fertile midwest-
ern fields and streams of my own
youth, in the teaming industrial
cities of the east, grimy but vigorous under the smoke and smog
of technocracy, in cities and
fields of the southland, along the
great Father of Waters, bisect-

ing the continent with his snaky
signature, on a far away eastern
seashore, in all these places I
could visualize America busy at
work and play, but armed and
apprehensive, pouring much of
her wealth and ingenuity into
nonproductive and sterile military effort.

The thought was inescapable:
why must Man, with his mastery
over physical things in full
bodied and present achievement,
fear his fellow man? Why must
great nations waste their substance and offer up their strongest youth in strife and struggle,
in battle and in fear of battle?
Why, with mastery over so much,
can Man not master his relations
with his fellow man?

From atop the Dearborn pent-
house, where I had climbed the
better to drink in the beauty
which surrounded me, I could
look down on the library. Under
that black-tiled roof, I knew,
were some hundreds of thousands of books, enough to well
reflect the complications and
fears of the times in which we
live, books to explain why citizens like myself were being
trained for a warning watch of
death and destruction from the
skies. Under that roof there reposed, I reflected, numerous volumes recording the understanding and mastery of things physical, how to produce more and
better foods, how to manipulate
and change the stuff of the world
to our liking and needs, how to
devise ever better, stronger, more
powerful machines, how to nurture and promote the longevity
of the human body, how to de-
vastate and tear apart the very
building blocks of the universe.

Under that single roof, I reflected, reposed a tremendous
amount of know-how patiently

WILLIAM HUGH CARLSON 15

but eagerly probed from his surroundings by Man, the searcher. Nevertheless, in all the volumned rows there were, I thought, relatively few books of wisdom, of insight into the nature and needs of the human spirit. And of these the best were comparatively ancient, the books of Confucius, Lao-tse, Buddha, and Christ, books all sprung from Asian soil and which I was acutely conscious, right then, of not having sufficiently read. Here, in my own failure to read, to ponder, and to heed the words of insight, of compassion, of understanding in these and similar books of wisdom, a failure which I know I share with citizens of the world generally, lay perhaps the key to the strains and stresses, the obsessions, fears, and dangers of our times. With thoughts such as these I surrendered the Skywatch to still another citizen.

On the Confusion of Tongues

The Children of Noah spread out over the world, multiplied, and prospered—but the Lord threw in a monkey wrench.

MAN, WITH HIS BOUNDLESS INGENUITY, has contrived to set down, in a wide variety of hieroglyphics and cryptic markings, most of the sounds he has fashioned for communicating his wants and his ideas. These markings he has put together in rich and wide profusion to record his achievements, thoughts, hopes, and ideals. So well has he thought of these records, so useful has he found them, and in many instances, so proud has he been of them, that he has brought them together, at considerable effort and expense, into the great storehouses we know as libraries. All of this, and particularly intelligent reading of the records, has been complicated no end by the wide variety of languages in which books are written. But it was not always thus.

We are told in Genesis that as the children of Noah spread out over the world and multiplied and prospered, the whole earth was of one language and one speech. Possessed of the brashness, inventiveness, and aspiration that has always distinguished Man from all other animals, these early ancestors learned how to make brick with which they built the city of Babel. Not satisfied with this, they undertook to construct a tower, the top of which would "reach unto heaven."

The Lord, looking down on all this busyness and scheming, perhaps with a mixture of pride and concern, said, "Behold, the people is one, and they have all one language; and this they begin to do: and now nothing will be restrained from them that they have imagined to do." The Lord

had apparently never intended that Man should have it so easy, so he decided to put a monkey wrench in the works. He confounded their language "and they left off to build the city."

What a monkey wrench! Gray's *Foundations of Language* tentatively places the total number of present-day spoken languages at 2,796, divided into nine major families. Thousands upon thousands of the books in our libraries are concerned with the efforts of Man to circumvent the Lord by communicating with his fellow man in spite of the numerous languages imposed upon him. And he has done pretty well at it, too, at least in technological fields, such as the tower building which started the whole trouble. Some of our most fascinating books are concerned with our languages. In spite of our progress, I doubt, however, that the Lord is much worried yet.

One has only to listen to translations of the wranglings in the United Nations to realize what a formidable barrier to understanding our languages are. Man, however, obstinate, tenacious, and inventive, never gives up. It could be that the Lord is keeping a wary eye on his efforts to fashion a universal language that will put him back to where he was when the plague of tongues was put upon him. Man is a great one, too, for machines, machines that will do instantly, or almost instantly, all of his most toilsome work. Even now his busy mind is at work to bypass the confusion of tongues with a machine, a machine which will translate instantaneously the printed page from one language to another. The Lord is probably not much troubled by this, but it deserves watching.

A Library Is a Living Thing

Books, like coral polyps, sustain themselves and are absorbed into the foundations of future growth.

IN THE THINKING of most people, perhaps, a library is chiefly an organized record of the past. And so it is. In our libraries, which, en masse, nationally and internationally constitute Mankind's most valued possession, on which his highly complex civilization rests, we do indeed have a record of what has been and what is. But the great mass of facts, aspirations, ideals, and ideas that make up the holdings of our libraries are far from a passive and dormant record, for within our writings lie the seeds of still greater growth, progress, and development. The modern library therefore needs to be and clearly is contemporaneous.

At the beginning of World War II, the libraries of the world were, of course, just as important, just as vital, and just as highly valued for and by the world of that time as are our library resources now. Even so, and I know some will dispute this, books published since 1940 are, at least in a scientific and technological sense, far more important.

Should libraries, by some stroke of ill fortune, lose every book acquired before 1940, they could still continue to serve the educational and research needs of the world, although poorly.

As of 1940 there would be little in their holdings, and that little dated and obsolete, about nuclear fission, supersonic flight, jet engines, television, cold sterilization of foods, and similar rapidly developing subjects. About those strange phenomena, the flying saucers, compounded of fancy, imagination, illusion, and just enough unexplainable incidents to suggest some substance, there would be nothing at all. Writings about hybrid breeding of animals and plants, artificial insemination, dental caries, miracle drugs, poliomyelitis, tuberculosis, and cancer, would, as of 1940 be so dated and obsolete as to be of only minor working value. Similarly in sociological, political, and economic areas and in international relations the research and instruction offered by universities would be seriously hampered. Best served, on the basis of 1940 holdings, but still very poorly served, would be instruction in literature, music, and fine arts.

I have often thought of books as corals, which grow from and sustain themselves on what has gone before, serve their purpose, and are then themselves absorbed into the foundations of future growth. While some of these corals continue, and have continued down through the ages, to have vitality and to nourish the mind and spirit of Man directly, most of our writings, once absorbed, are needed chiefly as the solid foundation. While it is bibliographical heresy, it is my increasing conviction that much that is so faithfully and meticulously organized and preserved in libraries, particularly from our fast-paced modern civilization, is not permanently needed even for the foundation purpose of sustaining the entire cultural heritage of civilization. I have predicted before, and do again, that our libraries and scholars, hard pressed by the fertility of the human mind and the grinding of the presses, will eventually be forced to recognize that much that has been written is dispensable, however unpleasant and difficult such recognition may be.

Contemporaneity is indeed essential in the modern library, and in America Uncle Sam's mail trucks are the lifeline by which it is nourished. Each day there arrives in quantity in every major library, books, magazines,

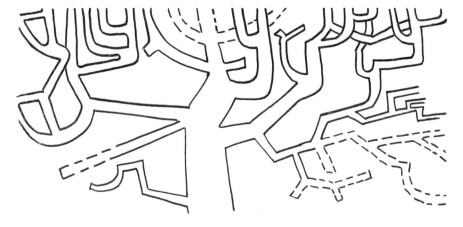

and other recorded data by foot carrier and truck, by package and by sack. So vital is this continuous inflow that if impeded for a single day, it is reflected in library service. Because journals and magazines are on the forefront of knowledge, libraries must be organized to check in current issues with the greatest possible dispatch and assign them to their respective posts.

Although these currently received materials may soon be obsolete and some of them possibly eventually even an unnecessary encumbrance, in the days, weeks, and immediate years of their issuance they are fresh and necessary daily nourishment, helping to keep the receiving library a vital, living instrument in the carrying on of research and instruction.

The Words of Man

Names became words, words begot words, ideas spawned new ideas, beauty inspired adornment, flights of fancy stimulated imagination.

THE THING that distinguishes Man, over and above all other of earth's creatures, is his ability to create languages. Georges Clemenceau, World War I Premier of France, has some interesting and provocative thoughts on this in the first volume of *In the Evening of My Thought*, the matured summation of his philosophy. It all began, says Clemenceau, with the "naming" of things. But it did not, Man being Man, stop there. The names or words created were as much alive as their creators, they became living things by and of themselves, with potential for growth and change.

Words, as created, caught up the dreams and thoughts, the practicalities and needs of their makers. In the continuing urge to understand and know they reacted, these emerging words, one on the other and on the makers and users of them. In

this process of growth and interaction Man's words, conceived in some 27,000 different languages, arranged themselves, without conscious effort of their creators, into families, systems, rules, and declensions.

Not until all of this had reached an advanced state did the grammarians and lexicographers, men concerned with words as words, appear on the scene. By this time vocal language had reached expression through symbols. When and as this happened, recorded words became increasingly abstract. Refinements were introduced. More and more attention was given to form and beauty, the dressing of fact and thought with majesty and grace which transcended the words themselves, uplifting the spirit, stirring up in the minds of both creators and users still other words and ways of using them. It is all, says Clemenceau, something like a game of tennis. Words fly from one man, or from men, to others, and back, obeying, in the process, complex forces which often elude us.

It is interesting to conjecture how all this must have begun in the slow eons of the dawning of human intelligence. The first words must have been crude, fumbling, no doubt inept. Little by little they would increase in clarity, in preciseness, in versatility. With each increase, each change as he achieved it, Man created for himself further tools of intelligence, tools which brightened and improved and assumed increasing usefulness the more they were used. With the monumental breakthrough to expressing words in symbols, Man was on his way toward the creative nourishment, across the generations, of his intellect. The miles upon miles of words now stored throughout the world in the great warehouses we know as libraries are the prodigious fruit of this nourishment.

In the beginning the first faint stirrings of intelligent thought must have been like the movement of air in an utter calm. Things were said that stirred the saying of other things. When the sayings finally reached the stage of being written, they could and did have meaning for others beyond the ken and time of the sayers. By this time there must have been a goodly breeze of intelligence moving, giving wing to more and more words, stimulating and invigorating all with whom it came in contact. More and more men were moved to write and to read and to attain the very considerable skills of so doing. As this went on thoughts and ideas were changed, horizons were widened, eyes and hearts and minds were lifted up to the hills and to the heavens from whence, even before the creation and mastery of words, Man must have drawn stimulus and inspiration.

In the time scale of an individual man or generation this process was slow, ever so slow, but on the evolutionary scale it must surely have been akin to the breaking of dams. Words begot words, ideas spawned new ideas, inspired beauty and adornment of expression, provided stimulus to further beauty, flights of fancy and imagination. This demonstrably went on over the centuries in continuing ebb and flow, action and counteraction. Each forward surge, or series of surges, could be stronger and more positive than those which had gone before. Accompanying it all, inevitably, was the search, continuing and unremitting up to the present moment, for better materials on which to write and faster and better ways to reproduce, read, store, and find, as needed, what has been written.

Now, in this the fateful century in which it is the lot of present generations to work and struggle, to think and write, the first faint stirrings of the winds of thought and intelligence have increased to gale force, casting up words, thoughts, ideas, facts, truths and untruths, mile upon mile, in orderly sequence, on shelves of libraries the world around. So increasingly vigorous and extensive have become the winds of knowledge that the meteorologists of the whole business, librarians, documentalists, abstractors, indexers, classifiers, and codifiers are sometimes heard to express apprehensive concern that the whole thing may break up in tornadic chaos. Man, intelligent enough to create the whole process will, hopefully, have the wit not to permit this to happen. That control will indeed require wit, ingenuity, and much common sense is increasingly and inescapably evident.

Simplicity as a Weapon

The simplest languages are the most efficient in a technologically oriented world.

THE OLDEST, most sophisticated and most enduring civilization to be developed on this planet has been by the Chinese. When the peoples of some of the so-called advanced countries of today were barbarians, the Chinese were thinking and writing and developing a high-level literature and a religiously centered philosophy. In this process they evolved an extremely complicated and complex means of writing in which the pictograph and the ideograph are basic.

It was the misfortune of the Chinese that they never achieved, as did the traders and merchantmen of the Mediterranean areas, a breakthrough from these characters to the simple markings that stand for sounds and which can be assembled in endless variety to represent words not even remotely related to the original ideographs and pictographs. Whereas the educated Chinese must master both the reading and writing of some 40,000 elaborate characters, the users and writers of the western alphabetic languages, having learned twenty-six or more alphabetic marks, can both interpret and write them with relative ease. So simple is this that the intelligent western youngster easily grasps reading techniques at ages of five and six and is soon using them with facility.

In one sense Chinese culture has been imprisoned within its complicated written language or at least proscribed or limited by it. Because learning to read and write is so difficult, illiteracy rates among these highly intelligent peoples are high. Also because of its complications and because it has been the tool of a relatively small educational elite, Chinese writing has endured with fewer changes than the writing of any other culture. The language barrier, because it is so formidable, has been important among the things which have kept China separate from the western world. It enabled her to retain her culture and civilization with minimum changes for many centuries.

Now, however, with the flowering of our technological age and the vanishing of the great distances that formerly kept peoples and cultures apart, this is not and can no longer be so. Nor is complicated ideographic writing a satisfactory competitive media of expression in a world widely equipped with a much simpler system. The Chinese, of course, have long been aware of the retarding technological restrictions of their writing. Within this century various reform moves for simplification have been undertaken. It has remained for the present Communist government, however, to push these with determination and persistence. In a long-range sense this may well be the most important thing going on in China today.

The language handicaps under which China now competes are tremendous. A Chinese typewriter, invented only after much effort, has proven so cumbersome that it is not yet being manufactured and marketed. All business and governmental directives and correspondence must therefore still be done by hand, copies as well as the original. This hand copying alone, even in our simpler language, would be enough to sabotage the United States Army and sink the Navy. Our business ways and procedures are now simply unthinkable without our typewriters, linotypers, and monotypers, all of which so quickly record whatever we have the wit to write.

Nor is the alphabetic organization of knowledge in card catalogs, indexes, bibliographies, and abstracts, which we take so for granted and which is at the very bedrock of our western libraries, possible for the Chinese. This but serves to emphasize the great indebtedness of the western world to the early Mediterranean cultures which achieved the greatest invention of them all, the simple phonetic alphabet. It is utterly amazing that these symbols, so few in number, can express all the thoughts of Mankind, in their infinite range and variety.

There are grave difficulties in drastically simplifying the language and system of writing of a great and rich culture. It can be done, however, as the French long ago proved in Indochina. It was attempted in China by the Communist government through the official adoption, in December of 1956, of a twenty-six-letter Latin alphabet. Experience proved that attempts to latinize the ideographs created more problems than were solved. The effort was therefore abandoned in favor of simplifying the characters so that they can be learned more easily. Substantial progress has been made in this with over 80 percent of the characters now in simplified form. Here indeed may be the greatest weapon China is presently contriving in its struggle with the West. There will, however, be great penalties in this simplification which at its best does not equal the simplicity of western alphabets. One is that it will tend to cut the newer generations of China off from the rich philosophical and literary heritage which is theirs. In the competitive technological sense, this may not disturb the present leaders who are breaking sharply with the past in many directions. Whether, ultimately, this be strength or weakness only the long future will tell.

Mother of the Liberal Arts

The Ages of Man and the liberal arts both spring from science and technology.

THERE HAS ALWAYS been concern, I suspect, at those institutions like Oregon State University, providing instruction predominantly in the sciences and the technologies, about offering to the young men and women who come to them for instruction at least the basics of those studies which have become known as the "liberal arts." At such institutions the "liberal" arts have often had to fight for a place in the sun. Sometimes, as at Oregon State, this has been by direction of higher authority. Sometimes it has been through intra-institutional policy.

There is a historic compartmentation in American higher education, and elsewhere too, between the arts and the sciences. Such a division has its base, at least partially, in the notion, mistaken it seems to me, that the liberal arts and the scientific and technical arts, being separate and distinct can therefore be advantageously taught separately. Far from this being the case, science and technology, as the mother and the father too of the liberal arts, need to keep these offspring within their province and to make every effort on a comprehensive basis to understand them and through them themselves.

All our history, from the dim and distant past to the present, shows science and technology as the maker of the liberal arts. Philosophy, religion, literature, the fine arts, the social sciences, these have all emerged from the crucible of science and technology, taking form, direction, and substance in relation to what has been discovered and understood, at first slowly, oh so slowly, but now with almost breathless, breakneck speed, about the natural laws of the environment in which we have our being. This has in fact been acknowledged by our thinking in a liberal arts sense about our civilizations and cultures. It is thus that we have the stone age, the bronze age, the iron age, and now possibly the atomic age, or is it the space age, all taking their names from the degree to which man has mastered, worked with, understood, and bent to his will the physical materials surrounding him.

In the circumstances of his long and increasingly successful quest for mastery of his environment, Man's philosophy and religion, his literature and his arts have their being. It is significant that we do not have, or at least do not generally think of an Age of Philosophy or Religion or Art or Literature. The whole though, from the known beginnings to the present time, could perhaps, in the history of Man on the planet, take the name of the Age of Reason since it all began with the emergence of man as a thinking, reasoning being.

Examples abound of the tremendous impact of science and technology in the areas at the heart of what we have chosen to call the liberal arts. The thinking of modern man, who through science and technology understands or thinks he understands many of the physical mysteries of the world about him, must be and is far different from the thinking and philosophizing of earlier man cowering in his cave before the onslaught of elements which he did not understand or, in happier circumstances, contemplating in awe the wonder and beauty of the heavens. Scientists in these later days have done more to shape the theology of our times than any of the theologians. Charles Darwin and his theory of evolution is but one of the more recent of the many examples of scientists under whose

thinking and study religious or at least Christian concepts have altered—often painfully and distressingly.

Literature too, and indeed the very words of which it is made and the use of them has altered and changed through the sciences, in content and viewpoint. Should some future man, divinely gifted in words, as was Shakespeare, walk and work among men he would not, in portraying the transitory and unsatisfactory life of an evil man be able to have him say, appropriately as Shakespeare so fittingly could, "Out, out brief candle!" We should not forget either that it is because of the technologists, from the chiselers of stone and the bakers of hieroglyphic-covered wet clay, from the fabrica-

tors of papyrus to the papermakers on down through Johan Gutenberg to the facile graphic arts of these days, that words, the basic machinery of the reasoning process and as such the building bricks of the liberal arts, now abound all about us in great wealth and richness, stored in organized and findable fashion in the warehouses of the word we know as libraries.

Yes, it is inescapable. The liberal arts spring from the womb of the sciences and the technologies. This being so, it is eminently appropriate and even essential that those institutions emphasizing science and technology, if they are to be whole and balanced, should offer comprehensive instruction both in the sciences *and* the arts.

Shaker of the Universe

Two boy babies born in 1564 grew up to shake the world, each in his own way.

THE REASONING of the foregoing commentary is confirmed, I feel, by two important births of male babies in 1564, one in England and one in Italy. Each newcomer was destined to have a tremendous influence, over the centuries, on the world he was entering, willy-nilly, through no choice of his own. Four hundred years later, in 1964, a grateful and admiring world did much homage, through festivals, articles, dramas, and exhibits to these two men who have grown and continue to grow in the esteem of all.

In these quadra-centennial celebrations it was, probably ap-

propriately, the dramatist, William Shakespeare, who was most frequently on the stage. In the fundamental sense though, Galileo, the boy baby the year 1564 brought to Italy, made the greater impact on the lives and times of succeeding generations. It was his destiny to literally shake the universe of traditions, concepts, and beliefs into which he was born.

The English language would, of course, have been great, but not as great, had Shakespeare never been born or had he been carried off young in the plagues and pestilences which were rife in his time. Science would have progressed and advanced dramatically, but not as dramatically or as quickly, without the perceptive and imaginative mind and incisive and often sarcastic pen of Galileo. It was eminently appropriate therefore that the great significance of these two lives should be so widely noted and celebrated in 1964.

Galileo, although making the greater impact in long-range terms, was not an original thinker. It was his great gift rather to be able to free his mind from the authoritarian concepts and traditions of his time, to bring the clear cool light of logic and reason to bear on observed facts, to follow them to where they seemed to him to lead, and to bring the disparate elements of the past and present into clear focus. It was his further great gift, shared with Shakespeare, to be able to present his ideas and theories incisively, clearly, in ways that challenged the interest and stirred the minds of all who read him. It was his misfortune that what he deduced and discovered and presented so clearly was at variance with the fountain-head, Aristotle, and with a literal interpretation of the scriptures.

The theory that the "sun is immovable in the center of the world and that the earth has a diurnal motion of rotation," so eloquently espoused by Galileo, had been advanced almost a hundred years earlier by Copernicus. The telescope he perfected had been known in Holland but only as a plaything. It was Galielo's genius to bring the Copernican theory to life. It was his further genius to perfect the telescope, to turn it toward the heavens, and to proclaim the startling results. These were the things that were to bring him to his knees before the inquisitors of the Holy Church.

In extending his own senses and the senses of all men through the telescope, Galileo began a process the end of which is not yet, nor possibly ever will be. In following facts, as revealed by vision improved a hundred-fold, to logical conclusions, regardless of what had been thought and said before, Galileo gave great impetus to a problem and quandary with which men have struggled throughout all recorded history—the conflict between the possessors and interpreters of revealed truth and those who see and interpret things not the way someone says they are but as their reason tells them they are. The yielding of the knowers of revealed truth before clearly demonstrable fact has been slow and grudging, even unto our day.

Many of us remember only too clearly the famous Scopes trial of the 1920's in Tennessee where a competent and dedicated young teacher was hailed into court in a kind of modern day inquisition for teaching the theory of the evolutionary descent, or ascent, of Man. The literalists, even at the highest levels, have gradually retreated from untenable ground, with no one now seriously challenging the theory of evolution or the revolution of the earth around the sun. The kinds of authoritarian mentalities which could and did motivate the earlier challenges are, nevertheless, virulent and long enduring, as is clearly evident in the extremists of our day, right and left, on the airways, in the press, and in the pulpit.

One of the prime reasons Galileo could so shake, loosen, and dislodge the basic intellectual and spiritual tenets of his time was that he could express himself so well. In his old age, blind and under close house arrest, he penned these moving and poignant lines, quite worthy of that other famous boy baby of 1564:

That sky, that world and that universe, which with my wondrous observations and clear demonstrations I amplified a hundred and a thousand times over what was believed most commonly by the learned of all past centuries, is for me now so diminished and narrowed that it is no greater than what my body occupies.

A Place of Involvement

Old myths and prototypes die hard.

ONE MYTH commented on in another essay is the concept of librarians as meek, mousy people jealously guarding their wares and shushing with pursed lips all who enter their sacred portals. Another is the idea of the library as a kind of ivory tower where, safely tucked away, one can escape the troublesome present in vicarious enjoyment of other times and places or of other people's thoughts and ideas. One need only enter any bustling academic library, any work-a-day period, to discover that these concepts, if they ever had validity, certainly do not have it now.

Rather than a place of escape and retreat, the modern library is, as Professor Reed Whittemore of Carleton College said at the dedication of the new Carleton Library building, a place of involvement. There is, he said, weather, real weather in a library. It is a place of exposure to the elements. Rather than a place of getting out of the world, it is a place to get into it.

The materials now flowing into libraries are direct evidence of this perceptive statement. The library of today does indeed gather in the intellectual, social, and political weather of the times—the troublesome, complex, complicated and seamy, of which there is an abundance, along with the pleasant and the entertaining. The breakneck record-ing of modern technology, as well as writings which are loftily intellectual, are everywhere appearing on library shelves in ever increasing quantity. As these things reach a library and are organized for use, they immediately attract readers. This is quickly apparent in the books and magazines which in any open-access library are daily pulled down from the shelves by the thousands for reading.

It has always been a pleasant privilege for me, in the libraries with which I have been associated, to greet the new weekly increments, all neatly lettered and readied for use. I confess, however, to mingled emotions as I have surveyed them. Pleasure and satisfaction have been predominant, but there has also been some sadness, a little frustration, and a bit of worry, too. The satisfaction has come from the sense of organization, order, and findability, at the root of all good librarianship, which the new books impart.

It has been pleasant, too, to conjecture as to what part these books, mostly bright and new, would take in the work of the university. Which of these pristine volumes would provide the background and understanding, the inspiration, spark, or idea, perhaps in no more than a sentence or two, for the beginning of a new search or bringing one already in progress to successful and brilliant fruition? Would one of them, perhaps, falling into the hands of undergraduate or grad-uate, provide the impetus, final or initial, which might decide a career and launch a lifetime of significant work? And would some, perhaps, nourish and broaden the spirit and restore courage and determination?

Sadness and frustration has sometimes arisen over lack of personal vigor of mind and body and eye to read more than an infinitesimal part of all the good things to read and over inability to know and understand. There has been scant comfort, somehow, in the reflection that even the most gifted and industrious minds can master only a small segment of the tremendous accumulation of knowledge, facts, and ideas that are the heritage of modern man. There has been sadness, too, because, in spite of all the facts, ideas, and know-how which we moderns put to print and so carefully organize in great storehouses, we are somehow neither wise nor good. Of that, the current world of strife, turmoil, war, and rumors of war is abundant evidence.

The impact of the writings available in libraries on young and formative minds, and on older ones too, is immeasurably great. Clear evidence of this is the breathtakingly rapid technological and scientific development of our times. The library, in generic terms, is the chief vehicle of these advances. It is not only a gatherer and a container of the factual and intellectual weather of the times, it is also a maker and breeder of it. Attesting to this are the commendatory bows which libraries and librarians so frequently receive in prefaces to books.

When we multiply the extensive reading which goes on in libraries everywhere in the world, and when we add to this the billions of dollars which are being spent to gather, organize, and make available the new writings cascading from the presses of the world in a growing array of languages, the place of the book as a breeder of the intellectual weather of our present civilization assumes tremendous proportions. Consciously or more frequently unconsciously, the book is central to this growth and evolution. Books assembled in great quantity and properly administered are, and always will be, not a refuge but a place of involvement.

When Stillness Reigns

WHEN MOST of the people who work in the acquisitional and administrative phases of a library have taken themselves off to their own firesides for the duties, pleasures, and the cares which there await them, it is then that stillness and quiet descend on the administrative quarters. The comings and goings have ceased and the clattering of the typewriters has died away. It is a time for reflection and for stock taking. Somehow, when all the bustle and scurrying which accompany the building and maintenance of a library fade away to await still another day, the purpose and pattern behind it all assumes greater clarity.

Sometimes, in the late hours, I have wandered through the cataloging, acquisition, and serials departments deeply conscious of work in progress, of the many files and records in the never ending process of being revised or added to, of books being unpacked, checked, or invoiced, of numerous book trucks filled with volumes receiving the ministrations of the catalogers, of the intricacies and the necessary minutiae of this work, of the new and vital blood being continually infused into the library by these many exacting and carefully meshed processes. Nearly always, in such excursions, I have encountered a department head or two, or other staff member, rounding off some phase of the day's work or, in service above and beyond the normal call of duty, ironing out some knotty wrinkle.

I have liked too to come to the library when it is closed over week ends or holidays. At these times, on occasion, in the various libraries I have served, I have walked among the mute and waiting stacks. How quiet the library when closed! For me it has been a vibrant quietness which heightens perceptiveness and awareness. The books, so carefully organized and stacked, in all their many thousands, have passed through the acquisitional and administrative processes, some recently and some by hands and minds long since done with earthly cares and pursuits. Their work and their efforts remain, nonetheless, in the careful marshalling of a portion of the world's intellectual and factual heritage standing waiting on the shelves. Knowledge and inspiration in waiting, this is a sense and a feeling that comes to me with particular acuteness when the library, in an almost overpowering quietness, stands closed.

Occasionally, at times like this, I have pulled down books at random to scan their title pages, to read a few paragraphs, and to inspect the charge-out dates. What, I have reflected, has been the impact and the value and the spirit of the withdrawals, numerous and in close time sequence on some volumes, few on others. Have these uses been merely a reluctant performance of lessons assigned? Have some perhaps brought insight, inspiration, new horizons, viewpoints, and outlooks that have changed a life or perhaps decided a career? How many have been sought out or stumbled on with no compulsion other than the instinct, peculiar to Man alone, to learn and to know? And what of those few books which have stood on the shelves undisturbed and unused from the time of their coming, save for the numerous shiftings which happen in every growing library? Would these dormant books perhaps also be called into use one day, possibly to speak across the years, or even the centuries, to those now being educated or to be educated or to those conducting that education?

These are thoughts and questions pertinent to the always exciting adventure of the academic enterprise. Always there has been the hope, particularly keen at the beginning of the yearly academic cycle, that the work of the years and of the present days has been done and is being done well and that the library will not be found wanting.

Crack-Pots, Oddities, Queer Ones

Free publications and writings, received by libraries sometimes depart far from accepted norms and current mores.

MANY LIBRARIES have a "freak" shelf where these unusual and often interesting publications come to rest. The bizarre writings that accumulate on such a shelf have certain common characteristics. Many of them are occult, mystic, or religious in nature. Often there is a weird jumbling of scientific and mathematical half truths and astronomical and meteorological lore. Some pieces are authored, undoubtedly, by honestly deluded men, others by shrewd exploiters of human credulity who thus manage to live well. In presenting briefly some of these curiosa, I am deeply conscious of the observation of the old Quaker who remarked to his wife, "Everybody is queer but thee and me, Rebecca, and sometimes thee is a little queer."

One author of a pamphlet extra-ordinary entitles it *From Evolved Beginning (i.e. A Hole Filled With Gastronomic Ingredients) To Involved Endment (i.e. A Whole Filled Out With Anatomic Particulars)*. Here is a sample of involvement that makes me dizzy. "The monstrous-exhibition, showing-off, as NOT-ME, i.e. that electrically engendered natural evolution of objectivity, that ingredentially fills in My-Eye-Cone-of-Vision, the bare consciousness of which reveals it, 'void as without form,' or as matter-per-se, i.e. that universal-thing-in-spatial-becoming, called: My Environment-in-General, and that menstruous-inhibition, known-on as YET-ME, i.e. that electively exgendered spiritual involution of subjectivity, that particularizedly fills out My-I-Zone-of-Vigor . . ." and so on for thirty-one pages.

A would-be benefactor of mankind was (and possibly still is) Richard Rodrian of New York City who in 1929 gave to the world a book *The Salvation of Mankind from Catastrophes*. Mr. Rodrian, with the cooperation of the Lord of the Universe, and the assistance of the United States Weather Bureau, unwitting no doubt, was engaged in the great and good work of "influencing and directing" the high and low pressure areas in their progress across the United States from Oregon and Washington, keeping them from getting mixed up and producing "devastating weather and natural catastrophes." Once having gotten them across the country without acting up, he harmlessly ushered them out into the Atlantic. What an opportunity for some Son of Satan to work this deal in reverse. Could the Russians possibly . . . Oh no, not that!

And then there is the Brotherhood of the Great White Temple which in 1942 purchased a "large, luxurious," three story building in the heart of downtown Denver. More appealing is their jumbo-mumbo, and more calculated too, perhaps. For instance Shamballa as described by Dr. M. Doreal, (a big wheel of the Brotherhood) who has visited it. It is a real place he says, seventy-five miles down into the earth, directly beneath Lahassa, the forbidden city of Tibet. Here it has been set aside by wave mechanics so that it vibrates "on a plane and an octave of vibration different from that of our material world, and even if the mountains crashed around this place and the earth fell it would still not be touched or shaken." Anyone trying to drop a bomb on this place "would find himself in another place so fast he would not have time to turn around." Tanks, big guns, and armies sent against it would vanish in the wave of shimmering light that surrounds it.

From Dr. Dorcal we learn that our wire and tape recordings of today and our projects for miniturization and computerizing of knowledge are millions of years behind the times and pretty primitive too. In Shamballa there is a vast room containing millions and millions of books on tiny little spools of metallic wire, each containing a complete book. These little spools are operated by motors made 5,000,000 years ago, and each, ever since its making, has been powered by a tiny grain of gold through radiation. When you press a "stud," the wire unrolls, portraying in word and person materialized into the air in three-dimensional space, "actual, living, historical events of the past world." Quite a thing, Shamballa. A good place to head for when the bombs start falling. I may not get in though after having written this.

Documents of Liberty

"Ah, Liberty, you look so simple crossing town."

WE IN THIS COUNTRY have approached some kind of zenith of ultra-carefulness and precaution in the enshrinement of our Constitution, the Bill of Rights, and the Declaration of Independence. These precious documents were transferred in December, 1953, from the Library of Congress to an elaborately prepared permanent home in the National Archives building. Twenty feet below the auditorium of that building there is a special vault of steel, two and one-half inches thick. In this vault the documents rest vertically in helium filled cases. At the touch of a button the massive lids fold back and the documents rise slowly into a specially prepared exhibit case in the auditorium above. There they are on exhibit daily under armed guard, returning to their vault each night. In this way they will be available, down through the ages, for exhibit and inspiration, untouched by human hands.

These documents have been successively in the possession of the Continental Congress, the State Department, and the Library of Congress before coming finally to their present bomb proof and fire proof home. Their existence has not always been so placid nor their care so elaborate. When the British were advancing on Washington in August of 1814, these three documents, along with other precious papers, were stuffed in coarse sacks and taken to an idle grist mill on the Virginia side of the Potomac. Later they were removed to Leesburg, Virginia, and kept there until the British fleet left Chesapeake Bay. Still once again they left Washington, under threat of war, going secretly and quietly, during World War II, to the gold vaults of Fort Knox, Kentucky. Now, presumably, they will remain in Washington, come what may.

The elaborate military precautions and dramatization of the taking of these hallowed bits of paper to their permanent home gives one pause. They were released by the Library of Congress to a detachment of the Marine Corps arriving in a heavily armored car with two accompanying tanks. While in transit, they rested on mattresses and the route of their passage to the National Archives was lined on both sides by personnel of the four armed services. The drama fouled up a little when one of the tanks, not quite equal to the event, broke down, but this was perhaps covered somewhat by the measured tread of marching young Americans and the skirling of bagpipes. In the new home the unveiling was marked by appropriate addresses by President Truman and Chief Justice Vinson. Once again, however, the military was not quite up to the occasion. This was when a woman of the Marine Honor Guard fainted during the address of the Chief Justice.

I could not help but wonder, in reading of this transfer and the attendant military dramatization what the authors of these documents, the men from whose minds they sprang and whose hands set down the immortal words, what these men would have thought of all this pomp and circumstance. Would they perhaps have reflected that it is only in the minds and hearts of people, generations past, present, and generations yet to come, that these documents and the ideals for which they stand can live and have meaning? Without this, the steel and concrete vault, the helium gas, the armed guards, the military drama, all these are as nothing. *The New Yorker* in commenting on the transfer expresses something of this thought in these better words:

A military escort attended them, an armored car bristled in the background, bagpipers squealed their delight and kindled the blood. How uncomplicated it looked, this physical act of guarding our greatest treasures! And how serene life would be if the essence of the documents could be guarded so easily, so precisely, and with such gay props as bagpipes and such exact ones as machine guns! Ah, liberty—you look so simple crossing town!

Books and Their Dedications

Librarians may be forgiven if, in moments of weariness, they sigh over the multitude of their charges and the things they must do to and with them.

EVEN THE MOST AVID book lover, as he handles the fiftieth book or the hundredth or the thousandth, may occasionally experience a sense of surfeit. Under these conditions, it is not surprising that for some persons engaged in bookish occupations books tend to become merely physical objects, to be bought from publisher or jobber, unpacked, checked off invoices, and paid for, or things to be quickly and neatly cataloged with all the attendant meticulous detail and in the least possible number of minutes, or to be charged out or discharged, fetched from shelves or returned to shelves, all with the least possible bother.

While book handling may and often does become routine, it is my belief that most of us who have the privilege of living by and among books find continuing and often uplifting interest, excitement, and sometimes deep satisfaction from and through the volumes with which we work continuously and in such numbers. This is so in part because books, even those which are technical and highly scientific, are essentially human documents. Behind each volume there stands a person who, even in the most intellectual documents, often shows through in preface or elsewhere to express his grati-

tude, in a very human way, to those who have endured or taken part in the agonies that sometimes accompany the birthing or who have lent a hand or sat in judgment or criticism.

Certainly when viewed in this aspect books take on individuality and interest. I have frequently reflected, as I have walked among the stacks surrounded by books, row after row, shelf upon shelf, about the lives and minds and spirits, from the earliest times to the present, which have produced these volumes, so quietly and patiently waiting to speak across the days or years or centuries to those who would hold converse with them. At what juncture did the inspiration or decision come to put pen to paper or to send the relatively few characters on a typewriter clattering into the meaningful assembly now standing on the shelves? By what travail and planning, industry, and sacrifice did these volumes achieve being?

One place where we sometimes get a pleasant hint of these things is in dedications where the author often bows politely to friend, colleague, or family, and even sometimes to librarians. These little tributes or inscriptions, are, happily, placed at the prow ready to launch the thoughts, facts, and ideas which follow on a cruise into the mind of the reader. Some dedications which have appealed to me as adding the human touch to books are these:

JOHN MacEWAN dedicates his *Between the Red and the Rockies:* "To Heather who was shaking the table much of the time when her Daddy was writing this story."

ROBERT NATHAN in *The Married Look* says appropriately, "For my mother—whose husband, my father, never lost the memory of his wife's young face."

GLENN SMITH's dedication of *Principles and Practices of the Guidance Program* is "To Cindy, who thinks her Daddy knows practically everything, and Her Mother, who knows better."

JULIUS GOLDBERG dedicates *Fabric Defects* to his wife in this husbandly way ". . . As a fitting reward for her unfailing loyalties, all my thanks, all my love—and, of course, all the royalties."

PHIL CARROLL in *Time Study Fundamentals for Foremen* acknowledges the influence of his father in this dedication: "To my Dad, who said, 'Always give a little more than they pay for and you will never have to worry about a job.'"

GEORGE SESSIONS PERRY in his very interesting *The Story of Texas A. and M.* has this perceptive inscription: "This book is dedicated, curiously enough, to something that never wholly existed in fact: The A. and M. that is remembered by its students . . ."

ROBERT HOPPOCK places practice over theory in his *Group Guidance* with this acknowledgment: "To my daughter Margaret Joan . . . who has taught her father a thing or two about the kinds of guidance that do not work."

It may be either condescension or tribute which impels T. H. BANKS to dedicate his *Milton's Imagery:* "To my wife whose profound and cheerful ignorance of Milton has been a Godsend."

CHARLES GRAYSON also acknowledges the parental influence in *New Stories for Men* in this breezy sendoff: "This is a sort of salute to my old man who thought a story ought to be something you enjoy reading."

There also is a dedication by SEYMOUR HARRIS in *The Economics of New England* which I particularly and naturally like: "To Robert Hammond Haynes, Assistant Librarian of the Harvard College Library, whose kindly helpfulness in serving scholars . . . has added much to American Scholarship."

WILLIAM HUGH CARLSON 27

The Quiet, Unobtrusive King

The basic stuff of libraries.

IN THIS COMPLEX and complicated civilization of ours we take paper for granted, as common and as essential as the winter rains of the Pacific Northwest. This cellulose fabric, which was once the precious stuff used only to record the writings and records of men, has now become so common and inexpensive that it has moved increasingly into the world of business and industry where it is lavishly, but nonetheless efficiently, used. Even so its prime and vital importance is still as the material on which men have and do record their writings.

Tons and tons of hieroglyphic-covered paper, recording the thoughts, the ideals, the aspirations and fears, the deeds and misdeeds, and the remarkable ingenuity of man, have been brought into the numerous great and complex repositories which we know as libraries. Without these rapidly growing reservoirs of print, the life we know could never have come into being. Many are the hallowed pieces of paper which met a great destiny by having set down on them the immortal words which have shaped and guided our thinking, our philosophy, our varied religions, and the development of our technology.

The early manuscripts of the Bible and the variant early printed editions, the writings of the great non-Christian religions,

the Magna Carta, our Declaration of Independence, the Constitution of the United States, Lincoln's Gettysburg address and his Second Inaugural and countless other writings, all these are carefully guarded in the libraries. There are the scientific writings of great minds too: of Galileo, Copernicus, Roger Bacon, Harvey, Newton, Faraday, Pasteur, Einstein, and many, many others, all of which have keyed and made possible this science-centered civilization of which we stand in awe, and now sometimes even in fear.

A world without paper is, in terms of our modern civilization, unthinkable. Some time ago a science-fiction writer created an intriguing situation around such a possibility. He wrote of a new gas which when liberated, caused the sudden and total destruction of all cellulose tissue everywhere. Passengers on suburban trains, reading their morning papers, suddenly held nothing in their hands. The contents spilled out of all paper wrapped packages. Newspaper and magazine stands all at once stood empty. Blueprints, mail, office files, wills, financial records, all these disappeared. This was as nothing though in comparison with the fact that all the libraries, great and small, special and general, immediately ceased to exist.

In the catacombs of the stacks which but a brief moment before had housed the carefully

ordered memory of the race, warm and alive, there was now suddenly nothing but steel and concrete, cold and impassive. The catalogs, abstracts, reviews, and classification schemes, so painstakingly contrived to compass and chart the multi-millioned volumes, these too were no more.

The result could only be hopeless and utter confusion. In every direction and in practically every endeavor the affairs of men were completely snafu, commerce impossible, transportation snarled, and educational enterprises completely impossible. Everywhere, completely and irrevocably, the fragile stuff on which a whole civilization rested was gone. It was then that men realized that while they had paid homage to the more spectacular iron, steel, and other metals, and spoken of themselves as living in an iron age that it had all the while been paper, quiet and unobtrusive, which had been king.

In Oregon the production of paper, in its many variant forms, constitutes a considerable segment of the economy as is indicated by the twenty-four hours per day operation of various paper mills. Recently I drove by such a mill in the black of a wild and stormy night. Lights aglow, surrounded by swirling rain, which half successfully obscured it from view, exuding steam, smoke, and varied vapors from numerous orifices along with unspeakable odors, this mill seemed to me like nothing so much as the headquarters for Hades. In the bright and rational light of day, it is of course only a modern streamlined manufacturing plant creating some part of the wealth by which the

Oregon Commonwealth, including its educational institutions and libraries, live.

Many of the Oregon mills produce the more plebian papers and cardboards, but they are blood brothers to those mills that do turn out the stuff which, in its great plentitude, has permitted our civilization to become so complex and complicated, so sophisticated and learned, and even sometimes, in the stormy and black tempests of the current scene, so terrible. It is in the dark moments that it is good to think on those hallowed and reassuring pieces of paper, so carefully housed, which record the ennobling thoughts of man in his upward climb. These are the writings which bring the rationality of the bright light of day and the sunshine of hope to all the affairs of men. God willing, these treasured documents and the more pertinent and valued of the tons upon tons of other writings will continue to endure in our libraries as Man's best monument to himself.

My active participation in and observation of the American library scene now covers forty years. The development and growth of libraries during these years, in America and the world around, can only be characterized as tremendous. Fantastic is perhaps a more appropriate and an allowable word.

In my beginning years few academic libraries exceeded a million volumes. Even the Library of Congress, probably the world's largest library then as now, had only 3,000,000 volumes. Now that library has well over 12,000,000 books and is heading lickety-split for 15,000,000. Million-volumed academic libraries with million dollar annual budgets are now commonplace.

In my first years it was quite often only the chief librarian in even the largest academic libraries who was well salaried. Usually only he could manage to have his way paid to conferences. Now every university library of consequence has a well established hierarchy of management personnel, travel budgets, and carefully devised staff organization charts. Much of this has come about in the post World War II years. All of it flows, both as cause and effect, from the phenomenal increase of learned publications. Concomitantly, academic and professional standards have advanced substantially. Education for librarianship has grown and developed and, I sincerely believe, in spite of many critical voices, improved in quality. Professional library associations have mushroomed. Specialization of libraries and of librarians has flourished.

All of this has perhaps more significance for librarians of my generation than for those who have more recently come on the scene, because we who are older view it from the realities and the sharp perspective of the depression years. The over-riding problem for most libraries in those years was to hold things together, to keep the very most basic materials and sets intact and growing, and to sever as few people as possible from the payroll. It was not then a question for young librarians, and sometimes older ones, of where will I work and how much will I be paid, but will there be work for me. In those days when job offers came, if they did, there was ready and eager acceptance and few questions asked. Perhaps it is the harsh but not unwholesome discipline of those lean years which accounts for the connotation of astonishment and amazement found in some of these pages.

While the essays which follow were, as is true of all the commentaries in this book, originally written only for Oregon State University readership and with no thought of publication, they do, in many ways, reflect the break-neck pace of library affairs and development everywhere. The immediately following essay however, probably would apply, at least as far as the title is concerned, to most keepers of the books from the very earliest assemblages of written materials to the present.

The Eternally Covetous Librarian

Both theme and title for this essay come from the facile mind and pen of my good friend Larry Powell, formerly Librarian of the University of California at Los Angeles, and later a teacher. A bookman first and last, Larry, eschewing the fancier modern titles such as Director of Libraries, takes pride in the ancient and honorable title of Librarian. Regardless of titles, Larry kept the relatively young UCLA Library he administered for a number of years growing vigorously and effectively in the service of a great university. For him, though, and for all the top-flight librarians really, librarianship both begins and ends with the book. There must of course, in a well administered large library, be organization charts, careful planning of work, concern about time and motion in executing the myriad minutiae of the acquisition and servicing of materials, analyses of costs, and attention to many, many other administrative facets and details of the total operation of acquiring recorded human knowledge in quantity and meticulously organizing it for use.

So important is the administrative machinery of a great library that it tends, in some quarters, to become the be-all and to increasingly remove administrators at the top levels from the book, the ultimate reason for their being. Some libraries have grown useful, possibly even highly useful, under such administration, but no library has ever grown great unless those in command, at all levels, root their activities in the book in all its manifestations and make it central to all their planning and all they do. The librarian as bookman never becomes enmeshed in and fascinated by the glories of his machinery as machinery. For him there is only one fundamental and stern test which every new gadget, machine, and device must pass, and pass convincingly, and that is, will this permit him to secure more books with the money he has and will it increase the convenience and decrease the cost of their use?

It follows from all of this that no library has all the books it needs and wants for the library has never been, nor ever will be, which can encompass all the books which have been and are being published in all parts of the world and in all languages. Nevertheless, many libraries, and

all true university libraries, have insatiable and usually, but not always, disciplined appetites. This is why Larry Powell, in a report made a few years ago in behalf of all the libraries of the Greater University of California from which I have extracted the above title, felt compelled to stress, even as he commented with satisfaction on the many riches added during the report period, that there are always more and ever more books which libraries need and covet.

Even though all-inclusiveness is an unattainable will-o'-the-wisp which even the richest and most covetous librarians know, with increasing certainty in these days of the unceasing spawning of the presses, they will never reach, some have, nevertheless, at least in comparative terms, made a pretty noble try at it. First and foremost among these is the Harvard University Library, which is among the greatest libraries of the world and certainly its greatest university library. This library has become great through the unremitting covetousness of its librarians, responding to a rich curriculum and to the stimulation and needs of a great and distinguished faculty.

It is significant that much of the Harvard richness and its growth to its present seven and one-half million volumes has been achieved in relatively recent years, most of it since the turn of the century, and much of it within the last few decades. In the eternal covetousness of its librarians and the resulting growth, which has brought it to a three million dollar annual operation, the Harvard Library has, in a sense, transcended its university to become a great national and world cultural resource of and by itself. An article in *Life* magazine of March 9, 1959, quotes the Shakespeare scholar, G. L. Kittridge, as saying, "You could destroy all the other Harvard buildings and, with Widener left standing, still have a University." In a converse sense, destroy Widener and you destroy much of the university and leave the world much the poorer culturally.

All of these things are, of course, relative. Libraries everywhere, in all the lands and nations and states of this earth do in their totality approach some kind of all-inclusiveness of the significant knowledge so painstakingly achieved and gathered together by mankind. Only because Man has been eager to gather and organize his knowledge into the volumed rows, mile upon mile, of the world's libraries, has cultural growth and technical progress been possible to the fantastic degree we have now come to take for granted. Among the libraries of world, nation, and state, the books assembled in the Oregon State University Library are a modest but nevertheless not an insignificant part. Of Oregon State, too, it could be said, destroy the other buildings and leave the library and it will still have a university, even though grievously wounded.

Throughout the years to come, even as in those of the past, librarians everywhere will, I am confident, continue to be covetous for books or for whatever other forms Man may devise for the recording of his thoughts and experience. Because of this, it follows inexorably and inevitably that they must also be covetous for the dollars required to secure graphic records and to house them in dignity and in beauty.

The Librarian's Hard Lot

"It is commonly assumed that the Chief Librarian of a place like the Bodleian or the British Museum has nothing whatever to do. He has gone through his period of storm and stress. He has catalogued; he has sorted out the new accessions; he has fetched and carried for readers; but at last he has been . . . promoted beyond the dust and trampling, into a region like that of the lotos-eaters where no labour is demanded . . . This prevalent misconception has at last stirred Bodley's Librarian to indignation.

"In the current number of the Bodleian Quarterly Record there is an account of what all Bodley's servants, from highest to lowest, have to do; and the list of duties is so terrifying that I feel, to use Sir Andrew Aguecheek's terminology, that I had as lief be a Puritan as a librarian."

THE ABOVE quotation from "The Librarian's Hard Lot," by Solomon Eagle points up the general human trait of being aware of only those phases of any enterprise with which we come in direct contact.

It is quite certain that most university students and many of the faculty are only dimly aware, if at all, of the intricate and continuing processes by which every research library lives and grows. To those who labor in the library the things they must do are neither dull nor terrifying. They are there by choice, the librarians, and most of them would "liefer" be librarians than anything. Those who work behind the scenes do many of the things which have surprised and terrified Mr. Eagle. They are things which must be done, nevertheless, if the teaching and research of any university is to be properly buttressed by book resources.

One thing of which every good librarian is acutely conscious is that he must keep on top of his work. Duties and functions neglected or evaded today, we learn by hard experience, become much harder to do on a tomorrow which, we are dead certain, will bring its own generous quota of problems, demands, and routines. Mail and express trucks, which constitute the lifeline of every library, arrive with certainty and precision. The materials they bring must quickly be reduced to order and system. The magazines received, arriving by the sackful in many and varied languages, must be opened, alphabeted, checked in, and forwarded to their designated posts in the service of the university. Those which should have arrived and do not must be pursued. The products of Uncle Sam's busy printing presses must similarly be processed. Books which have been ordered must be absorbed. Good things which have been variously acquired in duplicate must be organized, listed, and offered to other libraries from which important things are often received in return.

All this, if well done, involves much minutiae and detail. As this absorption goes on, librarians are also busy selecting from the vast literature of the learned world that portion which will serve the university best and which entrusted funds will encompass. This involves careful establishment of bibliographical data and the writing of numerous purchase orders. These the outgoing mails carry away to all parts of the world to bring still more resources and more work. The cataloging of books and the physical things that must be done to them before they can appear on the shelves goes on apace.

The only time the entire process becomes, if not terrifying, then worrisome, is when the work falls behind. If mail accumulates unopened, if book catalogs and trade tools go unread, if titles needed remain unsearched in quantity, if books pile up on shelves uncataloged; then confusion, the arch enemy of every library, begins to reign. Creaking and groaning of the closely geared machinery becomes inescapably audible and the results are soon, all too soon, evident in service departments.

As for a chief librarianship being a pleasant sinecure which permits the incumbent to lead a life of ease and to pursue various dilettante avocations, well, I know some chief librarians, but very, very few, who manage to do this and apparently with an easy conscience. While this has not been true at

Oregon State University and could not be true for long, I definitely know, because the library has such an able staff that the whole enterprise in all phases can carry on very nicely without me as indeed it is now doing. Any slight tendency I might once have had to feel indispensable

was completely dispelled by the beginning sentence in one department head's monthly report of some years ago. "January," she said, writing of a period when I was absent on a protracted eastern trip, "was one of the smoothest running months we have had in a long time."

On Education and Research

Academic librarians must also be teachers.

THE FUNDAMENTAL and central part of the library in the higher educational processes is clear, obvious, and well understood by all who are concerned with higher education, either as instructors or administrators. It comes as a shock then that some people and even some faculty members and university administrators do not recognize the teaching and research functions of college or university libraries or that the persons who assemble and organize the materials in them and assist in their interpretation and use are an integral part of and make definite contributions to the research and teaching of their respective institutions.

The concept of the librarian as merely a clerk who writes numbers on the backs of books, sets them on shelves in meticulous order, and goes off to get them when called for, stems, I suppose, from the fact that all these things must be done in libraries. It is probable too that the very great emphasis which earlier librarians put on these

housekeeping phases of their work has contributed to the image of the library as primarily a book-hoarding sanctuary presided over by stern watchdogs, male and female.

Far from this kind of an institution, the modern higher educational library is a dynamic educational agency which, if well run, is meshed in full gear with the curriculum, the research program, and institutional aims and objectives. In addition, the progressive library conducts, in various ways, educational activities of its own. It is chiefly in the present century, and particularly in the last two decades, that the library on nearly every campus has moved into direct participation in the education of students and support of the faculty in their research. The concept of direct educational activity and responsibility for the college library goes back well into the last century. As early as 1882 Professor Otis Robinson of the University of Rochester said:

A librarian should be much more than a keeper of books; he should be an educator . . . relation . . . ought especially to be established between a college librarian and the student readers. No such librarian is fit for his place unless he holds himself in some degree responsible for library education of the students . . . it is his province to direct very much of their general reading; and especially in their investigation of subjects he should be their guide and their friend.

This philosophy has been so fully accepted by modern college and university libraries that it may be said to be the very bedrock of present-day higher educational librarianship. It is expressed in the open access library buildings now so generally found in American universities; in removal, in so far as possible, of all barriers between students and books; in the work of readers' advisers and counselors; in instruction in use of the library, formal and informal; in direction of the bibliographical work of graduate students; and in assistance and support of the research of faculty members. It is expressed too in varying and interesting educational exhibits; in bibliographical research and publication by members of library staffs; in promotion of book ownership by students;

in service outside the library, through the mails; and in librarians educated in and competent in a subject field, or fields, as well as librarianship. In these and other ways, college and university librarians have moved steadily forward, ever since the late 1800's, toward direct participation in teaching, research, and counseling. In doing so they have sharply differentiated the clerical aspects of library operation from the nonclerical.

In all the work of our libraries, those librarians not often in contact with the public, who are busy selecting and organizing materials from all over the world and in a great variety of languages and subjects, are basic. Without their work, some of which is the most fundamentally intellectual of all the activities of librarians, the library would be a jumbled chaos instead of a smoothly functioning teaching and research agency. On these basic workers, too frequently unrecognized and unsung, rests everything that the library is and does.

Chicago, and diverse other points gathered in Philadelphia to found the American Library Association. Though few in numbers they built well and permanently. The Association they established now marches forward some 31,000 strong in membership and gathers itself into annual conferences with attendances of 5,000 and more.

There has indeed been a mighty flowering of the first organizational efforts of librarians. A marked American characteristic is the extent to which those of us concerned with similar activities and problems band ourselves together in formal organizations and go traipsing off to conventions hither and yon to speechify at each other, to listen, and frequently to come home with new inspiration and new ideas.

Whether or not librarians outdo the other professions in so coming together I do not know. I do know for a certainty that they will form a new organization at the drop of a hat. Thus it is that our parent American Library Association has proliferated into eight divisions, some of which are full-fledged associations in their own rights, with headquarters, paid secretaries, and all the other trappings and machinery of a strong association. And thus it is too that we have numerous other library associations reflecting the increasing specialization of our complex and complicated civilization.

Affiliated with the American Library Association but entirely independent in organization and usually convening separately, we have the American Association of Law Libraries, the American Merchant Marine Libraries Association, the Association of Research Libraries, the Music Li-

Librarians in Convention

Librarians organize themselves no less than books.

It is a hundred years now, and a decade more, since persons in this fair country of ours concerned with the assembling and organizing of books into libraries first undertook to bring themselves together into convention for a mutual discussion and a better understanding and handling of their problems. Eighty-

two persons from a dozen different states showed up for that first meeting held in New York City. The times were not quite ripe, however, for permanent and regular meetings of this kind, so almost a quarter of a century went by before another call went out for the librarians to gather in conference.

It was not until 1876 that men from Harvard, Yale, and Amherst, from Boston, New York, brary Association, the National Association of State Libraries, the Special Libraries Association, and the Theatre Library Association. In addition to these affiliated associations, we have eleven entirely independent associations and societies either concerned with libraries or with matters closely touching libraries. We also have numerous state , and regional library associations of which the Pacific Northwest Library Association is one proud example. The active and progressive librarian must perforce carry membership in a number of these associations.

While critics of the American scene might well lift their eyebrows over our numerous associations and their vigorous threshing of old straw to yield an occasional and solid new kernel, there can be no question that the organized and cooperative effort of librarians, stemming from their organizations, has been a tremendous factor in bringing American libraries to

what is universally recognized as high levels of excellence. Standardization and streamlining of cataloging and indexing procedures, including centralized printing of catalog cards, establishing union catalogs and bibliographical centers; coordination of the importing of research materials from abroad; library service to rural areas; promoting functional rather than ornamental library buildings; making surveys of libraries nationally as well as individually; establishing and improving professional education for librarians; drawing large sums of money, notably the Carnegie millions, and more recently Ford Foundation money, into support of library growth and improvement; these and many other things have been carried forward by the unified efforts of the associations. No university library can reach maximum effectiveness if it does not take an active part in these organized and cooperative efforts for better libraries and library service.

Professor of Library Science

The written record may become so massive that all intellectual workers may become librarians.

SOME YEARS AGO, in a paper dealing with cooperation among libraries and librarians I made the facetious statement that, at the present phenomenal growth of the writings of mankind and of the libraries into which they have been and are being accumulated we might well, in

three or four thousand years, reach a stage where the literature would be so massive that everybody would be busy taking care of it and no one would have time to produce it or read it.

This observation was based on library growth prospects which, at the growth rates of 1950 (and they are much higher now), would give the Library of Congress 323,000,000 volumes by the year 3000 and Harvard University 170,000,000 volumes. To

house these millions upon millions of books these two great libraries would, in the year 3000, I estimated, require 8,750 and 4,600 linear miles of shelving, respectively. I quoted Keyes Metcalf, now Director of Libraries Emeritus at Harvard, who, more than most librarians, had had to struggle for space for our burgeoning libraries and who had recently written as follows about the library situation in the larger educational institutions:

The gravity of the situation in many universities can be described bluntly: If libraries continue to grow as in the past, and if we have a reasonably stable economy and income, one or more professors will have to be dropped each year in order to keep the library going.

If Mr. Metcalf was right, and his is certainly both a respected and experienced voice in library and educational circles generally, then, I reasoned, each professor dropped in order to keep the library abreast of things, would mean one less producer of journal articles and monographs. On this basis, I thought, a predictive law or formula could be devised which would show, on a definite mathematical basis, more and more librarians, bibliographers, and indexers in proportion to professors until finally, in the dim and distant future the situation would come into a balance where all intellectual workers would be librarians and none would be teachers. We would then be at the long-predicted stage of complete suffocation with multitudes of people so busy taking care of the literature that no one would have the time to add new writings to it.

Some years after the above prediction, I read an article which made me believe that we cannot, under my proposed formula, get rid of the professors after all, at least not all of them. I was thinking only, in my paper, in terms of people concerned with the acquisition of written materials and their organization for use, and not at all about persons who teach users how to thread their way through the endless miles of the bibliographical labyrinth to items of momentary importance. Sixty years ago, while many persons were, in various ways, teaching the use of the literature of their subject fields, the professor of library science, as such, did not exist. But he exists now and in considerable quantity. This was made clear in a 1956 article in *School and Society*, in which the National Education Association presented its first effort to determine the number of full-time teachers in our colleges and universities. Of the 150,000 teachers listed in the N.E.A. statistics, 3,150 or 2.1 percent were engaged in teaching library science. It was not this figure by itself which impressed me so much as its relation to teachers of other subjects.

The 3,150 people teaching full time about libraries and how to use them, of whom perhaps less than one-third were in the professional library schools, were one-half as numerous as the 6,000 teachers of mathematics. There were more than twice as many of them as the 1,350 teachers of nursing, three times more than the 900 teachers of journalism, many more than the 2,100 teachers of philosophy or the 2,100 teachers of religion, four times more than the 750 teachers of chemical engineering, almost as many as the 3,750 instructors in economics, more than one-half as many as the 5,100 teachers of history, and many more than the 2,250 instructors in botany.

This is indeed quite an up-

surge in a species of professor which did not even exist sixty years ago. It lends further substance to the validity of a predictive formula such as I have suggested. It helps also to explain the increasingly acute shortage of professional librarians. While we will never, hopefully, permit ourselves to reach the absurdity of suffocation in our writings as long as Man continues to justify the name of Homo Sapiens, one

thing does, seriously, seem solidly and inescapably clear: The further we go along present lines, the greater will be the numbers of people, both quantitatively and proportionally, who will be required to accumulate and organize our writings and to help people find their way among the millions of books and the thousands of miles of shelving to the exact shelf, book, passage, or fact desired.

The Citadel of Reality

JAN STRUTHERS, the well-known author of "Mrs. Miniver," in a book of essays entitled *A Pocketful of Pebbles*, published in 1946, has this to say about librarians:

"It becomes clear that the Librarian, far from being remote from reality, is living at the very headquarters of it. He is the guardian of its citadel."

Miss Struthers was writing about the common concept of the librarian as a:

"quiet, helpful member of society, not very heroic, probably more than a little short-sighted, living in a dim, pleasant world that smelt faintly of dust and printer's ink and old leather, a world that seemed to us far removed from what we used to call the realities of life."

WRITING under the compulsions and the unpleasant realities of a world recently at cataclysmic war Miss Struthers said that it had been learned in a painful and difficult school that the supposedly solid realities of material goods and possessions had ironically become the most unreal of all. The only lasting reality, she said, is the world of thought as accumulated through the ages in books. Librarians as custodians of this world, she said, have a proud enough responsibility in ordinary times. Under the war-

time stress and danger which all who lived in the 1940's endured, and under the assaults on the citadel of reason and of fact, and the frenzied burning of books, as pressed and promoted by the Nazis and the Fascists, the responsibilities of librarians, as guardians of the citadel had become, wrote Miss Struthers, nothing short of stupendous.

Librarians are indeed living and working at the headquarters of reality in ways which Miss Struthers perhaps did not fully envision. More than in any other profession they are in a position to view, if not always to understand, the whole canvas and fabric of Man's time on this globe as a thinking creature recording his thoughts and acts and deeds, good and bad, in the wealth and profusion which constitute the libraries of the world.

Because libraries do, in their combined holdings, encompass nearly the whole of the written record of Man, not everything they contain is pleasant or noble. Rape, murder, pillage, theft, duplicity, deceit, lust, selfishness, greed—these and kindred things are all part of the human story, tier upon tier in the libraries, along, happily, with the sturdy virtues of honesty, truth, loyalty, self sacrifice, devotion to duty, and the offering up of life itself for friend or family or country. Fortunately these pleasanter things predominate in the libraries along with religious and ethical concepts so noble as to be God-like, and genius, vision, ingenuity, and a capacity to perceive and fathom out the secrets of nature so keen and understanding as to seem God-given.

Of all those who work in libraries, it is the catalogers who are in the best position to sense and be aware of the widely ramifying nature, from one extreme to the other, of the writings that come trooping in. This is so because it is they who must work intimately with every incoming book, inspecting it enough to know at least what it is about, assigning classification numbers and subject headings, and doing all the other things required before each book can take its place on the shelves. No one of perception can do this work without being aware of the tremendous range and versatility

of the human record. Graphic evidence of this range is the printed list of subject headings of the Library of Congress, running over 1,300 pages, which nearly all American libraries use in assigning subject headings to catalog cards. This fascinating book, to which I devote an essay elsewhere in this volume, would without question be a first choice for inclusion in a capsule to be shot to our planetary neighbors to show what kind of people the earthlings are. In hurling such intelligence into space there would be much to be proud of and a lot to be ashamed of too.

No one would claim, of course, that librarians understand or are capable of understanding every book they add to their collections. Nevertheless, they must know enough about them to know what they are about. They must have some kind of concept about what 'Angular Momentum (Nuclear Physics)" is before they can apply this subject heading to a book, or before they can devise it for application for the first time. They must brush the field of leprosy as they catalog a book dealing with it. Or the field of prostitution. They see a different facet of reality and history as they add a book requiring

the subject heading "Oil (in religion, folk-lore, etc.)" and make a cross reference for the searcher to see also "Extreme Unction." They may dwell pleasantly on a book dealing with "Love" as they provide see-also references to "Friendship" and "Courtship." They meet stark and unpleasant reality when they catalog a book such as Kraft-Ebbing's *Psychopathia Sexualis* and apply to it the subject heading of "Sexual Perversion" accompanied by such see-also references as "Exhibitionism," "Homosexuality," "Lesbianism," and "Nymphomania."

As they go about the never-ending task of creating and adding new subject headings for completely new knowledge or eliminating headings which have become obsolete or adapting and fitting old terminology to the new, librarians are kept continuously aware of the ever-expanding and changing fabric which constitutes the human record as set down in writing. Properly understood, worked at, and appreciated it is fascinating business, this profession of librarianship, even for administrators who are not among and with the books as much as most— well, at least *many*—of them would like.

On Lying Awake Nights

The aggressive librarian continuously pleads for more money.

ONE OF THE GREAT librarians of our time, active throughout the entire first half of this century, is Louis R. Wilson of the University of North Carolina. It was the good fortune, not only of North Carolina but of the library profession that when, in 1901, the librarianship at North Carolina was vacant for the fourth time in thirty months that the position was entrusted to this young student of English literature and member of the faculty of the German department.

While Wilson had no thought at the time that this would be a permanent position, he undertook his new duties with characteristic vigor. He carefully studied the then limited literature of librarianship with thoroughness and insight. He rapidly developed principles and policies which set the University of North Carolina on the path to developing one of the great university libraries not only of the south but of the nation. Only four months after he assumed the librarianship he placed a report before President Francis P. Venable emphasizing the importance of the library to teaching and research and urging the development of an adequate policy for its growth and development. He also made it clear that a permanent staff was essential and that the library could not be operated satisfactorily if librarianship was

to be handed around loosely among the faculty and at a small salary.

Wilson was quick to sense and understand that there is a common bond of problems and needs in all librarianship and that no library can live by and for itself alone. This brought him early into the work of the library associations both at the state and national levels, and quite as much in the interests of public library service as university librarianship. This wide range of interest and understanding was reflected in his effective work in establishing a state-wide library extension service in North Carolina.

It is not surprising that this man of vision, vigor, and dedicated belief in the importance of libraries should be drawn to a larger stage, that he should become one of the keenest and most articulate students of library problems and one of the most prolific writers in the profession, that he should be elected to the presidency of the American Library Association, and that the University of Chicago should seek him out in 1932 to direct its new Graduate Library School. It is understandable too that even in retirement, educational institution after institution has commissioned him to survey its library and make recommendations for improvement. His is a secure and an honored place among the statesmen of American librarianship.

From the beginning, Wilson

lost no opportunity to promote the welfare and development of the University of North Carolina Library. Maurice Tauber, of the School of Library Service of Columbia University, who has been closely associated with Wilson as co-author of *The University Library* and who has participated with him in numerous library surveys, narrates the following typical and illustrative incident in an article on Wilson on which this essay leans heavily.

In 1906 President Venable informed Wilson that he was going to pay the salary of both the librarian and assistant librarian from the income from a $55,000 endowment which had been raised as a condition for securing a Carnegie library building. Wilson went immediately to see the president and told him firmly, "You just can't do this." The president was equally firm and said, "Oh yes I can and I intend to do it!" Wilson then pointed out that the condition of the gift, signed both by himself and the president, provided that all income from the endowment must be spent for books with the university obligated to carry all administrative costs. President Venable was unhappy about this unescapable condition to which his librarian had been careful to bind him in the interests of protecting the book fund. When young Wilson was leaving, Venable said, perhaps partly in irritation and partly in admiration, "I believe you lie awake nights thinking of ways in which you can ask me for additional funds for the library."

There was truth in this observation. No library has yet grown great without expenditures of large sums of money. At more than one institution, people have been and are literally lying awake nights pondering where and how to find library money. Where this concern and drive and searching and asking has been sustained, as at North Carolina, a richness and strength and depth has been achieved which has infused the whole university program with vitality and effectiveness.

In many places, the continuing quest for library money has undoubtedly often caused administrative embarrassment and even irritation. It has, nevertheless, been a legitimate and inescapable quest inexorably conditioned by the extent and nature of the modern intellectual enterprise. Quite certainly, those institutions where the quest for library money has been sustained, unremitting, and successful have thereby been enabled to grow strong in many areas other than the library. Conversely, where there is no effective concern for the library and its welfare, there can be no great institutional vitality and strength.

Prestige and the Egghead

Wholesale wallops of death.

ONE THING that the American professor traveling in Europe is quick to note is the prestige, much greater than anything in this country, that people in academic circles enjoy. At first blush this seems somewhat strange. Lineal lines of descent for most Americans go back, sooner or later, to Europe. While I have read no learned disquisitions on this subject, I suspect that the lowly estate, comparatively, of the scholar and academician in our country may be due to the fact that Europeans flocking to this continent over the centuries had to be practical, doing men and women. No time for a book or for professorial counseling or theorizing in shooting a bear, repelling an Indian attack, getting an immigrant wagon up or down a mountain. So the developing and the plundering of a continent, the consuming of its forests, the exploiting and wasting of its rich soils, the building of its railroads and its cities was carried on, amidst the mingling of the blood streams, by impatient and busy people who had little time for the scholarly pursuits and the "book learning" of their time.

Nevertheless, the European tradition was there, although submerged; so the schoolhouse, the university, and even in a small way the library accompanied the pioneer as he conquered a new continent and took generously of its goods. The learned arts were respected and deemed essential and some of the new territories had universities, on paper at least, before they were states. However, the practical man, the man who could get a tree down the fastest or split the most rails or meet and foil the Indians at their own cunning or get a log house up quickly, was the man who counted. To a nation steeped in this tradition, it was a new experience, in the great depression of the thirties, to turn in considerable number to men in the colleges and universities for aid and counsel in controlling this economic upheaval. "Braintrusters," these intellectuals were derisively called. But all the while it was becoming increasingly evident that the world and civilization was becoming so complex and the products of the research laboratories and the libraries so fraught with both great good and terrible evil that, more and more, sustained scholarly application and study was essential for survival.

As more of the intellectuals came into government and public affairs, and as one of them with a singular gift for fluent expression and penetrating observation ran for President, came another term for the bookish people, *"egghead,"* disparagingly applied to the intellectual, the highbrow, the impractical idealist. But it has been precisely the intellectuals, the highbrows, the dreamers, who have achieved the atomic bomb, the hydrogen bomb, and who have sent new moons whizzing overhead. Once our frightened nation fully realized that even its survival might depend on its "eggheads" and the products of the laboratories and the writings in the libraries, prestige, recognition, and tardily in their wake, even financial emoluments, began coming to the eggheads. As always it was the perceptive poet who put these things neatly into words. as in "Mr. Attila" on next page.

On the Scarcity of Librarians

Rough on the administrator,
rough on the budget maker,
rough on the library staff.

IN 1962 it was my privilege to attend, in Miami, Florida, the annual conference of the American Library Association. As always I returned from this convention with increased awareness of the myriad problems facing the librarians of these mid-century years. One thing that came home to me with increasing impact, and I was pretty well shellshocked already, was the growing scarcity of librarians and particularly those carrying out what many feel, erroneously I have always thought, are the less glamorous features of librarianship, the classifying and cataloging of an abundant literature.

The birthing of the books goes on inexorably in quantity, in depth, in many strange and exotic breeds, and with a fecundity that this planet Earth has never before seen. It follows inevitably that the multifaceted gestative bibliographical processes are requiring more and more hands and ever larger buildings. All over the world these buildings are rising. And as they rise, the scramble and search for competent people to man them has grown more and more feverish, more and more competitive.

My mode of travel to the Miami conference, far beyond the wildest dreams of a Nebraska farm boy I once knew, was itself symptomatic of the times. As I hurtled through the skies at 600 miles per hour at an altitude of 35,000 feet, with the temperature outside the cabin wall 45 degrees below zero, as I could see perhaps hundreds of miles of the curving coast of Florida, it was not difficult to get an inkling of how Earth must look to the astronauts.

Nor was it difficult to achieve a mental readiness for machines and miracles for controlling the literature of the world approaching if not equaling Man's conquest of space. So far, however, books, in part because of their very multitudes, have stood fractiously and stubbornly against the mechanical and electronic processes, refusing mass submission, whether by computer or other gadgetry. It follows then that the need for more library hands increases in proportion greater than the book increase.

Here are some of the statistics, mostly guesses really, which have been bandied about. In 1959 somebody produced a figure of 10,000 library positions unfilled, with only 2,000 new hands appearing annually to fill them. One assumption was that 30,000 special librarians alone (mostly in industry) would be needed by 1970. By 1980 this figure was expected to swell to around 60,000. This was aside from the rapidly expanding need for college, university, high school, and public librarians. Perhaps no one has dared guess how many of them would be needed. Certainly great numbers, because it was also estimated that, as compared with 10 billions of dollars in 1962, four percent of the gross national product or about 28 billion dollars would be spent on research and development in 1969. At this same rate these expenditures would reach 40 billion by 1980. This, of course, would inevitably mean more reports, more articles, more books, and more, ever more librarians required to manage it all. Perhaps the facetious predictive formula in an essay above about all intellectual workers eventually being librarians is not so facetious after all.

Whatever the accuracy of the above projections, and whatever the possible future success of machine controls, the scarcity of librarians is obviously here and now. At the Miami Conference, a large curtained area of the Eden Roc Hotel was devoted to posting of notices, both by persons seeking positions and by librarians with positions to fill. Perhaps fifty or so librarians were offering themselves, thousands were being sought. Three sides of the room were filled with hopeful notices of positions open. These were a thing to behold and to contemplate. Climate, cultural advantages, glowing descriptions of work waiting doing, promotion opportunities, retirement benefits, salaries in alluring brackets for the most limited experience, and on up—these were being dangled before eligible librarians in great and varied array.

Come to our library, these notices said, sometimes with artistic adornment including, by the

imaginative librarians of the State of Washington, the Space Needle. "No barriers to creativity —horizons unlimited" said one notice. As I wandered about somewhat disconsolately reading these notices and shedding by the moment a comfortable illusion that we at Oregon State University had an excellent competitive salary structure, I saw one administrator busily taking down his placards. When I congratulated him on having filled his positions he said, "Oh no, I am only putting up notices that are more enticing!"

This is the way things were on the personnel front in the library profession in 1962 and the way they still largely are. Rough on the administrator, rough on the budget makers, rough on established library staffs and librarians spread too thin, rough on service too, without question but nice, very nice, at least financially, for the young librarians who have themselves to sell. For the young people of this generation the world is their oyster, in many directions. Many could do worse than heading for the library profession.

On Bibliothecal Reporting

Telling it in ways that make things better.

IN MY MORE than forty years in university librarianship, required reading for me has been the reports of other university and college librarians. Some seventy of these have reached me regularly in later years, arriving from universities and colleges of varied sizes and kinds, scattered throughout the United States and Canada, and since a European trip of 1957, including also a few from the Scandinavian countries.

Much of my education about libraries and librarians, other than that gained directly in the eight libraries with which I have been associated, has come from scanning, and more often reading in detail, these annual or biennial accountings of library doings and problems elsewhere. As is to be expected, these reports vary widely in treatment,

in spirit, and in format too, but whatever the approach they make it clear that the business of accumulating substantial portions of Man's recorded knowledge and organizing it for easy use by scholars is complex, costly, and fraught with many problems, both for the reporting library and for the institution whose cultural lifeblood it nourishes.

There are in the reports of university librarians everywhere, it seems to me in retrospect, two universal themes of not enough and too much. The not enough predominates. Not enough staff, space, books, even in some instances not enough use, all in varying ways arriving at the same common denominator, not enough money. I have yet to read a report from any library where enough of any of the above has been admitted or where the librarian has been content with what he has. "The

Eternally Covetous Librarian," one of the essays above, dwells on this theme.

The too much in library reports, sometimes only implicit, is inextricably interwined with the not enough. It is in fact a part of it. Too many books owned or recently acquired to be properly housed in existing space, too many students for the library seating space available, too many faculty members to be serviced by existing staff, too many good books being published or long since published, which cannot be acquired with available funds. More, more, more, and the need for ever more, in continuing refrain, and muted but inescapable, too much, too much; these Siamese twins are found in the reports of librarians from everywhere.

It seems clear to me that the too much will have to assume a more and more prominent part in the reports of librarians as the busy and inventive mind of Man produces more and more graphic tracks worthy of preservation. I have worked out no statistics, but whatever the applications of the Malthusian law to the human birthrate it can be quadrupled and quadrupled again as applied to books. There is indeed a tremendous cultural ferment and fecundity in these times. From it stems an equivalent bibliotecal ferment evident in the literature of all librarianship and significantly so in that important segment of it—the reports university librarians make to their governing authorities.

There was a time, within my experience, when the cries and pleas of librarians of not enough vanished, or at least were held in the background, unuttered, while a grim struggle to hold

together what had been achieved went on. A disciplining part of my professional education and experience was the necessity, during the deep depression years, of making do with less, very much less sustenance than the library I then managed had formerly had. During that period, I wrote two annual reports, while there loomed in the background as I wrote a very real and articulately voiced possibility that the university I then served would be closed entirely. Perhaps the ominous shadow was not real, after all, but it seemed real, very real, to all who were threatened by it. How happily times have changed is shown by the fact that that university not long ago dedicated a new million dollar library building, the gift of a generous alumnus. Such a possibility in the early 1930's seemed, and was, as remote as Mars.

Now, in the good years of affluence, the reporting of library affairs has everywhere grown more confident, more optimistic, and more demanding. Rare is the accounting which is not concerned with the problem of space. Occupancy of new buildings or bold plans for new ones (often with full confidence that they will be met), must be

met, are now found in all or nearly all academic library reports. The extent to which space needs are in fact being met, is shown by the erection of 283 new academic library buildings in this country in the 1956-1960 years alone. There has not been a library with which I have exchanged reports in recent years which has not either created new and modern library space or else has had ambitious plans for such space. None of these are long term solutions, however. The modern academic library just simply does not stay adequately housed, as experience everywhere inescapably shows.

One pleasant thing about library reports is that more and more they are interestingly and provocatively written. Some few are not much more than the uninspired bare bones of statistics. Others, in increasing numbers, dress these bones with living flesh infused with rich blood, and yes, spirit and soul too. Reports of this kind, and I have come to know from what libraries to expect them, I have always looked forward to. They have brought me encouragement, greater understanding and awareness, envy sometimes, and always increased pride in the profession of librarianship.

The Virtues That Characterize

Librarians must be responsive.

IN HIS ANNUAL report for 1957-58 Dr. Paul Buck, Director of Libraries at Harvard University said, "If the virtues that should characterize a library could be suggested by a single word it would be *responsiveness.*" I have pondered a good deal about this perceptive statement. I have tried to find some other single word which might be even better applied to the good library. This I have not been able to do. So I accept this word, *responsiveness,* with all its implications. I recommend it to all academic librarians.

What are some of the implications of being responsive either as an individual or an institution? Certainly a library, to be responsive, must first and foremost be *aware.* I have given some thought to "awareness" as the best single word to epitomize a good library, but it is possible to be aware without doing something about it. So another implication needs to be added, *intelligence.* But one can know what needs doing and understand both problems and consequences of

action and still do nothing. So still other factors are needed if responsiveness is to be complete. *Industry, application, dedication,* and *a will to serve,* these must all be found among those who work in a library if it is to respond fully to needs and opportunities. But even these are not enough.

A tradition of responsiveness, something to live up to, is helpful. Where this tradition has been created, over the years, by those who have gone before, the library is always currently found to be more responsive, and therefore better, than it would otherwise have been. Still another ingredient less tangible, but vitally essential nevertheless, is needed for effective responsiveness. This is *vision,* an understanding not only of what the library is and does today but what it may be and should be on the immediate tomorrows and in the years ahead. To all of these add spirit and courage and a modicum or more of aggressiveness. The library in which all of these things —awareness, intelligence, industry, application, dedication, a fine tradition, vision, and enough courage—are present, cannot escape being responsive. There are, of course, the material things, such as money and buildings. For the truly responsive library these things, as well as a wealth of books, will in one way or another within institutional limitations, come into being. They may come harder at some places than others, but they will come.

The Chinese have a proverb which says, "One kind word will keep you warm for three winters." This folk saying, carrying a fundamental verity as sayings born of the people always do, is one which particularly appeals to librarians and particularly to those who make their libraries responsive. This is so because the true librarian is a person who, rather curiously, enjoys helping others more than he does seeking to achieve, primarily and directly, himself. Not that librarians do not make direct contributions to scholarship and culture. They do, and often. The librarian nevertheless is happiest when either his services or the resources which he has carefully selected and organized are found to be of immediate and certain value to the individual user, be he citizen, student, or faculty member, or when the community or institution he serves clearly profits in its corporate capacity from what he has done or is doing.

Particularly when the busy people who use libraries pause for a moment to leave a kind word or a pleasant and appreciative smile, or all of these, do the intangible and warming rewards of librarianship come to the fore and make this work in the service of others deeply satisfying. And the users of responsive libraries, busy as they are, do so pause, quite frequently, to express appreciation for assistance received. Evidences of this are the statements often found in the forewords which authors use to launch their books and where they bow to those who have helped to make the neatly assembled thoughts and facts which follow more easily arrived at and also comprehensive and accurate.

In the Same Hut on Parnassus

"I have discovered that folly and wisdom occupy the same hut on Parnassus and that wisdom is not always at home."

EDWIN ARLINGTON ROBINSON to KERMIT ROOSEVELT, 1908

LIKE THE HUTS on Parnassus, libraries contain much that is folly, or a record of folly. This they must do because they reflect the minds and record the doings of men—and men have capacities that range from the wisdom of the sublime to the folly of the ridiculous.

From noble wisdom to utmost folly, from selfless good to great and selfish evil, the entire range is found in the library. The human record is there, from the time of print and even before, as ferreted out by the probing minds and insatiable curiosity of Homo Sapiens, both in terms of wisdom and of folly. There are no delphic oracles though. The books which stand on library shelves are limited and conditioned by the mind, personality, backgrounds, aptitudes, and instincts of those who come to read and who undertake to search. Because of this they often give the answers the reader wants to find.

Nothing illustrates the diversity of the human mind better than the reactions of those who use the books in the libraries, particularly in areas involving the emotions. From this use, additional writings flow. Examples are readily found, more so than in other areas, in religious writings: the Christian Bible, for instance. Here is a book with a tremendous number of interpretations, many arrived at with great zeal and conviction as the one and only final answer and interpretation. The words in the Bible are the same for all, but what a multitude of sects and churches and beliefs derive from them, nearly all well intentioned and sincere! There are also some atheistically inclined persons for whom the Bible is a set of beliefs and principles to be dissected and exposed in still other books designed to prove that the whole thing is mistaken. Such persons are relatively few though, as compared to those who find in this Holy Writ revelation, often many degrees and sometimes poles apart, of complete and final truth for all people.

But the record of folly, in many directions, also dwells on the shelves of libraries. Prime examples are the numerous volumes dealing with Hitler. These, headed by Hitler's *Mein Kampf* itself, were chiefly being added to libraries some twenty years ago. Here in *Mein Kampf*, a book still much studied by the students of Oregon State University, is recorded, as most but not all of the Hitler books point out, the folly of that strange, demoniacal, and irresponsible man who made a shambles of a great and able nation and, almost, of a world. There is a lesson here for these taut and bickering times and the present epic struggle between two so different philosophies and ways of life. It remains for the libraries of the future, possibly the near future, to record whether it will be the wisdom or the folly of the present moment which will prevail on Parnassus.

On the Anointing of Hands

"He that sells oil anoints his own hands."

SPANISH PROVERB

So GOES an ancient saying quoted by Frederic Vinton of the Library of Congress more than three quarters of a century ago, in an article in *Bibliotheca Sacra* about rare books in the Library of Congress. As with all proverbs, there is a fundamental verity in this saying. No one can operate a library or help in its operation, from the lowliest student assistant or page to the most erudite subject specialist, without some of the commodity he handles rubbing off on him. This is why most people who make librarianship a career find it an eminently satisfying profession.

Librarians have to be, and usually are, people who find the oil of facts and knowledge, as set down in books and other media, exciting and interesting. It is a part of their dilemma that once ensnared in the selling of these oils, so plentiful, so voluminous, and so continually gushing from the fount of the human mind, most of them have little time to be concerned, in any deep sense, with the oil itself.

Instead they find themselves enmeshed in the mechanics and techniques of its acquisition and its utilization, with how to find and deliver the most refined, specialized, and even exotic and rare kinds. Nevertheless, even on this basis there is a considerable and sometimes a satisfying anointing of the hands. There is

a danger too, in all but the highly specialized libraries, because any librarian who becomes too enamored of and interested in any one special variety of oil may well neglect others equally valuable and equally required by his clients.

The librarian, and in this sense I mean all who are concerned with the assemblage and usage of the literature, is more aware than any other functionary of our society, of the productivity of the human mind, of both the depth and width of its range, and frequently also of its abnormalties and its shallowness. Those who are concerned with the machinery of keeping the totality of our writings findable and usable through the mechanisms of classification schemes and subject headings, or in more fancy modern terminology, descriptors, organizers, and links, must confront the whole tremendous range of knowledge and also keep somewhere within speaking distance of its rapid development.

It is significant that the whole of knowledge, once the happy hunting ground of the philosophers, has long since been abandoned by them. The librarian cannot, however, so abandon it if he is to have any kind of unified chart and compass for the seas of print he must sail. He must, at one and the same time,

in the great libraries and in the comprehensive classifications, or in the computerized systems, if they achieve feasability, be increasingly specialized. He must also be continuously concerned that the whole of his organization hangs together with some kind of logic, however empirical, and that it makes some kind of sense. This means that his hands must be considerably anointed, and that he must understand at least the broad outlines of the knowledge and the literature of the times as well as of the past. Could he also foresee the future, his problems would be simpler and his inconsistencies fewer.

The implications of this, and of the increasing specialization of our times, is that librarianship must become, in its higher aspects, an increasingly intellectual discipline. We see this happening in the growing numbers of subject specialists who are now found in our larger libraries. We are beginning to see it, ever so faintly, in the hazy gropings for computerization of knowledge. We see it too in the smaller specialized libraries, where the librarian must be well anointed in the literature he assembles and services.

The logic of this is that those librarians who interpret the literature under their control will increasingly have to know it in a substantive sense quite as much and perhaps, even better than those who teach or do research. Nor will it be only those who service the literature who will need to be so at home in it. Those who classify, catalog, index, or abstract will have to know it equally well and also to be aware of its relationships to the sum total of knowledge. This will be particularly true if, as is now increasingly believed, literature controls are to be mechanized.

I am among those who believe that the machine will never completely, and in a comprehensive sense, master the organization of the totality of our graphic records. If it does, classification, organization, coding, and programming for the machines will require a far sharper knowledge of the literature and its relationships to other fields and areas than we now have among librarians or any other scholars.

Librarians have always, from the earliest times, anointed their hands in the handling of their wares. The librarian of the future must not only be anointed by contact, he must fully understand and know his product, in the particular and in the mass, its constitution, its nature, and its interlocking relationships. This brings him full circle to the increasingly awesome field the philosophers no longer cultivate, the totality of knowledge.

About Librarians and Hogs

A library service that reached the heart.

IN THE DEEP depression years of the thirties, Mrs. Margaret Hooper, until recently a researcher for the Primate Center of the University of Oregon Medical School in Portland, was working for Portland Public Library as a Bookmobile librarian. One of her stops was at a suburban acreage where a family which had met both health and financial reverses, with the husband ill, had established itself. The wife had courageously undertaken the raising of hogs as a means of family livelihood. As millions of people were doing with particular urgency in those days, she turned to the public library for aid and information. From Mrs. Hooper she had received good help. When a new book on the care and feeding of swine was acquired by the library, Mrs. Hooper at once set it aside for her rural patron.

When the book was delivered, this suburban wife (to whom hogs were bread and butter and a means of holding her family together) impulsively threw her arms around Mrs. Hooper and exclaimed "I just love librarians and hogs!"

Where but in America could this have happened? And why America? Because here people of vision early realized that only as the people are intelligent and well informed, can a democracy flourish and grow strong. So public schools came into being aided and abetted by the people's university, the public library. The first free public libraries of more than a hundred years ago were but tiny rivulets. Meeting a real need, they slowly grew to streams in which flowed the invigorating waters of knowledge and inspiration. About the turn of the century there came on the scene a man who, like Mrs. Hooper's rural patron, had drunk deeply of the waters of

knowledge in a library, and who had thereby grown in competence, in personality, and in wealth. This man, Andrew Carnegie, expressed his gratitude, as is widely known, by founding public libraries in his adopted land. Wisely he required matching funds and assurances of future support from each community to which he presented a library building. This opportunity was eagerly grasped in numerous places.

The result of the Carnegie benefactions was the establishment of more than 2,500 of the now familiar Carnegie library buildings. For them gifts of over $40,000,000 were made to communities throughout the length and breadth of the land. The consequent upsurge of interest and library development, in communities not receiving grants as well as those which did, increased the streams of free public knowledge to rivers and constituted the most rapid progress in adult education in the history of the world up to that time. Surely Carnegie, the poor and humble immigrant boy, was the good servant who invested his talents wisely and well. Surely too America is today stronger and better because of his numerous gifts. But even yet, all who would may not drink because many citizens of the nation are reached by neither rivulet nor river.

It was in 1956 that Congress, after some decades of effort and promotion by librarians and others enacted the now well known Library Services Act. Those of us who live in Oregon will always be proud that it was Representative Edith Green of Portland who introduced the Library Services Act in the House and who was foremost in promoting its passage. Now greatly expanded and liberalized, this enlightened legislation is helping to create the enlightened citizenry that every democracy needs.

A heartening feature of the enactment of the original Library Services Act was that it had the vigorous support of the young men of the nation to whom the future belongs. With sure instinct the Junior Chamber of Commerce adopted, as a national program, "Operation Library" in support of this Act. In Oregon the J. C.'s likewise made "Operation Library" a statewide project. From them the Board of Trustees of the State Library, which has statutory responsibility for promoting the development of libraries in Oregon and which is the responsible agency under the Library Services Act, received yeoman aid. With their help and matching state and federal funds Oregon could and did embark on a new period of library development rich in promise. Quickly, when the opportunity offered, it took the steps required to create more widely the environment and services which made possible that impulsive exclamation of depression days, in which was the very savor of the salt of good public librarianship, "I love librarians and hogs!"

world, the shape of things to come lies in the demands and partial success of the New York electricians.

For the scholar and intellectual of our times and of the future, the work and effort prospect is diametrically opposite. It is rather curious that the same

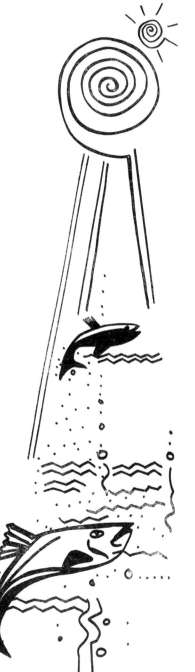

About Work and Weeks

More and more work hours per week—this is the prospect for intellectual workers.

RECENTLY we have been startled, some of us at least, by the proposal of a twenty-hour work week for electricians in the New York City area. Such an abbreviated week is nevertheless no wild dream. It but continues a well established trend which has come to full flow during this technologically oriented century. Sixty, 54, 48, 44, 40, 38, 36 hours, this has been the downward progression of the working week with the average now probably in the 38-to-40 hour range. Without question, what with the specter of automation hovering over many of the workers of the technological and scientific discoveries which make automation loom rather frighteningly for many classes of workers have simultaneously created a situation requiring more and more working hours of the scholar, the researcher, the scientist. Not that such people are, or ever have been, work-week conscious. Had they been, down through the ages, we would not now have serious problems flowing from automation or any other kind of scientific and technological progress.

For the scholar or researcher seized by an idea or a theory or a vision or the writing of a book and driving toward the goal, the only problem about time has been that there has never been enough of it. From time immemorial people so possessed have labored and experimented, read and written, early and late, often, in the more extreme cases, without thought of personal health or family welfare. We are increasingly reaping the resulting harvest, a harvest so bountiful, so fruitful that a twenty-hour work week for the technicians of the world begins to make some kind of sense. But not, definitely not for the scholars, the researchers, the scientists who have made it all possible. For such prime movers, it is essential to be grounded in what has gone before. There is, for them, so much to be learned, so much to know, that they find their noses held hard to an eternal grindstone, spinning ever faster, a grindstone consisting of the whole

scholarly apparatus of research, reflection, theorizing, experimentation, reading, and writing.

A quantitative aspect of the grindstone that sharpens and tempers and conditions the intellect of the world is our "multi-millioned" libraries—upward of 15,000,000 volumes in the Library of Congress, well over 7,000,000 in the New York Public Library and at Harvard, 6,000,000 at the British Museum and the Bibliotheque Nationale, and 20,000,000 (a rather dubious figure) in the Lenin Library in Moscow. Lesser millions and hundreds of thousands are in libraries all around the globe. A barometer of the fantastic rate of increase is 241,000 volumes added at Harvard in 1963-1964, 152,000 at California at Berkeley, and 276,000 at the Library of Congress.

Evidence of prodigious production of scholarly writing lies in the serial literature, a gushing fountain-head of growth. A striking example is the United States Department of Agriculture Library which receives and indexes in its magnificent tool, the *Bibliography of Agriculture*, 22,000 different periodical titles for agriculture alone. Even so this bibliography includes only about 60 percent of the total published periodical articles in the field of agriculture. Statistics equally impressive can be cited for other subject areas.

The fiscal and space problems of keeping the massive literature of agriculture, as only one example, under only partial con-

trol is evident in the present operations and the short-term plans of the USDA Library. That library, in 1962, estimated the cost of one professional man-year at $17,500, including administration, secretarial and sub-professional assistance, and the purchase of books. For its bibliographical and indexing activities alone it used 19.5 professional man-years. It estimated that within five years it would need 64 man-years. In 1962 its translating services consumed four professional man-years. A five-year projection brought this to 37.

Significantly, a program for analysis and coding for machine controls not present at all in the 1962 program of the USDA Library, would, it was estimated, require 44 professional man-years within five years. Similarly, facsimile transmission, not used in the 1962 operation of this library, would, within another five years, require annually four professional man-years. By then, however, the cost of a professional man-year might well have advanced, it was thought, to $30,000.

These Department of Agriculture Library growth, staffing, and financing costs, actual and projected, are relevant to every subject field and to all libraries. They lend a modicum of credibility to a statement elsewhere in these essays that librarians, having often been adjudged meek, may yet inherit the earth. But not on any twenty-hour week basis.

Part III
ORGANIZATION:
THE ABSOLUTE ESSENTIAL

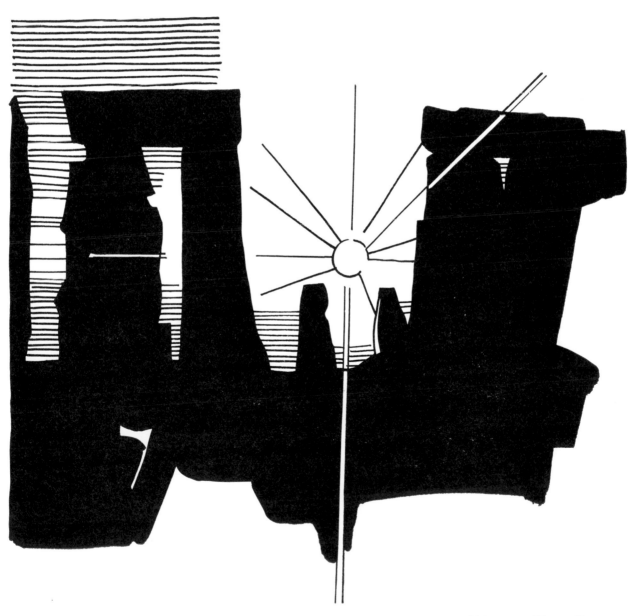

A basic and obvious fact is that Man, if he is to make effective use of his accumulated knowledge, must organize it in close detail. The fact is obvious, yes, but the solutions, the answers, the methodology, and the philosophy of satisfactory organizations have not been and are not easily reached. Far from it.

Libraries have struggled with the fundamentals of organization ever since books were brought together in quantity. Some have achieved satisfactory answers for their time and for their users, but no universally and generally acceptable plan of organization applicable over the years has ever been devised, nor, it can be predicted, will it ever be.

Efforts to range the physical books on a subject basis together in the stacks have been an abiding concern of librarians in many places and in many times. Notably in America, in the last hundred years, has there been varied, sustained and, on the whole, rather successful attack on these problems. In other places, chiefly in Europe where large libraries often grew over the centuries without any clear cut and sustained organizational plan, and under varied and changing administrative philosophies, subject organization of the physical books themselves became so varied, so complex that in some libraries books have been simply, in a kind of giving up, sent to the shelves merely in sequential order of acquisition. This is, of course, simplicity itself insofar as a place for the books to stand is concerned. The rub comes in that it places the entire organizational function on the catalogue or catalogues, which in themselves have often been the product of many minds, hands, personalities, and varied philosophies.

Nor do the newer prospects for some kind of electronic machine organization of knowledge offer any easy solutions. Under prospective machine controls, the problems of organization become more, rather than less, difficult, requiring a clearer definition of the nature of the library, who its users will be, and what the evolution of the collection or collections may be. There is only one certainty. This is that the materials to be organized are increasing rapidly and that they will continue to so increase.

The following essays are devoted to some facets of these knotty, complex, and difficult fundamentals of libraries and librarianship, so abidingly and inescapably present wherever Man's writings are brought together in any quantity.

Blondes, Brunettes, and Redheads

IT IS CHARACTERISTIC of our times that the organization of the totality of knowledge and the relationships of one group of phenomena and one branch of learning and thought to another and of all to the whole, which occupied the early philosophers extensively, is now left largely to librarians. Long before Plato and Aristotle, who thought about and discussed these matters, men no doubt pondered about observed phenomena and how these phenomena and what was known and believed about them were interrelated. Following the earliest philosophic concepts of knowledge, a long series of philosophers devoted themselves to plans and schemes for the organization of total knowledge.

The extent to which this problem occupied the minds of men is indicated by the following list of philosophers who thought and wrote in this field: Porphyry, 305 A. D.; Cassidorous, 550; Roger Bacon, 1266; Conrad Gesner, 1548; Francis Bacon, 1605; Descartes, 1644; Thomas Hobbs, 1650; John Locke, 1688; Immanuel Kant, 1781; Bentham, 1816; Coleridge, 1817; August Kant, 1822; Spencer, 1864; Alexander Bain, 1870; and more lately Karl Pearson. These philosophers acknowledged that classification of the sciences is a fundamental problem of philosophy, a necessary first step toward correlation and development of a positive philosophy of the sciences.

Classifiers, whether of books or of abstract knowledge, must recognize that the chemist, the physicist, the biologist, the theologian, or the poet, can all look at a flower or a waterfall or an atom (or books about them) and see very different things, although the basic phenomena of flower or of atom remain inexorably the same. Similarly, or more accurately, differently, the registrar might classify co-eds by intelligence quotients, while the man about the campus might classify them as blondes, brunettes, and redheads.

This may seem pretty remote from book classification, but it does illustrate that everything depends upon the point of view. This is why no classification of books (or of redheads) has yet been devised, or ever will be, that will satisfy more than its originator and quite likely he will not long find it adequate. This is why one man's classification scheme is another man's hodgepodge. And this is why, too, librarians spend a good deal of time explaining the use and application of their classification schemes to faculty members.

Book classification schemes can, although perhaps somewhat obscurely, trace lineal descent from the early philosophers, men like Roger Bacon, Conrad Gesner whose classification was bibliographical, Francis Bacon, and others. Melvil Dewey, whose "practical" classification is used by perhaps three-fourths of the libraries of America, professed however to have conceived his scheme in an intuitive flash when he was seated in an Amherst church "seeing" President Stearn deliver a long sermon. "The solution," he says, "flasht over me so that I jumpt in my seat and came very near shouting 'Eureka!' "

The Library of Congress classification scheme which has been adopted by many academic libraries, including, as of 1929, the Oregon State University Library, is an intricate and pragmatically developed framework for the organization of knowledge. It reflects, as does nothing else in our present world unless it be the list of subject-headings of the Library of Congress, both the diversity and complexity of the mental activities of Man, particularly during the last fifty years.

The intuitive flash of Melvil Dewey was not accompanied, unfortunately, by a clear vision of the extent to which science would proliferate and surge to a dominant position in the intellectual area. And so it is that Dewey's scheme, in spite of sixteen extensive revisions, has become an increasingly difficult straight-jacket for large libraries. Nor could the men at the Library of Congress who devised the L. C. Classification in the early 1900's foresee how the life sciences would merge and at the same time become, paradoxically, more minute, separate, and specialized, or that the mathematicians would devise amazingly accurate predictive formulae, and that physics, as a result, would move from the old "natural" philosophy to an exact science bringing us, in effect, to an entirely new age.

To contend with this largely unforseeable turn of intellectual progress, the devisers of any library classification scheme, bound by the basic framework they have adopted, must improvise, patch, expand, and correlate in the hope of maintaining coherence and some semblance of logic. It is the strength of the L. C. Classification that it *is* expandable. But the eager, inventive mind of Man is continuously and increasingly putting it to the test. In one way or another, this classification scheme of the world's largest library must adjust itself to new concepts, unexpected relationships, developments, and subject fields now undreamed of. *Must* is the right word, because with every new book absorbed under it this classification scheme fastens itself on the Library of Congress, and on the numerous research libraries which use it, more firmly, more inexorably. Pressed, as libraries are, to absorb the ever increasing significant literature of the world, the reclassification of the millions of books already present from whatever scheme presently used is formidable indeed. That is, unless the new electronic control systems can indeed, as some early machine enthusiasts implied, reclassify everything swiftly and painlessly. There have been many miracles during my lifetime but I, for one, do not expect to see anyone or anything, not even a machine, "rar' back" and pass this one.

On the Ordering of Knowledge

How to recognize a cataloger when you see one.

THE KEYSTONE but largely unsung workers of the library hierarchy are the catalogers. They are the people who stand between the acquisition librarians, busily operating their dragnets to draw into the library materials from all parts of the world, and the service librarians whose function it is to interpret and make easily available the totality of the library's holdings.

Of all the people who work in libraries, the catalogers and classifiers are the most clearly intra-library in their operations. They have no exciting contacts with librarians, authors, book dealers, and jobbers in the far places of the world. Very rarely do they see and participate in the satisfaction of the well-served library user, or conversely the disappointment and frustration when the library does not yield up the book or special bit of information required at the moment. It is their duty to reduce to order and system a vast miscellany of materials flowing into the library, on almost every conceivable subject, from all over the world, and in a great variety of languages. These materials, arriving in complete subject confusion, the carefully wrought ministration of the catalogers organize into easy findability. In nearly all American libraries, when books are released to the service departments, they are ready to take their places on the shelves in carefully designated sequence with previously acquired materials on the same subject. Hopefully, simultaneously with this release and in a planned coordination, cards fall into the catalogs to accurately describe and record these newest additions in all their subject ramifications.

Contrary to the opinion of many people, some librarians included, the things the catalogers do can be both exciting and satisfying. Catalogers sit at the fount, as it were, of the productivity of the human mind, reducing all to order and system. Working at the frontiers, they see and help to order the unfolding of knowledge. While materials come to them in quantity, they cannot be handled in quantity. Each book and each pamphlet must be considered and handled as a separate entity, and its content, regardless of language, sufficiently mastered to satisfactorily classify it both by numbers and verbally by subject headings, and to describe it so accurately that it becomes a unique bibliographical item which cannot be confused with the millions of other books of the world, thousands of which may deal with the same subject.

Fundamentally, cataloging is an intellectual process, sometimes, in matters of principles and policies, profoundly so. It is for this reason that persons of scholarly bent and orderly instincts make the best catalogers. It is for this reason too that many librarians who have shied away from the close application and meticulous detail of cataloging work find, to their considerable surprise, that once having taken the baptismal plunge, they like it.

Yes, of all the people who work in the library catalogers are the most basic. The efficiency and usefulness of the library rests on what they do in their daily work of absorbing new titles, of revising and fashioning the catalogs to keep them abreast of the times, and of eliminating outmoded subject terminology in favor of current usage. In a catalog department, poorly done work can often slip by unnoticed for long periods of time, but the effects are cumulative and the work of inefficient and careless catalogers, and of those who have not understood or been equipped for the fundamentally intellectual nature of the cataloging process frequently rises up to harass future generations of librarians and scholars. On the catalogers at all levels, clearly depends the ease or lack of it with which a library can make its resources available. Obvious yes. But recognized? Not often.

On Abstracting and Indexing

The work of scholars and scientists everywhere depends on the finding of controls.

ONE OF THE MOST difficult problems facing modern scholarship is the simple and efficient organization of the great mass of literature appearing in periodical form. While we have seen great progress in recent years in the preparation of a host of highly useful and indispensable periodical indexes and abstracts, in sumtotal indexing of this kind has been spotty and duplicative with some fields and periodicals covered several times, others not at all, and some with a serious time lag. The high cost of these tools too becomes an increasingly serious problem. Albert F. Blakeslee of *Biological Abstracts* has said that the greatest impediment to the advancement of science at present is the lack of effective means by which the finding of scientists, especially those of other nations, can be mobilized and put to work.

Librarians and scholars have been bestirring themselves to come to grips, far more effectively than has so far been done, with this gargantuan problem. In 1949 which is becoming ancient history almost in these fast moving bibliographical matters, an International Conference on Science Abstracting under the auspices of UNESCO was held in Paris. Preparatory to this meeting, a conference on science abstracting was held at the quarters of the National Research Council in Washington, D. C., under the auspices of the Council, the Research and Development Board, and the Department of State. Discussion at this conference, as recorded in the *Information Bulletin* of the Library of Congress, turned to specific proposals for the forthcoming conference. Said the *Bulletin:*

"It was the sense of the meeting that if a new international organization should be launched to effect coordinating measures in the field of science abstracting, it should also take cognizance of science indexing, since the two forms of bibliographic control are very closely allied.

It was also agreed that such an organization might well contemplate the extension of its coordinating function to fields other than the sciences, but that this should certainly be deferred until after success should be demonstrated in the more limited field. As to the establishment of such an organization, the meeting showed something less than enthusiasm.

It was admitted that the Coordinating Committee for Abstracting in the Medical and Biological Sciences had been launched under UNESCO's auspices out of a desire to reduce the amount of duplication in this field, but has not as yet succeeded in this objective.

It was also brought out that what U. S. abstracting services suffer from, specifically, is lack of money. Accordingly, the immediate desirability of a new international coordinating organization is in direct proportion to its prospective ability to command funds.

It was pointed out that, in spite of this gloomy outlook, there is great prospective gain to the scientific world through standardization of methods in abstracting and presentation . . .

One scientist spoke warmly to the theme that abstracting and indexing are parts of the overhead of scientific research which should no more be charged against individual scientists than are the costs of laboratories and libraries.

It was suggested that there are momentum and resources in the U. S. sufficient to solve the local abstracting problems on a national scale as a preliminary to attempts to solving it internationally.

On this note the Conference ended, resolved to meet again, perhaps in a more widely representative gathering, to attack the problem from a local point of view."

These were the problems in 1949. They are still the problems, largely unsolved, in 1966. Their solution, to the extent which they can be solved, will require much talk, argument, planning, and more than a few concessions by vested interests. The difficulties grow inexorably, by accretion, year after year, making the devising of satisfactory and not too expensive bibliographical controls increasingly urgent. In relation to the increase of materials, both in quantity and complexity, those seeking better controls are perhaps no more than running to stand still. Nevertheless, upon the finding of adequate controls depends the effectiveness of the work of scholars and scientists everywhere.

The Logistics of Scholarship

*The process
of reaching agreements
may in the end
be a step toward peace.*

MY THOUGHT, on reading the Library of Congress report quoted in the foregoing essay, was that while these controls are difficult internationally they are far from simple at the national or even the institutional level. One thing that is certain, I believe, and one which requires continued awareness by all scholars, is that what is done bibliographically at the Library of Congress, at universities and colleges large and small, in editorial offices of *Chemical Abstracts, Engineering Index, Biological Abstracts,* H. W. Wilson Co., and others, and on a larger scale by UNESCO, directly affects what the individual scholar can do.

It is perhaps an understatement to say that bibliographically the world has been and is in an era of "rugged individualism." The variety in scope, format, and plan of organization of the numerous attempts, successful and unsuccessful, to keep our writings manageable is about as wide as it conceivably could be. It remains to be seen whether librarians and scholars are pursuing a will-o'-the-wisp in their quest for greater completeness and uniformity, more simplicity, and less duplication in all matters bibliographical.

That the quest is not simple is indicated by the fact that even though planning efforts were pooled under UNESCO in 1947 and the work of bibliographical planners was speeded up and their enthusiasm increased the world over, progress was discouragingly slow. It amounted, chiefly, to nothing more than exploration, talk, and a fuller realization of the difficulties involved. We are still, in 1966, at the stage we were in 1940, when Fremont Rider, librarian of Wesleyan University and one of the most imaginative students of things bibliographical, said that every aspect of bibliographical work must be re-examined and reassessed, that the most careful investigation of bibliographical needs must be made, and that available methods and controls must be rationalized. In all likeli-

hood this will require new mechanisms and new approaches.

Matters are complicated by the unfortunate fact that many countries do not have a national bibliography, such as our United States Catalog of books and other numerous tools, so promptly and efficiently prepared and supplied to American and other libraries by the H. W. Wilson Co. In no other nation, I believe, are these important scholarly tools equaled.

Some of the knotty problems are, shall national listings be by author or subject or can we hope to have both, and how are archival materials and those newer adjuncts to the book, such as films, slides, and sound recordings to be listed? Also shall listings be complete or selective? Form, methods of cumulating, and arrangement are also matters in which scholarship would greatly benefit by uniformity. They are insistent and mounting, these problems. They will not wait forever for solution. On their solving rests scholarly progress throughout all the world.

One certain thing is that whatever the subject headings and classification schemes adopted are they will rapidly become obsolete. The handicap of atrophied subject headings must be anticipated, say the experienced commentators at the Library of Congress. If international agreement on these matters can be reached, capable of application on a uniform basis to the minutiae of bibliographical matters, scholarship will indeed have taken a long step forward. Possibly in the progress of reaching agreements on these things, the world may inch a little closer toward mutual interdependability, international understanding, and thereby toward peace.

More Than the Sum of Its Parts

A library, intelligently and systematically collected, represents not merely the titles gathered; it represents a useful synthesis, the having put together the books that belong together. This value of the library as a whole, in the estimation of some of us, far outweighs the value of the sum of the parts.

So, IN THE IMMEDIATE pre-World War II days, wrote Randolph Adams, Director of the William L. Clements Library of the University of Michigan, in a University of Pennsylvania Rosenbach Fellowship essay, *"Three Americanists."* All who have been associated with libraries, either in their building and administration or as users at the scholarly levels, will subscribe to this perceptive statement.

Which are the "books that belong together"? They are the books on zoology and botany, on chemistry, physics, mathematics, engineering, forestry, agriculture, on pharmacy, home economics, education, economics, business, and all the other subjects included in academic curricula and research programs. Through long years of thoughtful selection and purchase on the part of faculty members and library staff, books, in their many ramifications, have been brought together in the "useful synthesis" that constitutes a library.

Acquisition of books alone, however, does not make a library. Once acquired, they must be organized and grouped for ready findability and easy use. The degree to which this is done,

and it varies widely in different institutions, is, in the final analysis, the gauge or criterion of the value of a university or college library to its institution. The more logical and accurate the classification and cataloging, the fewer the barriers between the books and those who should and must use them, the better and

more complete the tool books and indexes assembled as guides to knowledge, the more valuable and useful the library.

To insure that a high degree of usefulness is achieved, a university library, in the modern sense, needs a staff possessed of knowledge and skills, of scholarly perception, and of judgment and tact equal to the best in the institution. A library staff of such quality, engaged in assembling and organizing the books pertinent to the work of their institution and interpreting and servicing them to faculty, researchers, and students, is a prime essential in bringing to a library that quality of responsiveness and usefulness which makes it considerably more than the sum of its parts, no matter how numerous and valuable these may be.

Old Things — New Names

A concise and simple naming of things is increasingly eschewed by a world growing ever more complex.

FROM THE TIME that men first wrote down ideas, facts, aspirations, or flights of fancy in enough quantity to make it essential to gather them together in some kind of grouping in order to preserve and effectively use them, these collections have obviously been recognized by everyone concerned, be he priest or potentate, teacher or student, as the place to go for knowledge and facts not within personal recall. As these collections grew,

and as the media on which the recording was done were standardized, as on baked clay tablets, papyrus, wood, skins or entrails of animals, or more recently on tremendous quantities of paper, the accumulators and keepers of the collections, as well as the users of them, had the ingenuity and wit to refer to them by a single precise and neatly fitting word.

In the Greek based culture "biblion," meaning an assemblage of books, as, for instance, in the Bible, came to the fore. In the Latin-derived vocabularies "liber," reflecting the media on which the writing was originally done, came to have universal application as applied to organized accumulations of knowledge. So in our western world we have the single word of library in the English and various applications of biblio, as bibliotheque in French, bibliotek in Scandinavian, and variants of the same word in other western languages. The accumulators, organizers, and keepers of book collections became known, naturally and succinctly, as librarians or bibliotekaries or some closely related derivative.

This eminently concise and simple naming of things, readily understandable by all, has become too simple for an increasingly complex world afflicted with what is, from my viewpoint, a considerable malaise of jargonese. For some of the accumulators and organizers of knowledge the ancient and honorable title of Librarian no longer suffices. They become instead Documentalists or even Data Engineers.

These differently named librarians, are, to be sure, apt to be pretty highly specialized functionaries concerned with information usually appearing in non-book form and less amenable to the controls established for codex books. More often than not the things they collect and administer are recorded in the typescript or near-print of company reports prepared in limited numbers. Maps, blueprints, charts, and similar difficult to organize materials are often found in abundance in these libraries. Whatever the nature of these specialized collections and the format of their holdings, those who collect and organize them perform exactly the same function as did the first librarian, that

is, to accumulate and organize knowledge so that it can be found and made available for use as needed.

The trend toward new and wordy names for old things is exemplified by the establishment in 1963, by the University of Pittsburgh of a "Knowledge Availability Systems Center." In describing this center, Mr. Allen Kent, its director, said:

The term 'knowledge availability systems' was chosen to characterize this field to represent an activity broader than 'information retrieval' and to indicate nothing less than the total problem of assuring availability of knowledge for desirable social purposes—whether current or in the future.

This is, of course, what librarians have been concerned with from the very beginning and what their objectives have been. Every library, small or great, is in accordance with its purposes and orientation, a knowledge-availability center.

What Pittsburgh will be doing in its ponderously named center is to seek new solutions, "both theoretical and empirical, idealistic and pragmatic" to the problems of coping with our too

abundant literature. The Center will be concerned with the criteria for systems design, comparative anatomy of systems, language manipulation, behavioral studies, hardware studies, media studies, and designs for substantive fields in specialized subject areas. A curriculum for teaching these things is also being developed.

These are exactly the same kinds of things libraries and librarians have always been concerned with, from classifying the first clay tablet or waxed board or parchment roll on up to the latest punched card or tape. The words are different and at first blush have an aura of newness about them, but they aim at the same basic and hardy old problems. Conceivably, and hopefully, solutions found by the Pittsburgh Center may be better and more easily and economically applied to our voluminous literature than are the present traditional methods. It is not a good omen though that so many words, those imprecise and variable arch enemies of the computer, are required to project what is intended.

From Aardvark to Zymase

Future civilizations may best learn what ours was like from a plow horse sort of book.

ONE OF THE most interesting books, in one sense, in our library and in practically all libraries, in America at least, is a large quarto volume entitled *Subject Headings Used in the Dictionary Catalogs of the Li-*

brary of Congress. This big book, now in its sixth edition, contains 1,357 pages and serves as a guide for the subject headings that go into the card catalogs of nearly all the major libraries in America and a goodly number elsewhere. It contains, outside of a five-page introduction, only a few connected sentences. Nevertheless, the numerous words and combinations of words it so carefully records are, I believe, more representative of our present culture and civilization than any other single book.

I personally nominate this volume as the book that could most logically be sealed into crypt, mausoleum, or steel capsule to inform future generations and civilizations what the western civilization of the twentieth century was like. I do this because this book lists, in alphabetical sequence with occasional chronological and other variations, all the myriad things and subjects about which books have been written. It is definitely a librarians' book, one of the increasingly numerous tool books essential to keeping track of all the other books. So true is this, that this book, which helps us catalog the other books, rarely gets cataloged itself in libraries, nor do librarians generally treasure and carefully house its various editions since it is always only the latest edition that is of value to them in their task of keeping the knowledge of the times organized and findable. Even so, this work-a-day, plow-horse kind of a book might well be a rare find for an archeologist of some far century or for the men from Mars when they come to see how the Earthlings live or lived.

The complexities of Man communicating to Man, in our times, is reflected in this book by twenty-seven distinct languages or dialects recorded for the Philippine Islands alone, languages distinct enough to have books either in them or about them recorded in the Library of Congress. We need only multiply this by the world situation to bring home to us the confusing maze of the ways in which men make or try to make themselves understood. That this problem, one of the real obstacles to world peace, has been and is occupying many minds is shown by the recording of thirty-four separate artificial languages of which one, appropriately for those familiar with English, is Gab.

The numerous subjects about which books have been written might well give a distorted view of our civilization to those who come after us, distorted, that is, in the sense that it is the black sheep of the family that gets the most attention. At any rate only one-fourth of a column is required to record the subject headings under *Peace*, whereas *War* and its subdivisions requires more than three pages, while the European War, 1914-18, requires four pages, and World War, 1939-46, has accumulated enough subject headings to require almost five pages of headings.

Similarly, *Crime* and *Criminals* require three pages, including references to such subjects as abduction, arson, assassination, body-snatching, forgery, homicide, infanticide, kidnapping, lynch law, pirates, rape, rogues and vagabonds, suicide, thieves, thugs, wife beating, and many others. And in the agonies of World War II came a newcomer to this infamous lot, genocide, to point out the trend of the times.

Small wonder that some future scholar or student might well conclude that so-called Homo-Sapiens was a singularly quarrelsome and vicious species. Further examination, however, of such headings as *Justice, Love, Friendship,* and *Affection,* even though not numerically so well represented might, let us hope, at least temper this opinion somewhat. It is doubtful though that any conclusion would ever be reached that this was a man's world, for the headings *Man* and *Men* require less than a page, while *Woman* and *Women* require three pages. Nor will there be any wonder, in distant days, that a race prolific enough in the writing of books to require this large tome just to record the subjects written about found need to include in it a cross reference from "Scrivners' palsy" to "Writers' cramp."

Entrepreneur to the Learned World

Halsey Wilson looked more like a banker than a printer-bibliographer-publisher.

IN THE LATE eighteen-eighties a young man, Halsey W. Wilson, intent on educating himself at the University of Minnesota, was filling every waking moment outside classes with whatever revenue-producing activity he could put his hand to. He worked for a time in the Minneapolis Public Library; he did Christmas clerking in book stores; he was the janitor of his church; and he delivered morning papers. But this was not enough, so he entered into a partnership with his roommate and the firm of Morris and Wilson was established to supply fellow students at the University of Minnesota, then only some 300 in number, with textbooks and supplies.

This embryo business, operated from the partners' bedroom, was founded with a capital of $100, some of which was borrowed. From this humble beginning, Halsey Wilson moved in steady progression to full-scale operation of a bookstore and on to become the greatest bibliographical publisher of all time. When he died in March of 1954 at Craton Heights, New York, in his eighty-fifth year, the H. W. Wilson firm, child of his industry, sure business instinct, and fertile mind was publishing some twenty-two indexing and bibliographical services without which scholarly work, as we know it on this North American continent, could not go on.

Wilson's success and his great contributions to scholarship and research are in the best sense a part of the great American saga. His daily routine at Minnesota included rising in the small hours of the morning to walk into town, in advance of the opening of the horse-cars, to collect his papers at 5 a.m. Then he walked an additional five miles making his deliveries and hurried home to devour breakfast and rush off to an eight o'clock class. Only Sundays were different. Then he had to get up an hour earlier to build a fire in the church furnace. Even after he entered his book selling partnership, he continued this rigorous work program as a means of securing added capital. It is a part of the American saga, too, that of young

Wilson's companions in his 5 a.m. daily trip to the newspaper office come rain, snow, or blizzard, one became a professor at Dartmouth and the other the editor of *Living Age*.

Wilson quickly encountered, as he moved into book retailing, the exasperating difficulties of finding all the pertinent facts about a book. Seaching for these items in varied catalogs and lists was tedious and costly. To eliminate this inefficiency for himself and other book stores, he decided to publish a cumulative monthly catalog of books, optimistically hoping for 500 subscribers at $1.00 each, with himself and his wife doing all the work at home. These ideas came to fruition in February of 1898 in the first number of the *Cumulative Book Index*, the progenitor of a long and increasingly numerous list of Wilson publications. Next to be published was the *United States Catalog of Books in Print*, 1899, followed by the *Readers Guide to Periodical Literature*, the *Book Review Digest*, and a host of additional publications.

All this meant expanding quarters and staff for a business solvent but not then, or ever, spectacularly profitable. Wilson's success in one of the costliest forms of publishing and for a limited clientele was due to efficiency, sound common sense, and ingenuity. To cumulate his publications he left the type up for all entries, interfiling linotype slugs for quarterly, annual, and biennial cumulations. As the business grew and migrated to the great publishing center of New York City, the firm came to have, under this plan, literally hundreds of tons of metal up in type.

A second and fundamental part of the Wilson success rested on service basis subscription rates, whereby libraries pay for the various indexing services in proportion to the number of the indexed journals to which they subscribe. Under this plan, the large libraries pay more, much more, but obviously they also get more. While some large libraries have been restive under this arrangement, it has without question increased tremendously a widespread use of all the Wilson tools. American librarianship has been the direct beneficiary.

Halsey Wilson was a quiet, pleasant man who looked more like a banker than a printer-bibliographer-publisher. He was an accepted and substantial part of every national library conference. He was indeed a giant whose enterprises grew quietly, unobtrusively, and naturally to the completely indispensable stage. As his publications increased and cumulated, esteem and honors for their founder also cumulated into growing recognition of and appreciation for his very great services to scholarship. His life was one that counted and will continue to count. Through the research tools and services he brought into being, tools essential now and for generations yet unborn, he achieved the kind of immortality which is the bibliographer's Valhalla.

How Do You Work This Deal?

Every student wants to know.

ON A PLEASANT morning some years ago I happened to be in the lower foyer of the Oregon State University Library when a freshman student, obviously ready to conquer the world in fifteen minutes, burst through the front doors, took a quick, somewhat nonplussed look around and then said to the nearest available person, who happened to be me, "How do you work this deal?" This young student, intent at the moment on finding some books on speech, soon had them. He had worked the deal successfully in his very first approach in part because he had not been reluctant, as too many freshmen are, to ask questions.

We can be pretty certain that this student departed unaware of the full implications of his question. How indeed is the deal worked? Well, it has gotten to be a pretty complicated and expensive proposition, in the sense of supplying needed information and books quickly and efficiently, to users at all levels, and particularly for serious research. A whole relatively new profession has had to come into being both to create the deal and to make it work. It costs money, too, quite a lot of it, as the multi-million dollar library budgets of numerous universities show. And the larger the deal becomes the more it costs.

A knotty and on the whole a poorly solved problem in higher education is how to indoctrinate the undergraduate student into the bibliographical mysteries, how to teach him to easily find his way to that portion of the written and otherwise recorded heritage of Mankind which has special relevance to what he means to do in the world. A few colleges and universities meet this problem head on by requiring each freshman to take a formal course in use of the library, sometimes for credit and sometimes not. I have yet to hear of such a course which is, in my opinion, worth the time, effort, and money that goes into it.

It is a rare instructor indeed who can, in a mass situation, relate use of the library to the student's primary ambitions and purposes. Also, when taught en masse, library instruction presents all the problems of sectioning and finding of competent instructors, at low rates of pay, that is found in other required freshman subjects. And in student motivation, creation of a realization in the student that it is important for him to learn this thing well, teaching about classification systems, call num-

bers, subject headings, cross references, periodical indexes, abstract journals, books of quotations, year books, encyclopedias, financial and legal services, and similar matters presents unusual difficulties.

Most universities have brushed the problem of instruction in use of the library rather lightly and some not at all. Our efforts at Oregon State University have included, in various years, a film on library use presented to all freshman English sections, accompanied by lectures by library staff members; a series of locally prepared slides similarly presented with lectures; tours of the library in Freshman Week; seminars for the English instructors at which library staff members have explained the fundamentals of the organization of the library and some of the more important reference tools; voluntary library tours; class instruction in the library or in the classroom, as and when requested by individual professors; and more recently a video tape on the library to present to all freshmen English sections.

It is at the graduate level that we became acutely aware that many, perhaps most, American students reach advanced educational levels without having learned to use the literature effectively or how to systematically record where their searching and their reading has taken them. It is also at this level that we become aware, and I say this softly, in lower case, that some members of the graduate faculty, drawn from universities everywhere, have reached their present station without having mastered the bibliographical intricacies, without having learned to impart really good instruction in use of the literature or even to use it effectively themselves. Nevertheless, the quality of theses, bibliographically and otherwise, is improving. This becomes readily apparent when we compare the more recent theses with those of the earlier years of graduate instruction. We like to think that instruction in use of the rich bibliographical heritage will improve at all universities, for both graduates and undergraduates, that libraries everywhere will, at all levels, better teach their users how to work the deal.

Part IV
BOOKS THAT SHOULD AND SHOULD NOT BE IN LIBRARIES

The principles and philosophy of modern librarianship I am least certain about are the right and the wrong of which books should not, because of the nature of their content, be admitted to the shelves of a library, whether public or academic. Not, I emphasize, books dealing with political, economic, and sociological ideas. In these fields, which I consider to be the basic freedom of speech and expression areas, I have always felt and maintained that any soundly conceived and sincerely expressed book, whatever the extremities of its political views, deserves a place on library shelves and ready availability for reading.

It is the books, chiefly novels and plays, which emphasize, extoll, portray, and dwell, to the point of nausea, on sex, perversion, and licentiousness of all conceivable kinds which trouble me. In my forty years as a librarian, the library trend in books of this kind, reflecting the changing morals of our times, has been toward more and more extremes and more and more so-called four letter words—the vulgar words of the street, the gutter, and the bawdy house.

I have always felt, rightly or wrongly, that many of the books in the vanguard of this trend, some written by men or women who have achieved a kind of fame and best sellerdom thereby, are deliberately salacious, that they are written so obscenely, not because of a legitimate need to create suspense or to honestly portray emotions and the development or the growth or the decadence of a character, but because the author feels this is what is needed to sell his or her book. I have suspected too that these authors, and their publishers, have counted the day lost when they could not produce a book creating an uproar of protest with all its attendant publicity. To the extent that these things are true, if they are true, authors of this ilk, and I think of some well-known names, are, in my opinion, in exactly the same category as the under-the-counter purveyors of pictures portraying the sex act under a variety of provocative conditions.

I have never shared, nor been in sympathy with, the shrill and almost hysterical defenses which librarians have cast up around such books in the Intellectual Freedom Committee of the American Library Association and elsewhere. From my point of view, there is, for librarians, a considerable professional tragedy in this situation, the tragedy of mistaking licentiousness for freedom of thought and of vulgarity and just plain nastiness for freedom of idealogical expression.

It has been and is my personal dilemma, as I suspect it may be for many librarians, that it is difficult indeed to know where to draw the line, to know where true dramatic skill and artistry ends and outright, deliberate, and calculated salaciousness and pornography, as a formula for sales, begins. Always too, as has been emphasized over and over again, one man's pornography may be another man's true dramatic art. So I have remained quiet, but troubled.

There must be, nevertheless, I have continued to feel, some kind of standards. Surely too, a national literature admitting unlimited, extreme obscenities, vulgarities, and fornication without end must be a decadent literature. I am by no means alone in these concerns. In 1935, at a time when standards were very much higher than they are now, Ellen Glasgow, author of wide repute, said this:

"Few things however are more certain than this. The literature that crawls too long in the mire will lose at last the power to stand erect. On the farther side of deterioration lies the death of a culture."

It has seemed strange to me, as the levels of taste have steadily lowered, that all who defend the sex- and passion-obsessed books—lawyers, jurists, publishers, and librarians—do so in conventional and polite words of good taste. If we are indeed to have our literature, or a portion of it, on gutter levels of vulgarity, then why should not that portion, I have wondered, be defended on this level, in its own nasty language and nauseating vulgarities.

The essays which follow do not, except indirectly, express the above convictions. The commentaries fall instead, largely in the field of idealogical freedom of expression. In this, by far the more significant area, I do have convictions, clear and unyielding. These, the immediately following pages variously express. The second essay is printed exactly as originally written.

The War of Ideas

THESE ARE TIMES of atomic bombs, of inter-continental missiles and anti-missiles, of submarines which can lurk in the depths of the oceans indefinitely and emerge, on command, to send death-dealing instruments speeding to far distant and unsuspecting targets, of space satellites which will circle the earth endlessly to spy out the military installations and secrets of enemy countries. In spite of all these modern military marvels of death and destruction, it is becoming increasingly evident that a simple weapon, the idea, will outrank and outdo them all.

Long ago it was written that the pen is mightier than the sword. Curiously, the very efficiency of the modern and awful physical weapons of war, those present and in prospect, has demonstrated the fundamental importance of ideas and the necessity of winning wars in the minds of men and not, in the ancient military tradition, through the killing of their bodies.

Now that it is certain that an aggressor loosing the mighty weapons in the modern military arsenal will destroy not only the enemy but himself, he is constrained, as men have never before been, to hold his weapons on leash. He may threaten and assume frightening postures; he may practice brinkmanship, but only in suicidal mania can he give the final command. So information, the idea, the fact, come to the fore as the only safe way of winning wars in the modern world. This places some pretty unlikely soldiers, in the traditional military concepts, on the battle front. All who are concerned with the idea, those who create and expound it and those who communicate and disseminate it, these are the new infantry and the new artillery.

Vital among the troops of this warfare are the librarians, a folk traditionally thought of as gentle and harmless. That librarians are indeed on the front, immediately and actively, in the clashing war of ideas, in the marches and counter-marches, is shown by the fact that the United States now maintains over 150 "Information Centers" in 64 countries. For the "soldiers" who man these centers, this is not always a genteel and quiet service. Too often the aspects of physical warfare intrude. In recent years our information libraries have been either burned or bombed or mobbed or otherwise attacked in twenty or more countries. Quite literally the librarians who man them are on the battle front.

Violent destruction of the idea, and the means of disseminating it, is a delusion as old and older than civilization. From the days of the primitive witch doctors, those whose ideas departed markedly, or often even slightly, from the accepted mores and patterns have frequently been dealt with harshly. Because Man is the contradictory and strange creature he is, these persecutions and restraints have served, more often than not, only to fertilize the ideas meant to be suppressed.

Two thousand years ago those who did not like his ideas nailed a man to a cross on Golgatha hill in Judea. They killed his body, but his ideas grew and flourished. Eager and dedicated followers wrote them down and carried them to all parts of an expanding world. Often they died for them as courageously and unflinchingly as the bravest soldiers on the military field of battle. Today, these ideas, which it was thought a dying gasp would still forever, are a strong and vital part of the spiritual mosaic of the total civilization.

Instances are legion of men and women who have been pilloried and imprisoned, who have been tortured and ridiculed, who have been drawn and quartered or burned at the stake because of the ideas they held. Man's long struggle upward from the jungle, both spiritually and scientifically, is marked by the stubborn and tenacious men who had different ideas and who were not deterred by the most fiendish tortures their detractors and persecutors could devise. The fearful ones thought, always, that if they could but still the disturbing mind and tongue and spirit, by imprisonment or, if necessary, by killing, the accepted and comfortable way of life would, for them, go on.

Often this warfare extended not only to killing bodies but also to killing the hated ideas, as put to writing. So books too have been burned at the stake, publicly and with acclaim. Always, eventually, the fearful ones have lost. A recent and vivid instance for many of us was the banning and the burning of books by Hitler and his Nazi cohorts. Little did these stupid and unperceptive men realize that they were only nourishing the divine will and gift of man to think independently.

These things are all relative. We see them in lesser degree in the current hysteria about communism, in red scares, in deliberate smirching of reputations, in loyalty oaths, in suppression of newspapers and magazines, in censorship and book banning. While our librarians in our information centers around the world are on the front line of this eternal warring by and for the human mind, the battle lines are present, usually more remotely and in politer terms, wherever the minds of men clash. In a sense all librarians are a part of and party to this never ending struggle. This is but another aspect of the profession of librarianship which gives it interest, vitality, and significance.

Cancer of the National Psyche

December 1963

JUST ONE YEAR ago, plus one month, this Cover Comment was devoted to the direct confrontation of the United States and in effect, through it, of the Free Western World, with the Communist World as represented by the Soviet Union. Now, these brief few months later our young President, whose calculated, courageous and forthright leadership then turned the tide and averted tragedy lies dead, victim of an assassin's bullet aimed not by the Communist nations but, according to overwhelming evidence, by one of our own young citizens whose whole life had been one of resentment, frustration, and maladjustment.

In its grief and humiliation our nation has turned to deep introspection, such as it has seldom known in its history. How could this, the foulest deed of our century, be done? What were the incidents, the beliefs, the convictions, the hatreds, and the bitter passions which festered, fused, and amalgamated in the mind of the assassin, leading finally to the fatal moment of release of the bullet which struck down the smiling and unsuspecting young President? How could this monstrous thing happen in the land of the free and the home of the brave?

Out of all the individual and national self analysis which has welled up among us, at all levels, in the wake of the President's brutal murder, has come a deeper realization of the extremism, the hatred, and the venom which has, in these recent years, been injected by extremists of the right and the left into the blood stream of national consciousness. Never has it been more evident that these extremes, as they move from passion to passion, from fear to fear, finally come full circle to meet on the common ground of blind intolerance, sometimes calculated, often unreasoning, of all thoughts, facts, motivations, and beliefs which are not in accord with the extreme, whatever it may be.

The ultimate extreme then becomes loss of freedom of expression, of action, and even of life itself for all who do not agree with the phobias of the moment. Among the millions upon millions of words which have followed the tragic events of November 22-25, have been many which have said that we must somehow draw off, neutralize, and cleanse away this national illness, manifested in bitterness and hate, so evident in so many places in these troubled days. But how?

Our dilemma is that the vehicles of this venom, this bitterness, this unreasoning hatred, are words—words spoken directly to individuals or groups, words sent winging over the airways, words set down in print. If we are to maintain our sacred freedom of expression, these words, except for possibly the most direct threats and exhortations, cannot be killed. Who is to judge which of the expressions of hate and extremism are so extreme that they cannot, in behalf of the common safety, be tolerated. And even if such decision is reached how are these things to be suppressed?

These knotty questions all apply directly to our libraries where words, wild and malicious, no less than those which are wise, kind, and understanding finally come to rest. Is it symbolic, perhaps, that the murderer's rifle was braced, as he cooly awaited his quarry, on a pile of books? Innocuous books, very likely, these which helped direct the

fatal bullets, but behind them were other books which had been read and pondered and which had festered into this nightmare harvest. These were the books which in a very real sense sustained and aimed the rifle, which led to the final mad moment of squeezing of the trigger.

Into our library and into all free libraries there come, if not daily, then at least in substantial quantity, words and ideas which, falling on the fertile soil of warped or resentful minds, might well lead to further deeds and actions just as monstrous as those of November 22 in Dallas, Texas.

My own predilection is to eject these words from our library summarily, as encountered. When I read of the "evil men manipulating the Congress of the U. S.," of the "treasonous bribery of a *willing* Congress," about the Jews *boasting* in the Talmud that "they gave Christ five deaths and he had sex relations with animals," about Ike the Kike, and about the "Burma Rat" who directs the United Nations, my immediate reaction is to discard out-of-hand all these bits of venom as well as others of their ilk. Any western librarian who does this, however, falls prey to the persistent malady of intolerance which has always afflicted Man and which is now so virulent among us.

We, and by "we" I mean all the world, can only hope that the wise, good, and strong words which have come flooding from all the world following the murder of our attractive and intelligent young President will literally drown out the evil words. This is the only effective antidote for the national "cancer of the psyche" so evident in the hate and venom of our times.

WILLIAM HUGH CARLSON   67

Communism and Capitalism

If Marx and Engels can look back they must be saddened to learn they were wrong about many things.

SOME YEARS AGO I undertook to talk to a local group about the Communist Manifesto. I did this because it has always seemed to me that, while the word communism is ominously ever-present in our daily press, on the air waves, and in angry and partisan bickerings in our legislative councils, many of those who raise shrill and hysterical voices about it have never stopped to read the Bible of this philosophy, the Manifesto, or to measure it against things as they now are.

Coming home from this talk I picked up a pamphlet, "General Motors Builds its First Fifty Millions Cars," received in the mail that day. The Manifesto was fresh in my mind. The casual glance I had intended for the GM pamphlet was turned to sustained reading by the superb skill and artistry of those who wrote it and who made it so visually attractive. As I read on the thought was inescapable: Here indeed is striking demonstration that much that is in the Manifesto has been, and is being, increasingly disproved.

Karl Marx and Frederick Engels, who wrote the Manifesto well over one hundred years ago, while still in their mid-twenties, were intelligent young men of fervent social consciousness. When they wrote, the industrial revolution had been in progress for some one hundred years and, from their point of view, had reached an advanced stage. There was much to give substance to their revolutionary philosophy which is shaking our world of today. The laborer, they said, had become a mere appendage of a machine, his work bereft of all individual charm and character. At the mercy of his capitalist employers, the bourgeoisie, he must sell himself piecemeal to them, the pawn of all the vicissitudes of the capitalist system. As the uses of machinery and division of labor and the repulsiveness of his work increased, his wages decreased and his burden of toil was increased either by prolongation of working hours or amount of work exacted in a given time or by increased speed of machinery. Under these conditions, he was sinking and would sink deeper and deeper toward pauperism.

But capitalism, thought Marx and Engels, had within itself the seeds of its own destruction through overproduction, through recurring depressions, each more severe than the last, and through grinding into defeat and absorption into the proletariat many of the lesser bourgeoisie who could no longer compete with the larger capitalists. The time was already imminent, they felt, when this process had proceeded to the point where the proletariat would be so numerous that they could rise up and strike off their shackles, abolish the oppressor bourgeoisie, and emancipate society at large by establishing something that has never yet existed on this earth, a classless society without private property.

What Marx and Engels did not foresee, and what the GM pamphlet so strikingly demonstrates, is that far from being exploited and impoverished by the machine, the worker has, through his increased productivity, gained in compensation, in stature and in dignity. They did not perceive that the machine, increasingly complex and complicated, would itself raise up, as a new aristocracy of workers, those who understand it and direct it to perform its miracles. Neither, it may be assumed, did they envisage the possibility that capitalism could adopt and thrive upon the then revolutionary doctrines which they, in the Manifesto, were willing to accept as way points to the eventual and inevitable classless society; such things as a heavy graduated income tax, centralization of credit and of transportation and communication in the hands of the State, bringing wastelands into cultivation and improving the soil, combining agriculture and manufacturing industries, and providing free education of all children in public schools. All of these are now things which are part and parcel, unquestioned, of our current capitalist society.

If Marx and Engels can look back from that "undiscover'd country from whose bourn no traveller returns," they must certainly be saddened by the obvious fact that the chief country where their philosophy has been given a trial, in the revolutionary sense they advocated, far from having attained a classless society, is today a despotic bureaucracy where the lot of the laborer does not approach that of his fellows in the capitalistic countries. Seeing the prosperous capitalistic workers of today and a society which in one nation alone has been able to absorb over fifty million motor cars from a single manufacturer, they must surely know that they were wrong about a good many things.

One such thing is the extent to which money flowing from capitalistic enterprises has been turned to the social good through the work of great foundations, such as the Rockefeller, Ford, Mellon, Carnegie, Guggenheim, and thousands of lesser philanthropic foundations. Not the least of the beneficiaries of bequeathed capitalistic wealth have been the libraries. There is not a library in America which is not, in countless ways, daily benefiting from freely and intelligently given capitalistic wealth.

Struggle for the Minds of Men

Continuous exposure and trial provide the most effective weapons against unscrupulous propagandistic techniques.

ONE OF THE ominous possibilities of the future, with direct implications for libraries, is the possibility that unscrupulous men may be able to control the thoughts and ideals of large masses of Mankind through astute and scientific use of all the media of mass communication: newspapers, radio, television, libraries. We have seen this done with varying and sometimes frightening success in Nazi Germany, in Fascist Italy, and now, on a tremendous scale, in and by communistic Russia in her efforts, so far apparently somewhat successful, to control and indoctrinate the populations of her satellites. And we see elements of some of these techniques in our own country.

We like to think, and in the main it is undoubtedly so, that our side of the struggle for the minds of men is sincere, honest, decent, and not deliberately perverted. It is easy and tempting, however, for our *Voice of America,* and even the U. S. Information libraries which we maintain at numerous points abroad, to fall into the easy practice of fitting the facts to whatever case we seek to establish.

Nor are we free in our own national life of the dangers of systematic thought control. Our newspapers often stir uneasily over the possible loss of freedom of the press, the great bulwark of free man. Our public libraries, too, and possibly some college and university libraries, fortunately not very frequently so far, are being brought under pressure and criticism for having freely on their shelves the literature of both sides of controversial problems. The extent of these forays against a free literature is indicated by the fact that the American Library Association Committee on Intellectual Freedom is increasingly busy.

Even in local community affairs, we are not free from vicious propaganda techniques. In so simple a matter as fluoridation of the municipal water supply, unfair name-calling and racial prejudice, standard stock-in-trade of the unscrupulous propagandist, raise their ugly heads.

At least one great statesman refused to accept the possibility of continuing and systematic thought control. When the Massachusetts Institute of Technology had Winston Churchill there in 1950, he had this to say:

"In his introductory address, Dr. Burchard, the Dean of Humanities, spoke with awe of 'an approaching scientific ability to control men's thoughts with precision.' I shall be very content, personally, if my task in this world is done before that happens. Laws just or unjust may govern men's actions.

Tyrannies may restrain or regulate their words. The machinery of propaganda may pack their minds with falsehood and deny them truth for many generations of time. But the soul of man thus held in a trance or frozen in a long night can be awakened by a spark coming from God knows where, and in a moment the whole structure of lies and oppression is on trial for its life.

Peoples in bondage need never despair. Let them hope and trust in the genius of mankind. Science, no doubt, if sufficiently perverted, could exterminate us all, but it is not in the power of material forces, at present or in any period which the youngest here tonight need take into practical account, to alter permanently the main elements in human nature and restrict the infinite variety of forms in which the soul and genius of the human race can and will express itself."

It is, I am confident, the hope and ideal of all American librarians to so administer their libraries that they may continuously supply the information and the spark which will keep the "structure of lies and oppression" of unscrupulous propagandistic techniques continuously exposed and on trial.

Happy New Year!

Lowering of artificial barriers between peoples promises to make the coming years more fruitful and happier in the storing and use of knowledge.

In February one year our library received belatedly a "Happy New Year!" card. More startling than its lateness, however, was the fact that it came from Mezhdunarodnaja Kniga, the Soviet agency in Moscow that presides over the Russian foreign book trade.

It seemed but yesterday that our efforts to place subscriptions for and claim back issues of Russian scientific journals through this agency or its New York City affiliate, the Four Continent Book Corporation, had been turned aside with pointed phrases such as "Will not be exported from U.S.S.R." Our check cards for these journals consequently showed vacant blocks through the years 1950-54, varying, according to title. By mid-1954, however, a new policy was clearly in effect. Since that time, the current issues of all the Russian journals we subscribed for had been arriving regularly. And now came friendly New Year greetings too!

What had happened? Was this card, inscribed "with all Good Wishes" and attractively depicting the beautiful new and spired Moscow University, with a statue of Lenin standing tall in front to dominate the scene, was it a last petal from the Geneva Spirit that bloomed so hopefully

for a brief moment? Or did we have here, as later events seemed to confirm, a harbinger of more permanent policies of intellectual and cultural cooperation in which Russia and her satellites would move further into friendly participation in an enriching give-and-take in the world of ideas and of undistorted facts and figures?

Should this be true, as it now seems in at least some part to be true, then the curtained countries should be more than welcome, for the task of promoting international understanding is great. The impediments and barriers of language, national traditions and psychologies, of illiteracy and poverty, these are enough, and more than enough, without officially maintained barriers.

One of the things that has characterized the postwar Western World has been the surge back toward international cooperation in all things cultural. While this has of course been promoted by the United Nations and UNESCO, much of it would have happened anyhow by sheer necessity and the logic of events. This cooperation, to which the book in all its forms and manifestations is inescapably integral, is exemplified by the *13th* conference of the International Publishers Association meeting in Zurich, Switzerland, in 1954. Before that convention, attended by 300 delegates, among whom, I suspect, the Russians were conspicuously absent, Dr. Gustav

Keckeis of Switzerland, newly elected President, said this:

Let us not forget that we are . . . men of good will drawn together in the spirit of our profession . . . Let us in everything we undertake, in the many languages in which our books are written, bear witness to the fact that we are servants of the humanitarian spirit and sow seeds of understanding the length and breadth of the world that today has shrunk to such small proportions. Which body of men is more called upon to perform this task than ours?

There is, it may be answered, one body of men "more called upon" in these areas than even the publishers, and that is the librarians. For while the publishers prepare and sow the seeds, it is the librarians who husband and nurture them and through whose help, in large measure, they bear fruit.

That librarians have been and are responding to this responsibility is shown by their international awareness and activities long before the birth of that child of bloody conflict, the United Nations. It is evident in the International Federation of Documentation and the International Federation of Library Associations. Postwar library emphasis on cultural cooperation is further reflected in the organization and meetings, for the first time, of an International Congress on Medical Librarianship in London in 1953, the International Congress of Libraries and Documentation Centers in Brussels in 1955, and the International Association of Agricultural Librarians and Documentalists in Ghent, also in 1955.

These are all organizations which have done and continue to do much to promote intellectual cooperation and international understanding. Even so, the way things are, they operate in only half a world. When the carefully contrived curtains of iron and bamboo come down, as hopefully they eventually will, and Russia, and more particularly China and the Asiatic countries under her influence, come into these and similar associations and groups, in friendship and good will, sincerely and without guile, then indeed will greetings of "Happy New Year!" from them be rich in meaning and in promise of a better world.

Schizophrenia Among the Soviets

Independence of thought and action required for scientific progress must inevitably spill over into the social sciences and the humane arts.

THE FOREGOING essay reflects on freedom of thought and expression, or the lack of it, in the USSR and her satellites. There can, it seems to me, be no sharp, precise, and impenetrable iron curtains in the human mind, at least among those devoted to intellectual endeavors. People free to read and think and study in the areas of the sciences, as are the intelligentsia of the Soviet-dominated countries, with the blessings and substantial encouragement of their governments, will inevitably develop independent patterns of thought in areas beyond the precise sciences which, fundamentally, know no politics. Sputniks, atomic test blasts, astronauts, and Nobel prizes to Russians, seem to confirm these thoughts. Food for further reflection comes from papers presented at a University of Chicago Graduate Library School 1958 conference, "Iron Curtains and Scholarship: The Exchange of Knowledge in a Divided World."

In the Chicago discussions, Dr. Lawrence Dertick, then U. S. Commissioner of Education, who had recently visited Russia, was quoted as expressing amazement about the USSR commitment to education as a means of national advancement. "Everywhere we went," he said, "we saw indication after indication of what we could only conclude amounted to a total commitment to education." Among the evidences of this commitment, Dr. Dertick found complete acceptance of the book and making it "absolutely accessible to all the people" as the best and chiefest means of education.

Here are some of the facts: In 1913 half a book was published per person in Russia. In 1957 this figure was five and one-half as compared with a world average of two books. Book stores covered the country to its most remote corners; from 1949 to 1957 these increased from 3,474 to 6,331. Including bookstalls and department stores, there were 25,000 bookselling outlets, as compared with only 2,500 in 1913. A number of networks of libraries, distinct by type and function and with separate networks for the several ministries, also blanketed the land. These are headed by the great Lenin State Library in Moscow with 20 million items and the Saltykov-Shchedrin State

Public Library in Leningrad with 12 million items. Altogether there were 147,412 libraries in Russia, in 1956, as compared with 17,225 in 1922.

Hand in hand with the tremendous increase in Russian publishing, in book stores, and in libraries, giant strides have been taken in control and organization of these rapidly accumulating writings. This is managed through the All-Union Book Chamber, with subordinate branches in the various republics. Now, without exception, all published materials are listed in the bibliographical organs of this Chamber. Perhaps the greatest achievement of all was the development, in 1953, of Referativnyi Zhurnal, a gigantic abstracting service supplying in one single service, the Soviets believe, all the major informational needs of the scientist and the engineer. A comprehensive unified abstracting service of this kind for the less regimented countries of the western world continues to be a desirable but elusive bibliographical will-o'-the-wisp.

Now the Russians are reaping the bitter-sweet fruit of this tremendous emphasis on education. Sweet to them are the Sputniks and the Moon shots, and the Astronauts, and their rapid advances in atomic research and other scientific matters. Sweet too, and proudly accepted, was a Nobel Prize in Physics. But along with this came the bitter, the reviled, the unwanted, the spurned Nobel Prize to Boris Pasternak for his novel, *Dr. Zhivago*, unpublished and unpublishable in his own country. In this ironic situation, Russia stood publicly and dramatically impaled, for all to see, in Russia as well as out, on the twin horns

of her dilemma. It just is not possible to place the minds of a great and well-educated nation in water-tight compartments, with full intellectual freedom permitted in the a-political sciences, and in them only.

Inevitably, the independence of thought and action required for scientific progress must spill over into the social sciences and the humane arts. There are numerous evidences, other than the Pasternak award, that this is happening in Russia. When in the post-Stalin "thaw" the authorities encouraged the intelligentsia to "greater flexibility, greater daring," writings exceed-

ing what was acceptable came into being so quickly, some probably out of carefully guarded files, that the deep freeze was again turned on, and quickly. Nevertheless, under the icy surface, we may be sure, ferment and unrest continue. This received fresh and potent fuel from the repudiation of the Pasternak Nobel award. Behind the curtains of iron and bamboo, quite as much as elsewhere, the deep world-wide political significance of this absurdity will grow in ways which will yet completely strike off the already yielding and weakening shackles on Soviet minds.

Proceedings Against Readers

East Germans have already endured the Soviet yoke longer than they did the evil pall of the Nazis.

AT MIDNIGHT on September 7, 1961, a delivery van belonging to the East Berlin "Buchhandelgesellschaft" came barrelling down Unter den Linden at sixty miles an hour headed toward the Brandenburg Gate. It burst like a tank through the red and white barrier between East and West, went crashing through the barbed-wire entanglements and came to a halt three hundred metres to the West, in the British Sector, safe from the pistols of the startled People's Police. At the wheel sat a twenty-three year old bookseller. He was but one of the millions in the Soviet sector who have risked their

lives in a flight to freedom. He was nevertheless "special," because he was a dealer in a very dangerous commodity, the book. Dangerous, that is, to all who would shackle the human mind and spirit.

A small trilingual booklet, Prozess Gegen Leser, "Proceedings Against Readers," prepared by the Borsenverein des Deutschen Buchhandels E. V., telling of this dramatic event, and the reasons for it, reached the Oregon State campus and presumably the campuses of universities throughout all our land. Two copies were sent me by faculty members with the thought that I might, as I did, wish to use it in my New Booklist comment.

I had a curious feeling of "this is where I came in" as I read this documented analysis of the prostitution of the German book-trade and of how men of conscience and spirit, such as the brave young driver of the van, have been fleeing, and continue to flee from their galling degradation. This was in part so because the first article I wrote for a national library journal, in 1936, dealt with this very same theme, the shaping and distorting and marshalling and manipulation of facts and ideas, as expressed in books, to support an ideology. In 1936, however, it was Adolf Hitler and his henchmen who held all of Germany by the throat, who menaced and strutted, screamed and ranted about Lebensraum and Nordic superiority.

A short ten years later, a fleeting instant in the troubled history of Homo Sapiens, the unhealthy and unholy world these madmen had sought to build had come crashing down about their ears, taking all the chief architects to suicidal death, to the ignominy of prison, to insane asylums. They, like the Communists now in control of East Germany, had planned to shape the minds of men through the book, had created ministries and agencies, issued directives, established inspections, all to assure that only literature favorable to their cause should be available in the bookstores and in the libraries.

It was with these efforts that my 1936 paper, "Preparers of the Mind and Heart" was concerned. I pointed out in it that every dictator who rules by force and not by popular will, cannot be tolerant of hostile political philosophies and the free expression of ideas, that he or it or they must of necessity stifle facts or thoughts or ideas not favorable, that the Nazi directives, rules,

and regulations could be transferred directly to Russia with only the change of a few words, making communistic and socialistic literature the desired type and its opposite the "unerwunschtes" and hostile literature. Now for the unlucky millions of East Germany in the Soviet sector this has come to pass. They have but exchanged, or been forced to exchange, the Nazi darkness and tryanny and ruthlessness for the Soviet kind. A different type of literature is now under attack, to be sure, but the methods and the ultimate purpose remain exactly the same.

The Prozess Gegen Leser comment, taken from official East German sources, makes clear the degraded function of the bookseller and by implication of the library. The bookseller is ad-

monished about his high responsibility for educational enlightenment. He is warned against pernicious attempts "to distract people from the order of the day." He is told that his chief task is to "educate enthusiastic builders of Socialist Germany" and to popularize "the great achievements of the Soviet people in building up Socialism in the factories." He is given a quota of political literature. He is told that the book is not a commodity in the usual sense, that development of socialist culture is a question of the security of the state (as it unquestionably is), that all inimical ideas and facts must be relegated to the "poison cupboard," and so on and on and on.

To me it has been a shock to realize that the East Germans have already endured the Soviet yoke longer than they did the evil pall of the Nazis. It may take longer to escape this time, possibly some generations, but I have great faith that the Human Mind cannot be permanently held in bondage. I believe we are beginning to see this in relaxations of restrictions, however minor, in writing and in expression in Russia.

I am mindful, as I think of and sympathize with the unfortunate East Germans who have suffered the same tyranny from two opposite extremes, that we here in America, safe America, are not free from the undertones and overtones of the German plight. We too have our book burners and our witch hunters, few but ominously present at both extremes. Among us too there are those who initiate, and sometimes carry out, albeit so far abortively, praise God, Proceedings Against Readers.

About Truth and Bigotry

Only the weak fear free expression of ideals, thoughts, and phobias.

WHATEVER ELSE librarians who are concerned with the building of libraries in our western countries have to be, they must be people who can make up their minds, freely and unhindered. This is so because libraries, even the greatest libraries with their multimillioned holdings and their hundreds of miles of shelving, grow by accretion of small individual entities.

All of these things, each volume that reaches the shelves to stand in orderly and waiting sequence, each pamphlet that goes into the vertical subject file, each map, each picture, each microfilm or micro card added to the collections is there because someone, usually a librarian, has decided that by being there it will help to fulfill the ultimate purpose of the library. This is to place in the hands of the user, be he learned savant or scholar or the lowliest freshman student, the information or stimulus or inspiration he needs. This is by no means a guessing game. It proceeds, for the most part, in disciplined fashion, closely coordinated with or geared to curriculum, institutional objectives, and ambitions or to whatever clientele the library serves.

Nor is this entirely a positive process because librarians must not only decide what books and related materials should be in the library; they must also decide what should not be there. Nearly always this is more difficult than deciding what should be added. This is so, has to be so, particularly in the areas of literature and art and the abiding political and ideological conflicts between right and left, because emotions, passions, personal backgrounds, phobias, and enthusiasms tend to govern.

Librarians are no more free, personally, from these complexities than other folk. Nevertheless, every library in the current American scene and throughout the western world at large attempts to deal impartially with, and fairly represent, the extremes.

Attack and criticism, if it comes, always emanates from the extremes. In our country this is now happening with increasing frequency, particularly among the public libraries, by attack from the militant far right. From this source, materials are flowing, unsolicited, toward the libraries. These extremists, though, are more concerned about what should not be on the shelves than what should be there. With increasing frequency we hear of organized efforts to flood meetings of trustees of public libraries, to manipulate the elective processes, to assume control, all in the interests of making a prevailing extreme philosophy, or phobia, or belief dominant not only in adding materials but in removing those books, already present, deemed to be offending. For the most part, if not universally, such efforts have not been successful. They have resulted though in some stormy standing-room-only library trustee meetings, usually among the quietest and most decorous of all meetings of public bodies.

Fortunately, these emotional conflicts have not been much evident among the academic libraries. They would be, however, and quickly, should either of the two extremes be successful in high places. We have had continuing instances of this down through the ages, for these conflicts are no new thing. They go back to the beginning of libraries and beyond. In this century we have had tragic demonstration of the certainty of what is right, in Nazi Germany, with its futile, almost childish burning of the books, and more successfully perhaps, in the Communist countries, with sharply devised and careful controls of what people are permitted to read. Public press and libraries alike are subject to these controls, with retribution swift for those who deviate.

For librarians in totalitarian countries, as well as the press, life is simple. Simple that is in the sense that the functioning of a robot is simple. And also just as unexciting. What is right is right, so there need be no troublesome and soul searching choice such as the western librarian frequently faces. While the totalitarian controls, at either extreme, seem and look, in the moments of ascendancy, to be evidences of all-conquering strength, they are actually a weakness—for only the weak must fear the whole range of human emotions and passions.

The splendid progress of the western democracies are evidence, checkered, troubled, and uncertain sometimes, eclipsed in long nights occasionally, but clear evidence nevertheless, that where truth and falsehood are free to grapple, truth always wins eventually. This is what makes all the communication processes of the western world, including librarianship, difficult, trying, but also rewarding and satisfying.

The tragedy is that the extremists of both right and left are always so sure that they are right. There are, of course, knaves among them playing adroitly on human emotions and passions for selfish ends. The rank and file, however, without whom there can be no substance, are sure, so sure, that they are right. Rabindranath Tagore, with the calm understanding of the eastern philosophers has perceived their unwitting quandry in this notable line:

Bigotry tries to keep truth safe in its hand with a grip that kills it.

the land in places where it was rich in succulent earthworms and where the climate was fair. These ancient ancestors were the founding fathers who established the dress a proper robin should wear and the mores and rules whereby nests were to be built and worms were to be pursued. All who conformed gained, no doubt in varying degree, status and acceptability. Now, centuries later, here was this poor little hen robin who through no fault of her own was different and who, because of it, was much persecuted.

The White Robin

Something there is in nature which does not like differentness.

IN MY EARLY years at Oregon State a snow-white robin was one of the curiosities and attractions in the library area. For several years, three or so, this robin, probably a hen, arrived regularly in the annual migrations to spend the summers in and about the adjoining shrubbery and lawns. She was however hard to observe closely because she led a harried and unhappy existence. Apparently, and this obviously was because of her color, or lack of it, she was not socially accepted in robinhood. Her moments of peaceful worm hunting were few and wary. She was fought, chased, and set upon by the other robins.

Perhaps there were among the indignant robin aggressors direct

descendents, pure and unalloyed, of ancestors who had come across the Bering Straits or up from the jungles or out of the forests primeval to establish a hold on

We have in this harried white robin an illustration of one of nature's laws or traits for the countless millions of her animate creatures, including Man. In a Robert Frost kind of way, it can be stated as Something There is Which Does not Like Differentness. Nature, we must believe, knew what she was about in arranging things this way, but as her creatures proliferated and evolved and changed, and as degrees and shades of color and other distinctive changes appeared within species, problems and difficulties grew correspondingly.

This has been particularly so for Man, presumably the most intelligent and certainly the most articulate of all of nature's creatures. This articulateness has resulted in quantities of books on the shelves of libraries everywhere, some profound, many reportorial, and some outright ridiculous, all dealing with the conflicts and complications rising from physical differentness. Tribal battles, growing in our later years into great wars, have been fought about it. One entire nation is governed by a ruthless doctrine of Apartheid through which the dominant robins keep those not dominant, even though they were there first, strictly and remorselessly under careful controls. In our own nation a great civil war has been fought over this issue, brother robin against brother robin. Now a hundred years later the end is not yet, nor doubtless will it be in another hundred years. Hopefully we can believe, however, that progress is being made, no matter how distressingly slow to the immediate protagonists.

Nature has other and contrary laws, strong, primeval, and not to be denied. One of these, perhaps the strongest of all, is the biological urge to reproduce. Our library robin demonstrated this too. There came a spring when we looked for her and found her not. But we did find one, possibly more, partially white robins. Obviously, in spite of her harried and persecuted life, the white robin had been integrated, at least biologically. Perhaps it was a basic fear or instinct that spurred and activated the aggressor robins, the horrible possibility that robins generally might become all white when obviously red and brown and black, as established by the founding fathers, was such an eminently proper and satisfactory color.

Certainly among men, wherever the races mix, the biological urge has its way. This has been demonstrated in our own country where, in spite of the negroes beginning as slaves and being held in inferior status for so many cruel years, a person of pure negro blood is becoming increasingly rare. It has been said too, with sound basis of fact, that some of the best white blood of the nation is in the negro race. Obviously, as a nation we have

gained much from the negroes. Their great gifts in music, from the beginning, and increasingly in athletics as they have more and more opportunity, attest to this. Nor are they lacking in the sciences and in literary abilities, as books and other writings in libraries everywhere increasingly show.

The single little white hen robin of our library was quickly absorbed into the dominant blood stream, just as the American Indians are increasingly being absorbed. Perhaps there can be encouragement in the fact

that all predominantly white people, or nearly all, now bearing American Indian blood in their veins are very proud of it. Perhaps from this we can believe that nature has a grand design not easily discernible in the immediacies of the racial strife and conflict now going on, as it has, in varying degree, ages on end, not only in our country but the world around. Prayerfully, we can hope that the library shelves of the future will contain a happier and more humane record of the conflict over physical differentness.

Fantasy From Another Century

The All-Wise One lays devious plans to control Planet Earth.

It is the year 2165. Homo Sapiens, the knowing one, has completely dominated and exploited the planet Earth in all its parts. He has long since given up the ambitious concepts of two hundred years earlier when his forebears dreamed and experimented and devoted great substance to exploring the uni-

verse. These primitives did indeed travel to the moon and back only to return broken in mind and body and bearing tales of a small globe, airless, waterless, and inhospitable beyond belief.

Journeys out into the planetary system of the sun, these too had been undertaken with results even more sterile. The earliest of the interplanetary explorers never returned at all. They managed, nevertheless, to send back to Mother Earth messages relaying thoughts and observations experienced as they drifted through space toward capture by high gravity systems. When finally the most sophisticated space vehicle of them all, embodying the ultimate in thrust and speed did make it back from no greater distance than Mars, its broken occupants were only able to gasp out the futility and hopelessness of it all before falling dead in Earth's dense atmosphere. It was then that Man finally, and reluctantly, accepted the inevitable fact that he was solely an Earth creature, stuck with his little planet and it with him.

Having bowed finally to the inevitable fact that he was after all not God, that he could not change the laws of the universe, and that he would have to be content with his little planet, Man turned his fertile and often scheming and evil mind to completely and absolutely mastering the world he had. This had indeed been going on all the while the space experimentation had been under way.

In the two hundred years since the first space flights, the humans of Earth had multiplied and multiplied again and again. The Caucasian races, dominant and dominating in the early twentieth century had now become Earth's minority and exploited peoples. The traditions of freedom and democracy and the worth of the individual which they had developed and nurtured over some centuries had persisted nevertheless to trouble and annoy the new leaders, the great and all-wise ones.

The multiplying of people had been as nothing in comparison to the multiplying of the books they wrote. In the year 1965 these writings had numbered some 200 million volumes. By the year 2000 they had grown to a billion. By 2065 they had reached five billion. Now in the year 2165 they had grown to 20 billion, which, even in miniturization far beyond anything known in the primitive days of 1965, presented grave management and housing problems.

These micro-reduced materials existed in great national and regional warehouses. Reading and receiving rooms equipped with batteries of finding and reading consoles dotted the world. Technicians and librarians to manage it all had in a sense inherited the earth. They alone of all the occupational groups had never, in the two preceding centuries, been in over supply.

In the materials these librarians managed and guarded, coding and classifying with great skill and ingenuity, there still endured, in original hand and letter press form, the documents of liberty, the Magna Carta, the Declaration of Independence by England's rebel colonies of the New World, the Constitution of the United States, the Bill of Rights, Lincoln's Emancipation Proclamation, and millions upon millions of books either supporting or attacking these ancient expressions of human ideals and hopes. The great rulers of the one world had always wanted to dispose of these troublesome relics of a once free world but how to do it?

Came now a new and shrewd young great leader. Like his predecessors he too wished to rid the world of these dangerous ideas. Unlike them he had a plan. It was based on the vulnerability of mechanized knowledge to government control. Under the guise of friendliness to the

liberal ideas of earlier centuries, an edict went out to assemble all the hallowed documents of freedom and all the books supporting them in a great One World Freedom Library. So these documents came forth from their various shrines with pomp and circumstance presaging a safe and glamorous new home. The millions upon millions of books supporting them were quickly computer-extrapolated from the billions of Earth's other books for placing in the Freedom Center.

All the freedom literature was now in one place, in originals and on tape. When all was in readiness there came, in the still and quiet of the night, great rays that consumed it all. The new young great leader, the all-wise one, had accomplished what no tyrant before him, and many had tried, had been able to do. He had rid the world of all the physical embodiments of the doctrines of freedom. Even so, he could not be content or at ease. The words of one of the greatest men of all time, who had in 1965 been buried with great and richly earned honors, these words even though now all destroyed, continued to sear and rankle in his mind. This man, a Caucasian, who had stood staunch and strong when freedom was, in his own time under attack, had eloquently maintained that people in intellectual bondage, whatever the odds against them, would one day rise up to throw off their shackles. In spite of all his technological controls, the new young all-wise one could, therefore, not rest easy. There was, for him, no escape from the haunting fear that this confident prediction of two centuries earlier was indeed true.

Part V

SHELTER: ONE OF THE THREE BASIC ESSENTIALS OF A LIBRARY

The impact of Man's great and growing graphic record, and its vital importance in all his affairs, and particularly in higher education and research, has required, has forced in fact, detailed thought and planning to the housing of it all. Sustained thinking and planning and erection of library shelter has consequently, in these more recent years, gone on all over the world. This has necessarily included libraries of all types and kinds: governmental, public, private, those maintained by business and industry and also, of course, those required by academic institutions.

Perhaps the planning and erection of library shelter has been more detailed and possibly more efficient for the academic libraries. Or possibly it may only seem so to an academic librarian because, in America at least, such a tremendous number of new academic library buildings have been erected, particularly in the last two decades. By the law of averages, if for no other reason, some of these should have been, as some indeed are, pretty good.

The following essays deal with some general aspects of the housing of academic libraries. It is inevitable that some of these commentaries should be rather highly personalized in terms of Oregon State University. I believe and hope, however, that the Oregon State experience will have applicability to academic libraries generally.

A Building Is Not a Library

WHEN the Gothic tower which houses the Yale University Library was nearing completion in 1931, Andrew Keogh, then Yale Librarian, is reported to have said that the inscription over the doors of this imposing building should be: "This is not the library; the Yale Library is inside."

Here is the nub of a philosophy by which those who operate libraries in buildings that are something less than the heart's desire may warm themselves while the better structures they hope for continue their being somewhere in the nebulous future. A building, good or poor, is nothing but bricks and concrete, steel and wood, without the things it shelters and the spirit, enterprise, and devotion of those who work in it.

The wry humor of Andrew Keogh's remark was called forth no doubt by the fact that administrators and architects had, as has happened in many other places, run away with his building. Intent on making a striking architectural monument, they were little concerned, or only secondarily concerned, that it be so built that the housing of the books and their increase and servicing could be carried out with a minimum of inconvenience and a maximum of efficiency. How far architects have sometimes gone astray in library buildings is pointed up by the remark of the little four-year-old girl who with her mother entered the vaulted reading room of a magnificent Gothic library building. After a quick look around she said in a hushed voice, "Mama, when do we sing?"

At Oregon State University there certainly could not be complaints about architectural overemphasis in the library building of 1918. By the standards of its time, the building was a good one, not tradable even for some of the million-dollared architectural show pieces. Nevertheless, the librarians working in it and the faculty and students using it were, by modern standards, surrounded by and operating under many building-imposed difficulties and inconveniences. Some of these, to be sure, resulted from the fact that the building was required to house far more books than it was ever designed to contain.

Corners, corridors, low beam rooms, book-lift chute, fan room, reading room alcoves, nearby Shepard Hall, all these had been invaded by books. The elevators by which these books were reached were temperamental and erratic. During quiet vacation interims, they worked perfectly. They sensed the busy spots and picked them as a nice time to grow recalcitrant.

There was a continuing stream of complaints about reading rooms being stuffy and either too hot or too cold. Ventilation was nonexistent as the vapors of the reading rooms, when well filled, made only too evident. Books and mail arrived and waste materials left awkwardly and inefficiently over a public entrance sidewalk. The catalogers were far removed from the catalog which they were creating and ministering to daily. Traffic of book trucks moved with difficulty up and down ramps and on elevators which rarely stopped on level. These were things which, with variations, the less well-housed libraries all over the country were having to contend with. But they were all only physical inconveniences. They were not the library.

What then was the library? What is any academic library? It is the books and the people who have and do select, organize, and administer them. It is inescapably both these components; for books without competent people to manage and interpret them are a bibliographical chaos of little value. An academic library is all the people, librarians, administrators, and faculty, who have been concerned over the years that it be a strong, good, and vital teaching and research agency. All who went before, university presidents, faculty members, library administrators, rank and file library staff members, and students too, all these are in varying degree for better or for worse and usually for better a part of the library. And of course the library is also the current faculty, librarians included, whose brains and interest are daily being built into it and who also daily take out dividends of the exact bit of information, the comprehensive subject backgrounds, the philosophies and thoughts of great men, the inspiring message needed to carry the teaching and research of the day successfully forward. Yes, every library no matter what the condition of its housing could honestly inscribe on its sheltering walls, "This is not the library —the library is inside!"

On the Storage of Books

Most space in a library stack is filled with nothing but empty air. Unique solutions for filling up the emptiness have been proposed.

IN EVERY LIBRARY with which I have been associated, two paradoxical and, in one sense, opposite problems have always been present. One of these has been a need for and a drive for many more books than the library owned. The other, as regular and as inevitable as the rising and setting of the sun, has been a battle for space to house the books already owned and those newly acquired. Because of this background, shared by most university librarians, I greeted with enthusiasm a book published in 1950 by Fremont Rider, librarian of Wesleyan University, devoted to the subject of compact book storage.

Mr. Rider, now deceased, was definitely one of the more imaginative and inventive of the mid-twentieth century librarians. He was also, I state appreciatively, the possessor of one of the most gifted pens in the profession. He pointed out in his little book that most of the space in a standard library stack is filled with nothing but empty air.

This, of course, is obvious to all who have thought analytically about the stacking of library books. Mr. Rider's significant contribution was that he sup-ported the general observation with facts and figures and arrived at least at a partial even if radical solution. He said that 65 percent of all space in a library stack is devoted to aisles, and only 35 percent to book shelves. Within the shelves themselves, however, only 35 percent of the space is utilized due to the variant heights of books. Of the total space in a library stack, he estimated that only 10 percent is actually occupied by books.

Mr. Rider cited earlier studies which had statistically demonstrated that 21 percent of all books are above ten inches high. His solution for the great amount of vertical space required for the interfiling of the higher books with the shorter ones was the simple one, used to some extent by all libraries, of shelving books turned down. Rather than a haphazard turning down of books as expediency may require, Mr. Rider, characteristically, approached the problem systematically. He found that when measured by width, rather than height, practically all books are less than nine inches wide. He applied turned down shelving to the less used research books in his own library by grouping books into six compact storage sizes by width, shelving them separately, and prefixing the call number for such books by an Arabic numeral indicating which size group it is shelved with.

Some of the turned down books, all of which he rested on their spines, received call letters directly on their bottoms. Some were trimmed for this purpose. A larger number he shelved in specially manufactured boxes, for the six size categories, with each of the six box sizes supplied in fifteen different widths to fit books of variant thickness. By application of the turned down shelving, Mr. Rider estimated that he would reduce the annual cost of housing his books by as much as six cents per title while increasing the storage capacity of his stacks by 50 percent.

Mr. Rider has in his book a Rube Goldberg chapter for the purpose, he said, of stretching the mind on the assumption that the fantastic sometimes evolves into the practical. He envisaged books shelved in a ferris wheel order, in self righting shelves, with a control to bring any desired shelves to a single floor level and at eye height. Then he compresses this wheel vertically, to have book shelves moving up and down vertically, as required. Elevators in each stack aisle moving the user up and down, as well as laterally, were also suggested as a possibility, as well as the lateral moving of book shelves on a belt principle in short shelf units, to permit turning of corners.

In all this one can see a solution for that hardy perennial, the departmental library problem. The university of the future can now be honeycombed underground with book tunnels, much like present heating tunnels, although, of course, in gleaming tile, well lighted, and with perfect humidity and ventilation.

Each of these tunnels will carry book tracks and shelves from a central store—the equivalent of the present central library. Faculty members and graduate students requiring specific books on any subject will then only have to press a control button to have whole shelves and sections of books come sailing through these tunnels, at subway speeds, and pop into seminars, laboratories, and offices, ready for use. Gone then will be a present impediment to research and study, the great, the tremendous, the onerous distance from faculty office to library.

"Too Damned Library-Like"

A true library cannot be un-library-like.

ONE OF THE more imaginative librarians of these mid-century times is Ralph Ellsworth, Director of Libraries at the University of Colorado, Boulder. Mr. Ellsworth has had the unique experience of having formerly been the librarian at Colorado and of planning the building which now houses that library and then leaving the University for fourteen years of service as Director of Libraries at the University of Iowa. During this period, he planned and put into operation a first unit of a new library building for Iowa. Now back in command at Boulder, Mr. Ellsworth naturally views the entire library situation there, including the housing of the library, in a different light than he would have or could have had he remained continuously at Boulder.

Looking at the Colorado Library from the vantage point of his fourteen years elsewhere, Mr. Ellsworth said in his annual report for 1957-58, the first since his return, that the trouble with the library was that "It's too damned 'library-like.'" The basis of this pungent remark was that the *Colorado Daily,* in an article on study space being arranged in the Colorado Memorial Union had said that this space should be "un-library-like" in character. This, Mr. Ellsworth thought, puts a finger on the shortcomings of the tone and atmosphere of the Colorado Library. I judge that what he had chiefly in mind are the physical attributes of housing and furnishing for which he had personally been chiefly responsible.

If the Colorado Library is too "library-like," and suffers therefrom, then this must be true much more sharply of many other academic library buildings very much less adequately and pleasantly housed than is the Colorado Library. I for one do not admit that it is bad for a library to be like a library, particularly since there has been and is progress in the housing of libraries as there has been and is in all other affairs of higher education. The things that make a library like a library are first and foremost books and people, simultaneously present. Without people, administrators, faculty, library staff, students, there can clearly be no library.

Remove the people completely and entirely and earth's best university library becomes only so much concrete, steel, and cellulose. It is only through and by people that meaning, life, and substance are given to the books in a library. The way the books are acquired, the amount of money made available for library purposes, the ability and interest of the faculty, the quality, number, and dedication of the library staff, the methods adopted and evolved for organizing materials, the rules and regulations governing use of materials, these are the things that determine the quality, the tone, the personality of a library.

That Library is best, and also most library-like, which possesses and is continually acquiring the books required to support the curricular programs and objectives of its institution and which can surely and quickly lay its hand on these materials. If in addition these books can be made pleasantly available under easy and liberal regulations, in comfortable and attractive surroundings, this of course enhances the excellence of a library and increases both the pleasure and effectiveness of its use. The basic essential of a library, nevertheless, is to have the books, to know what and where they are and to produce them, surely and quickly, to whatever extent the work of the day, or the year, or the decades may require. The library which can do this is a good library, regardless of its housing. To the extent it so responds, it is, the externals of housing and regulations aside, library-like.

A good library, if it is to remain good, can surmount the handicaps and hindrances of inadequate housing. This has, by ingenuity and good management, been done at numerous institutions. The notoriously poorly housed libraries, of which the University of Iowa was one before Mr. Ellsworth went there, are rapidly, and happily, disappearing from the academic scene of modern America. In every instance, poorly housed libraries have blossomed and bloomed and yielded increased harvest as they have moved into adequate and modern quarters carefully designed to promote the easy use of books.

Many academic libraries inadequately housed have far outstripped and outperformed sister libraries well and elegantly housed. They have done this by being very much like libraries—active, vibrant, responsive to user needs, alive. When and as they have achieved modern quarters in well lighted and ventilated buildings, equipped with faculty studies, staff rooms, photographic laboratories, typing rooms, map rooms, microfilm rooms, and all the other apparatus required to facilitate and add pleasure to navigating through the ever increasing sea of print, such libraries have universally taken on added vitality and effectiveness. From being good library-like libraries, they have often moved forward to becoming damned good ones.

Something to Pat

"I know, Jo, but . . .

AT THE ANNUAL conference of the Oregon Library Association in Coos Bay in 1965, one of the featured speakers was Jo Pardee, the able and dynamic librarian of the new North Central Regional Library headquartered in Wenatchee, Washington. Miss Pardee, whose main theme was the need for and efficiency of larger units of public library service, spoke of the difficulty of making appropriating authorities understand the need for increasing the operating expenditures of her library. She told of one of her commissioners who invited her to come to see the new county fair facilities in the process of construction at substantial thousands of dollars.

As this superior was, with pride, showing Miss Pardee the new buildings and telling her what they would cost, she asked him, "How is it that you can spend so much money for these buildings and yet you cannot find an additional $12,000 for operating our library?" Shoving his hat back on his head and scratching his ear, he finally said, "I know, Jo—but this is something I can pat!"

This apt reply hit squarely on the head the nail of the very natural human reaction and psychology of liking to see something real and concrete, in physical terms, for dollars expended or effort made. It is always, as contrasted with the intangibles,

easier to support and demonstrate the need for physical facilities. If then, by good fortune, success is attained, the results stand for all to see.

This is true of all human effort, public and private. It is particularly true of every enterprise supported by the public purse, federal, state, and city buildings and streets, college and university campuses and the buildings on them. It is true, naturally, of the new building which since 1963 has sheltered the Oregon State University Library. This structure stands on the campus centrally and, we like to think, gracefully. All who pass can rest their eyes on its physical presence, hopefully in appreciation. Those who are so moved, and some of us may be, can pat it, either literally or figuratively, and say, *this* is the library. It is not, however, really the library. The true library is, as is emphasized in a foregoing essay, the books and related materials the building houses, the people who use them, and the staff which services them.

The care and wisdom with which an academic library accumulates books in numerous languages, from all over the world, its painstaking organization of them for use, its intelligent interpretation and servicing of its resources, these are the things which make the library, any library, go. They are the things which infuse a library with soul and spirit. They are not physically demonstrable in budget requests. They cannot be patted. They are in effect very fragile. They could easily and quickly be destroyed by only a few unfortunate key appointments. The ready smile, the courteous answer, the patient interpretation, and the skillful handling of confused and often fumbling questions, professional competence and knowledgeability, readiness to go more than halfway, whether in the establishment of policy, the acquisition of books, or making them quickly available or in marshalling resources dealing with a specific subject; these are the vital factors found in a busy, happy, and useful library.

These things are real and precious. No one, least of all the librarians, can pat them but they are there infusing spirit and pleasantness into everything the library is and does. Happily, all these attributes are enhanced and given added dimensions when conducted in the attractive and efficient library quarters now increasingly found on the university campuses of America.

Once in a Lifetime

Librarians face a continuing and unrelenting battle for space and more space.

IN THE AUTUMN of 1963 it was my pleasant privilege to attend the dedication of the beautiful new $4.5 million addition to the Henry Suzzallo Library building at the University of Washington. As I stood with Kenneth Allen, Associate Director of Libraries, where the new meets the old, and as we looked out into the beautiful and functionally right new space, crowded with students, he said, "One building like this in a lifetime is enough."

Mr. Allen had carried, with marked success, the chief responsibility for both the planning and the equipping of this very fine addition, so much more successful than anyone would have deemed at all possible only a few short years ago. If I detected a note of weariness in his voice, he probably was thinking, perhaps subconsciously, of the long hours of discussion, of thinking, of planning, of struggling with the knotty problems of adding a functional, streamlined wing to

an unfunctional cathedral-type parent building which is just about the epitome of the library buildings of the first one-third of this present century in which architectural grandeur and ostentation had free rein.

In these earlier buildings, architecture came first. It was the order of the day to give only secondary and limited thought to the primary purpose of the building, the efficient acquisition, preparation, storage, and servicing of books and related materials. Mr. Allen may have been thinking too of the very considerable obstacle course which planners and architects for governmental agencies must run, if not always, then certainly nearly always, in creating new structures under abundant regulations, both legal and administrative.

Regulations at higher levels are of course essential. Undoubtedly, they do sometimes keep planners from going off the deep end in the direction of extravagance or in becoming legally involved with contractors and suppliers. Indeed this sometimes happens within, and sometimes

even because of existing regulations. As an example, one major university library building was delayed the best part of a year while the state adjudicated between contending contractors. By and large, however, it is my conviction that, at least in the library field, in the present state of building planning and know-how, that if the planners could be freed of many of the regulations which so closely circumscribe their efforts they would create better and more efficient buildings, better equipped and for less money. Certainly their work would be accomplished with less stress and strain and wear and tear on nerves and dispositions both at the planning and regulatory levels.

All this aside, one thing is, in the present state of things bibliotecal, certain. One major library building in a professional lifetime is no longer enough at any major academic institution. With books pouring from the presses with abandon the world around, with a million dollars or more per year being spent for acquisitions by the larger universities, with their libraries growing as much as a million volumes per decade, the creation of space to contain it all must go on, willy-nilly, in increasing tempo. The special demands of inflowing materials in all libraries will of course be reduced, is being reduced, by acquisition in micro image. Great multitudes of things do not, however, lend themselves to such reduction, at least in the present state of the art.

More and ever more new library space—this is the handwriting on the wall for this articulate civilization of ours. So much so that any young person entering the academic library profession today can expect to be associated with several major library constructions during his professional lifetime. Indeed some of the presently active people have already been involved in a number of such constructions. Some universities, as a matter of fact, now have several major library buildings rising simultaneously.

For most librarians of my generation, one major creation of new library space has been enough to maintain and upgrade the current programs at least on a nominal basis. Everything that has happened, is happening, and promises to happen indicates, as has been emphasized here, that it will not be enough for the younger librarians now in the field, to say nothing of those to come. For these younger people there can be only a continuing and unrelenting battle for space and more space with all the accompanying problems, trials, tribulations, and, if they are lucky, deep satisfactions.

Blood on the Moon

It took fifty years to get the classrooms out of the library. It may take fifty more to get them back in again.

BLOOD ON THE MOON! This was the exclamation of a startled faculty member in 1953 as he walked into the lower foyer of the old library building at Oregon State University and saw the ceiling turning into a vivid pink under the ministrations of the painters. Another member of the faculty, because of this colorful ceiling, awaited momentarily an investigation of the library for reasons which, in the climate of mid-twentieth century public opinion, need not be elaborated. Certainly the pinks, greens, corals, greys, and browns which were then going up on the walls and ceilings were a drastic change for a dignified old building after some thirty-four years of nondescript and colorless institutional buffs and tans.

Too startling, too much of a change, too different for an old building long accustomed to a less vivid interior, said some people. These old walls and pillars, long accustomed to going unseen, unnoticed, could easily be imagined as gasping under this sudden onslaught of color, raising a friezed and pinkish eyebrow, Walt Disney fashion as it were, and exclaiming, one to the other, "What goes on here!" Once the initial shock was over though, they began, we think, to admire themselves a bit. The new colors were, of course, a part of the trend to bright and colorful interiors which is a distinguishing characteristic of newer or renovated library buildings, as can be immediately noted in the numerous new postwar college and university libraries of this country.

It could be said that the use of color in the modern library is symbolic, that it reflects the emergence of a passive, rather aloof agency, withdrawn from the hustle and bustle of the classroom and laboratory, existing somewhat for itself but willing to serve those who would come quietly and circumspectly to avail themselves of its services. Transition from this state into a positive, dynamic agency eager to be noticed, to be helpful, to take an active part both in teaching and research, this has been marked.

Such a vital function is the aim of the modern, divisional, open stack library with its various subject areas under the direction of subject specialists who are at home both in the subject content of their shelves and in the methods through which they can be most effectively used. These li-braries are a far cry indeed from the quiet, secluded, largely non-circulating academic library of earlier decades, surrounding its books with numerous barriers. How different the modern library, with students roaming through the stacks at will, with typing rooms, conversation rooms, seminars, faculty offices, smoking rooms, music listening rooms, photographic laboratories, coke bars, and what-not. With these changes has come a change of emphasis in libraries nearly everywhere from acquisition and conservation to utilization. As one college administrator has shrewdly observed, the librarians of America spent fifty years getting the classroom out of the library and they will probably spend the next fifty years in trying to get it back in.

This Old House

Simplicity, harmony, and adaptability made it the "most artistic building on campus."

IN THE AUTUMN of 1918 there was deep satisfaction at Oregon State College and particularly at the Library. This was so because after ten years of planning and urging by "Mother" Kidder, the then librarian, a new library building had, through the efforts of many people, come into being. To be sure it was not complete, awaiting installation of a central stack unit and other furnishings. The 35,000 cataloged books constituting the collection had, however, by the volunteer work of the men of the faculty, been moved from crowded and ham-pering quarters in Benton Hall to their new home. At last the library was functioning in the beauty, ample space, and dignity of which many people had dreamed.

Mother Kidder of course was prejudiced, but she was perhaps right when, in her annual report for 1916-18, in celebrating the completion of the building, she said, "From its simplicity, harmony and adaptability to service, I cannot but consider it the most artistic building on the campus." In the intervening years many changes and many new buildings came to the campus. Perhaps not even Mother Kidder, were she here, would now claim her library to be the most serviceable and beautiful of the structures within which the university now functions.

Times changed. Architecture became more functional and the library grew apace. As it grew, other college services and departments it once sheltered were required to find other and better quarters elsewhere on the campus. More quickly than anyone had foreseen, and this was within a well-established American pattern, came the time when the building was chuck-a-block.

A new wing was needed. With the assistance of the Works Progress Administration, it was erected in 1941. This wing too was rapidly filled with readers, books, and the people acquiring and administering them. As the printing presses ground merrily on and the college struggled to secure that portion of their output essential to carrying on its work, the cry of more room for books, for staff, for readers once again went up with increasing insistence. This too was within the American pattern for academic libraries. It is a pattern not established by administrative choice. It flows from the unescapable facts of the current academic scene. Every college, if it is to be strong, vigorous, and successful, in teaching and in research, must have a good library. For Oregon State this required collections and services which could no longer be satisfactorily encompassed in the building which was so abundantly ample in 1918.

All this was in no way a disparagement of the old building which had served so well. The dignity which Mother Kidder saw in it was certainly there, amplified through years of service and accumulating and crowding memories. The years took their toll, as they do of all material things. Rotting window sills in the main reading room required replacing. The roof nearly always leaked somewhere, and drip buckets were often busy catching that part of the Oregon mist which chose not to go down the drain spouts. In spite of all this, the building, like some old houses, had, at least for many of us, a certain charm and appeal not always found in the sleek, modern, streamlined libraries being erected in such numbers on the college and university campuses of our country.

This New House

Streamlined, sleeker, more colorful, the new building quickly fitted into users' habits.

THE FOREGOING commentary, written in 1956, was directed, appreciatively, to the library building of 1918, even though a case was being made at the same time for a new building to take its place. These efforts were, at long last, successful. The time came then, in 1963, when the "Old Building," which served so well for its time, and for which I have both love and affection, stood dark and empty against the evening sky, bereft of the busy pulsing life of almost half a century. Taking its place was this "New House," the first unit of the new home dreamed about and planned and worked for so long. Streamlined, sleeker, more colorful, tripling the user capacity of the "Old House," it rapidly fitted itself into student and faculty work and study habits. Even in its very initial service, it gave promise of contributing more, for its time, than did the old house for its.

One thing we quickly knew for a certainty. In this new home, use of the Library would increase tremendously. And not simply in a study hall situation, although such use is, as we had expected, a significant motivation among the students who come thronging to all reading areas. Evidence of increased use of books in the Library, as contrasted with charge out for home use, is that student assistants are kept continuously busy clearing the tables and reshelving books taken down for table use at a rate running into the thousands daily. Additional statistical evidence of increased use was an upturn of 27 percent in reserve book withdrawals in the first month of service.

There is, I think, no academic institution of significance any-

where in our country which has not recently created entirely new space for its library or expanded existing library structures or which, failing this, does not hopefully have plans on the drawing boards for such additional space. And in every instance such space is and has been desperately needed. Indeed, Oregon State has been a come-lately in the continuing parade of new library construction and then only on a limited basis as this first unit of the new home barely suffices for the moment.

Out of all the busy and costly building going on everywhere has come an exciting evolution of library architecture departing, sometimes drastically, from the conformity of the three first decades of our century. Low buildings and tower buildings, buildings that are square, rectangular, ell shaped, round, some with several levels below ground, some entirely without windows, others with liberal use of exterior screens, as in our building, these are now to be found everywhere, in increasing numbers, from the smallest colleges to the greatest universities, many of which now have an extensive complex of library buildings. Gone entirely are the expensive high-vaulted, cathedral-like reading rooms of earlier years.

Almost universally the new buildings share one characteristic. This is a lively concern for functional efficiency, for aesthetics, for reader comfort, for economy of operation and maintenance, and for a minimum of barriers between students and books. We like to think that in all these things the Oregon State University building, achieved at one of the lowest square-footage costs in the country, is not the least.

Thanks and Farewell

Sorrow and nostalgia accompany departure from the comfortable "Old House."

As we reached, at Oregon State University, the final fulfillment of the long held dream of a new home for the Library there was elation, of course, and deep satisfaction. Our new building, even as we were in the process of occupying it, gave promise of coming close to everything we had hoped for. Curiously, however, and unexpectedly, I found my most poignant emotions centered at that moment, not around the new building, but the old.

It was, somehow, a profound shock, when after a full day in the new building, assisting with the moving-in operation, I walked into the old main reading room to find it entirely devoid of books and its stacks being vigorously and effectively attacked and dismantled by two industrious young student workers. Amidst the banging and the clanging and shouting, my first reaction was one of desecration, my impulsive instinct to cry out, cease and desist! There was a tear, literally, even as I realized how ridiculous I was being. Obviously one cannot have one's cake and eat it too.

Common sense notwithstanding and in spite of pleasure over the new building, these same emotions returned, again and again, as I came back to the old building to find more and more of its life blood carried away. It was a shock, equally, to suddenly see the central reference room bare, its books transported to their new environment, its busy catalog, nerve center of the entire Library, no longer there. To be able to suddenly look right through the stack well, to walk, without the comfort of surrounding books, over its glass floors, and to hear footsteps echoing hollowly in the emptiness—this too was a shock. In the eagerness for the new home, I had not been prepared for any of this.

A prevailing refrain in these commentaries is that a building, of and by itself, is not a library. Books, the people who collect, organize, and service them, and the building that shelters it all, these, I have said, in one way or another are the triumvirate of the total library. This fundamental truth came home to me with increasing impact in the time of moving to the new building. Two of the basics were steadily being drained from the old building, which, for almost half a century, had so well served the college and the succeeding university.

As the books departed, truck by truck, and as the library staff left, the service librarians first, the life blood and the very soul of this comfortable old house, from whose McDonald room, bare of books, this essay was written, was inexorably withering away. The building would, of course, have a new and a good life. Soundly conceived plans for its transfiguration for other purposes were on the drawing boards. This was as it should be. It did not alter the fact, however, that in the month of September 1963, it was, as a library, slowly dying.

Many and proud were its memories. Forty-five graduating classes had trod through its halls, gathering knowledge and inspiration from its books, making love in its convenient nooks and crannies, and literally wearing out its marble stairs with their busy comings and goings. Once capacious enough to house the College Auditorium, the Speech Department, and the Office of the Dean of Women, this building saw these agencies and functions depart, one by one, that it might better serve its primary purpose. This it did to the utmost, yielding up surprising amounts of extra space, in the plenum fan room, on the elevator bridge, around the periphery of the stack well, on the reading room floors, even in toilets, for the books which, continuously, and without let, came crowding in. No building could have done more and given more. It experienced three administrations of its resources and services, each following the other smoothly and harmoniously, to permit it to continue its serene although increasingly crowded and eventually inadequate service. One memory it had all alone, of all the academic libraries of this land. It was without doubt the only library where the Librarian of its planning and early occupancy lay in state at the time of her death.

I was not alone in nostalgia for the old house. On a late afternoon of the moving time, as I walked with one of the student helpers from the new to the old and as we entered the lower lobby to find the central reference room suddenly bare and despoiled, he sighed and said "The poor Old Library. I had grown to be very fond of it." So had we all. So in behalf of us all, students, staff, faculty, I could and did salute this comfortable old home and say to it, humbly and gratefully, "Thanks! thanks and farewell. You have richly earned our respect and our love!"

There are, it seems to me, two chief implications in the tremendous increase of Man's recorded knowledge. One of these is the sheer physical impact of the quantitative growth, the problems of housing and storage. With this these essays and indeed much of the current thinking and writing of librarians and others is much concerned. The problems of the evolving library architecture discussed in Part V, how best to make books available for use, these all flow largely from the mass of materials to be processed, preserved, and delivered for use as required. This is the easy, or at least the easier part, of Man's effort to cope with his mounting knowledge.

The other and far more important aspect is the intellectual implications of it all. What does this great and growing graphic store portend for current and future generations? Will it indeed, as some have feared and predicted, be intellectually suffocating? Can large portions of it be discarded now or eventually? What are the prospects for continuance of the intellectual and technological developments which have come about through the careful storing of and organization for use of knowledge from ancient times up to the fast-paced present.

While Man has continued, in a series of ups and downs, to move forward in his understanding of the world he lives in and all its physical and biological phenomena, it has remained for those of us now on the stage to be present at and to participate in a sensational breakthrough scientifically and technologically, a breakthrough, unfortunately, not equalled in sociological and psychological areas and in Man's understanding of himself.

I am quite convinced that the books added to academic and research libraries in the past two decades have recorded scientific and technological discoveries and achievements which will never again be equalled in the history of mankind. The literature of this period has been climax, or the beginning of climax, to the centuries of probing, thinking, writing, and reading, to the intuitive, ingenious, and persistent efforts of Man to know the unknowable.

The antibiotic drugs, the conquering of many of the most stubborn diseases, many of the wonders and miracles of electronics, the further conquest of space and the universe through rockets and missiles, planes tripling the speed of sound, and, ominously or by providence as the years to come will tell, the finding of the key to nuclear energy; all of these things have either come newly on the scene or been brought to perfection during the two decades through which these essays were written. Certainly, further discoveries and miracles will come. Planes will go faster, computers will become more versatile, new drugs will do even more wonderful things, the moon and possibly neighboring planets will be visited, the far reaches of the universe will be explored in detail, but the pattern has been set for what nature's laws will permit. The limits are definite and discernible.

One megaton or fifty, the bomb is the same. Planes and rockets will almost certainly, at the maximum, never achieve more than one-tenth of the speed of light, as compared with one-hundredth of that speed now. Man, the prober, has opened the vistas wider and looked further into lands of the once unknowable than might ever have been hoped. He will achieve new and important scientific and technologi-

cal conquests but along lines now pretty clearly established. And in it all books will continue to be, as they have been, basic. Never again, however, will Man experience the wonder, the excitement, and the awe which has been reached and recorded in the books added to libraries everywhere during these mid-century years. This will be so because all research and discovery now, contrary to earlier times, goes forward in a climate of rising expectations.

The following essays particularly, and in a sense all the essays in this book, are grounded in beliefs such as this. It seems appropriate, as historical setting, that the first essay in this series should be devoted in part to reactions of earlier generations to the increase of books.

Too Much to Know

"The multitude of books is making us ignorant."

So said Voltaire in the eighteenth century when the product of the printing press was still, as compared with present times, a mere rivulet. What Voltaire meant, I suppose, was that there were getting to be so many books in the world that neither he nor other men of scholarly instincts and aptitudes could know them all. But the concern of Voltaire, who himself contributed significantly to the multitude, availed not at all, as one can surmise he did not really wish it to avail, against busy minds and moving pens and the click of the type-setter's stick.

Somewhat over a century later we find Washington Irving, another fecund contributor to the library heritage, coming at the same problem:

But the invention of paper and press have put an end to all . . . restraints. They have made every one a writer, and enabled every mind to pour itself into print, and diffuse itself over the whole intellectual world. The consequences are alarming. The stream of literature has swollen into a torrent—augmented into a river—expended into a sea . . .

Unless some unforeseen mortality should break out among the progeny of the muse, now that she has become prolific, I tremble for posterity, . . . let criticism do what it may, writers will write, printers will print, and the world will inevitably be overstocked with good books. It will soon be the employment of a lifetime merely to learn their names.

Many a man of passable information, at the present day, reads scarcely anything but reviews; and before long a man of erudition will be little better than a mere walking catalogue.

It is doubtful that even Irving, who spoke in awe of libraries of three or four hundred thousand volumes, foresaw the speed with which our writings would increase. Symbolic of the rampant flood of print is the Library of Congress now growing at the rate of more than seven linear miles of codex books per year, 700 miles in a century, and in 500

years, just once again as far into the future as the invention of printing is into the past, 3,500 miles.

Against this flood there stands throughout the world a small army of librarians, bibliographers, abstractors, indexers, valiantly striving to keep Man's literature satisfactorily housed and in findable order. Small wonder that they seek and fasten with alacrity on all devices, such as microprint and microfilm for reducing the physical size of the book, that they are beginning to plan, however reluctantly, to pool their books into vast regional and national reservoirs, that their catalogs and indexes are becoming increasingly cumbersome and unwieldy and that some librarians typical of their age, cry out for a machine, a machine which will organize, classify, and select from out of the vast multitude those books and articles needed at any given moment or on any given subject.

The multitudinous spawning of books does not make too fanciful the article, published in 1947, by Garrett Hardin of the then Santa Barbara College in which he depicted the publication, in Mars, of the content of some steel plates found near the site of worldly New York, plates portraying the unsuccessful attempt of one benefactor to reduce the size of the world's libraries. Mr. Hardin makes the *Martian Morning Revelation* say:

With the discovery of these plates we have, for the first time found evidence that a few of the Worldlings tried to fend off their doom . . .

What a strange quirk of fate that these people, who titillated themselves with visions of destruction by atomic power—which to these primitive folk seemed a wondrous thing—should instead have perished peacefully, inexorably 'suffocated' as one of their prophets put it, 'by their own intellectual excreta.'

Retrieval Is Retrieval Is Retrieval

A FUNDAMENTAL and ancient problem of libraries, going back to the time when writings first began to be gathered into collections, is to know what is owned and to quickly lay hands on whatever writings may be needed at any given moment. In earlier and simpler times this was not much trouble. Librarians often simply remembered what books were owned and where they were. After the invention of printing and the rapid proliferation of writings of stature and significance, this became increasingly impossible.

The obvious solution when this stage was reached was to catalog the books for easy finding. Such catalogs have taken many variant forms throughout the world from ancient times to the present. In this country they have evolved into the well-known author-title-subject card catalog, usually filed in a single alphabet. This is the tool, along with intricate classification schemes, by which nearly all American libraries keep track of and find their books. The pioneer American librarians of the latter half of the nineteenth century, who evolved and laid down the principles which still largely govern American cataloging processes, were reasonably well satisfied with their creation. Writing in 1877, C. A. Cutter, one of the great catalogers of his time, said this:

> The subject-catalogue grew up in the same way as the librarian's memorandum . . . It is costly, but it is cheaper than men and women intelligent and learned enough to be its substitutes, and it does not die or get married, as men and women do; it is never tired and forgetful; it requires no vacation, and is never sick . . .

The catalog of which Cutter spoke, and its companion apparatus of abstracts and indexes for the journal literature of specialized fields, such as chemistry, medicine, physics, and many other disciplines, are the chief keys to the holdings of even the greatest libraries. Under the impact of a literature which has made multi-millioned libraries common, these tool devices, which have served and are serving well, have come under increasing strain and are steadily becoming more costly and less satisfactory.

Vannevar Bush, World War II director of the Office of Scientific Research and Development, a good many years ago voiced the shortcomings of our venerable literature controls in these terms:

> The summation of human experience is being expanded at a prodigious rate and the means we use for threading through the consequent maze to the momentarily important item is the same as was used in the days of the square rigged ship . . .

Small wonder that under these circumstances the librarians and scholars of a machine-oriented world, in seeking relief, began hopefully turning to the machine which so completely dominates our current civilization. A considerable literature devoted to the machine controls of our writings has grown up in the past two decades. Bush himself envisaged a "Memex" desk for the individual scholar in which most of the literature he will need will be stored in coded and micro-reduced form ready to yield itself up merely at the pressure of the proper button.

Edmund Berkeley, in his "Giant Brains, or Machines That Think," confidently and rashly, as events are proving, predicted that these machines, which are already fantastically successful in sorting, analyzing, and digesting data and quickly arriving at answers that would require many man-years of mental effort, will also one day think intuitively, make brilliant guesses, and leap to conclusions. In doing this, says Berkely, they will determine *all* their own instructions. It is already theoretically certain, even though these machines are still only in their infancy, that they can, as applied to the literature of specific fields, know what is in a library and retrieve it as needed. Theoretically possible, yes, but practically? Not yet.

I have in my own lifetime seen our civilization emerge from the primitive days of an earth-bound man, the horse and buggy, and the coal oil lamp. I have long since determined not to be surprised at anything. I am quite prepared to see a machine-centered library in which some mechanical marvel will efficiently retrieve and retrieve and retrieve literature as required. Some especially gifted machine may even write creatively, with imagination and verve. I can easily visualize a machine on a literary binge joyfully, endlessly, and with variations, writing, à la Gertrude Stein, *retrieval is retrieval is retrieval is retrieval* . . . In spite of my resolution to be sophisticated, I am going to be faintly surprised though, in an Emily Dickinson sense, if a machine attains the delicate perceptiveness to write, and then modestly hide, for the delight and applause of the eugenically perfect test tube denizens of the full-fledged machine age something like the lines below.

A little madness in Spring
Is wholesome even for a King
But God be with the (Machine)
(Which) ponders this tremendous scene—
This whole experiment of green
As if it were (its) own!

David's Attack on Goliath

Confronting the Monster of Massiveness.

In 1956, I noted, in these essays, the establishment of the Council on Library Resources created through a substantial supply of Ford Foundation dollars for the purpose of attacking and bringing under control and effective organization for use, the massive and exploding literature of our time. I likened this new Council with its few millions of dollars, to David attacking Goliath.

In the intervening years I have appreciatively and with keen interest followed the work of this Council as recorded in its annual reports and elsewhere. I have done this because I have felt, as I am certain most librarians have, that it is at grips with one of the fundamental problems not of libraries alone but of our entire culture and civilization. Over and above this, I am particularly interested in the Council because, along with millions of other Americans, I have a proprietary interest in it. I too have added my grain to the fortune from which the Council draws its sustenance. A brass radiatored Model-T of 1917, kept clean and shining in spite of Nebraska mud and dust, this was the pride and joy of my teen age years, bringing release from weary country miles and victory over numbing cold. After 1917 I went through five products of the Ford factories, each improved but none so wonderful as that first one. Each of these obviously brought black ink, in however minuscule a quantity, to the Ford ledgers.

They were relatively simple times bibliographically, those days of 1917. Even those who knew about books and libraries, which I certainly did not, were not then deeply concerned about the massiveness of the world's literature or about controls. The librarians of those days, largely untroubled by visions of surfeit, had chiefly a burning zeal, even as now, for more and more dollars to accumulate more and more books. Had Henry Ford been told, in those years, that the profits he was piling up so handsomely would one day be used to help solve the problems of libraries he would probably have been impatiently disbelieving, possibly even horrified. Nevertheless, the fruit of the Ford seed dollars so astutely planted early in the century is now being used, in some small part, to solve the bibliographical complexities of our wordy and highly literate civilization.

It is our good fortune that, as the annual reports of the Council show, this is being done wisely and well. The Council, however, is somewhat like but in a far more difficult situation than was David facing Goliath. Before its very eyes Goliath grows bigger and bigger. With each passing day the conquest becomes more formidable. Nor can any single stone be flung for immediate and dramatic victory. Instead the Council has filled its arsenal with an assortment of pebbles, possibly even a small stone or two. These are being peppered at the monster of massiveness from all directions. Many of them are merely improvements and refinements of traditional library techniques and methodology. Others, and these may be pebbles of telling effect, look to machine controls, automatic indexing, density storage, and greater cooperation among libraries in a common attack.

Ever since I have been a librarian, I have amused and sometimes startled myself by calculating the growth rate of libraries. Each time I have made these calculations, the figures, reflecting the rising flood, have been more impressive. I have disturbed some of my colleagues by suggesting, partly in fun but with some seriousness, that faced with the tremendous bibliographical store we are piling up so rapidly, which as estimated above may bring the Library of Congress 3,500 linear miles of books by the year 2560, the learned world of the future may throw away, completely and irrevocably, some thousands of miles of its books.

Recently I have been thinking of these things this way. The best estimates are that our planet Earth is five billion years old. Only for the last million of these years, however, has Man been present and only during the last six thousand years has he been making the meaningful marks through which his high culture has been attained. Only during the last 500 years have these marks been duplicated in quantity to create great libraries. Our little planet, however, reliable estimates say, will be habitable for another five billion years, or once again as long as it has already been in existence. This places us at high noon on the cosmic clock. In the split second during which we have, in the cosmic scale, been on the globe as book-writing and book-storing creatures we have created endless miles of books. But we still have five billion years to go.

We are then in the merest infancy of our bookishness. It is not to be expected that those in the ages to come will retain all the writings of this infancy. Believing this, I attach great importance to one small stone being directed at Goliath by the Library Council. This is a project euphemistically called "Selective Book Retirement" carried out by the Yale University Library. Professors, under the stimulation of Ford dollars, have systematically combed the Yale stacks, library shelf list in hand, to finger those books which might be safely retired. Those deemed less vital have, as professorial judgment has dictated, been retired to a kind of second class citizenship, storage. This I believe is a harbinger, a very gentle one, of things to come. Somewhere within our next five billion years, possibly within the next few cosmic seconds, an additional brutal but inevitable step will be taken. This will be, and it makes me shudder, to replace the euphemistic "retirement" of millions upon millions of books by their death.

The Holy Grail Evades the Search

For two decades and more, efforts to harness the machine to control our massive literature has gone on at increasing tempo.

A STEADILY MOUNTING number of highly skilled man hours and an impressive expenditure of dollars have been and are being devoted to this task. Librarians, documentalists, (really librarians sailing under a different flag), engineers, chemists, physicians, biologists, physicists, mathematicians, all supported by foundation grants and/or generous industrial dollars have been bending energies and talented minds toward a search for the Holy Grail, a machine or machines which will yield up quickly and economically whatever portion or item or fact in the mushrooming graphic store which may be needed at any given moment. A major index, but by no means the only one, of the tempo of the search is that the Council on Library Resources has, as indicated in the foregoing essay, devoted a substantial portion of its dollars to the quest. This has, in terms of specifics, been more grant money than has been devoted, since time began, to the perfection of traditional library controls.

The search, or so at least it seems to me, has proceeded in three phases. First were the blythe and confident beginnings. This was a time marked by fuzzy thinking and extravagant promises, when men new to the field and unaware of the magnitude and complexities of the problem, the Edmund Berkeleys and others, had visions of machines which would not only yield up whatever facts or literature or documents might be desired but would largely determine their own principles and directives. These mechanical marvels, however, were always, as they indeed still are, somewhere over the horizon. The talking and writings of this period were rife with such phrases as "can be," "is possible," "will be," "could be." The clear words of concrete achievement, "is," and "does," these were conspicuous by their absence, as they still largely are.

Gradually there emerged a

second phase in which predictions became less positive and less extravagant. This was a time of reappraisal, or recognizing, meeting, and learning to contend with the bibliographical facts of life in all their complexity and magnitude. The searchers were now discovering, the hard way, what all experienced librarians have learned, often the hard way too. This included recognition of the infinite variety of ways and words in which men express themselves, the unexpected relationships and inter-relationships between concepts, facts, documents, and the necessity to provide for these in any finding system. The curious and oblique ways in which people approach a library for the literature and the answers they seek were also beginning to be realized. More and more it was being recognized that the organization of the world's knowledge is a deeply intellectual process.

Sober reappraisal and better understanding led to a third and more fruitful phase, the full realization that literature control is a tough nut not easily digestible by the machine. Concrete achievements are being made in this, the current phase, but often not in the direction that had been expected or promised. Easy push-button location of specific knowledge in the mass continues to evade the search. Instead has come application of punched cards and magnetic computer tape to indexing processes and to the clerical details of acquisition and cataloging. Real successes have been scored. The "is" and the "does" have arrived in such things as computer-prepared concordances, book catalogs, and other indexing.

Two stubborn facts face all who seek to turn the machine to literature control. First and foremost is the sheer quantitative mass of the materials to be digested even currently to say nothing of retroactive application. A second major problem is that most of this mass consists of words, and words as we all know are nonprecise, variable, delicate instruments too often misinterpreted, as the whole history of Man shows. Their meaning is often determined by their context or the way they are spoken or who utters them, even though spelling and pronunciation is, in each instance, identical. The word "democracy" for instance, how varied and sometimes diametrically opposite are its uses and its meanings. Or the word "love." We love our wife or sweetheart but we also love pumpkin pie and playing golf. We are admonished to love our neighbor as ourselves but we can also say, if occasion warrants,

that we would love to sock him in the nose.

Unfortunately for men and machines alike, the devious mind of man sometimes uses the word white when what is really meant is black or black when white is meant. Owen Wister recognized the realities of the ways of words when his Virginian said, "When you call me that, smile." Obviously, any practical scheme for mechanical organization and delivery of knowledge must cope, as have the traditional controls, with semantic realities which often confuse and defeat the most subtle minds. Computers, however, "love" only precise terms and symbols which they handle with incredible dexterity and speed. Because the words man uses so copiously, in some 27,000 languages, are neither uniform nor precise, the quest for the Holy Grail of findability by machine, within literature in the mass, promises to be long and arduous indeed.

Librarians or Icemen

The machine has almost replaced the horse. Will it also replace the librarian?

FROM TIME to time in recent years an uneasy stirring has been noticeable among librarians over the prospects of having much that they do performed by machines. This reaches the stage sometimes of fretting about will the machine perhaps displace the librarian? One such expression, not so much of concern as of the implications, is by Aaron Fessler in an article "Librarians or Ice-

men" appearing in the 1960 spring issue of *Sci-Tech News.*

Mr. Fessler says that just as the iceman has been displaced, the machine will indeed displace the librarian, unless he becomes an "information scientist" or a "documentalist" or a "machinist" or unless he secures degrees in mathematics or physics or patent searching or electronics. He says librarians must enslave the machine to their purposes rather than to "permit the reverse to happen."

These suggestions exhibit the

tendency, present in all circles of our society, to confuse what is done with the name applied to it, or more precisely, to give status and dignity to what is done by assigning some kind of prestige name to it. Thus the janitor becomes a "custodian" but he still has to do the same old sweeping, scrubbing, and cleaning even if, happily, with the aid of machines. The name changes not one whit what he does or needs to do. Similarly librarians, whether they call themselves "information scientists" or "documentalists" or as has been suggested "data engineers," still have the basic function of accumulating, organizing, and servicing the world's literature. And an honorable and essential function it is, fundamental to our complex and highly articulate civilization. To the extent which the machine can be bent and harnessed to this work it may be executed better and more efficiently, but it will still be exactly the same and more and more people, whatever they are called or choose to call themselves, will be required to carry it out.

Since time began, in the memory of the race, technological advances have caused unease and concern. The maker of bows gave way, with grumbling and unease no doubt, to the gunsmith; new vistas, new enterprises, and expanded work resulted, moving rapidly, in a historical sense, to the propelling of missiles into space. Nevertheless, the object and purpose is still the same, to throw something from one place to another. The primitive man who first shaped and sharpened a likely stick to hurl at animal or human is quite certainly grandfather of the modern missile man

firing satellites on endless journeys throughout the universe.

The missile hurling process now, however, involves quantities of people, many of them not even conscious of being a part of it. Fundamental to the process is something not needed by the first spear maker or the first bowman. This is the written fact and word and theory accumulated into libraries, row after row, tier upon tier. The function of those who gather, organize, and preside over these materials is exactly the same, whatever they are called, as that of the first librarian with only a shelf full of books.

The iceman, with dripping ice block on shoulder, whom greyheads of today like myself easily remember, is completely extinct, but his function, far from being extinct, has taken on new dimensions. Far more people are involved in the making of ice today than ever before, and ice, once a luxury reserved for king or potentate, is now a commonplace essential of our way of life. Similarly, in the recording of knowledge, the scribe gave way to the printer, thereby making possible the massive writings which have

brought librarianship, in the modern sense, with all its complexities, into being.

Actually the evolution of management of the literature is the reverse of that indicated by Mr. Fessler. Rather than the librarian becoming physicist, or engineer, or doctor of medicine, people in these occupations often become either librarians or else assume some other aspect of producing or managing the literature. We see this happening all the time as men and women engaged in medicine or law or chemistry or other professions assume fulltime responsibilities for editing journals, for directing abstracting and indexing, or for managing libraries.

A specific case in point in the field of medicine is the Institute for Advancement of Medical Communication. This institute, begun under the direction of Dr. Richard Orr, an M.D., is concerned with the increasing inadequacy of the traditional methods of medical communication. It hopes to cut across present editorial and abstracting lines to make the findings of medical research workers available with an economy of words and much more quickly than the present eighteen months. In this professional evolution of being drawn off or partially drawn off from direct practice of his profession to tending its literature, Dr. Orr has the company of thousands of men in a wide variety of professional fields. Moreover, this is a trend which is accelerating, willy-nilly, as the literature grows ever more voluminous. What the people who direct and manage the literature are called is not so important. What they do is all important. The ancient and honorable title of Librarian, though, is a good one.

Automatic Library of the Future

*Knowledge unlimited,
books without cost
—a dream for 1980.*

IMAGINATIVE AND PROVOCATIVE forecasts of what the library of the future will be like have, in recent years, occasionally appeared in books and journals. All of these have had a substantial basis in scientific discovery and the application of the miracles of electronics to reproduction of the written or printed page and the rapid transmission of the image of it over considerable distances. Experimental devices which will do this have been developed along with machines that will permit micro-reduction of the graphic store of knowledge for reproduction, in normal size, as needed.

In *Scientific Monthly* of February 1951, Colonel Fred L. Walker, Jr. published an article, interesting and imaginative but also naive and lacking in perception, in which he visualized streamlined, mechanistic library service of the year 1980. The cover of this issue of *Scientific Monthly* portrays J. D. Doakes, a character imagined by Colonel Walker, sitting at ease before a gooseneck video screen, reading literature which he has called up from a central library merely by punching a nearby control panel. Samples of the whole gamut and background of the human heritage of recorded writings make up the background of this appealing picture.

One of Colonel Walker's ideas which is particularly curious and naive is that this kind of use of written records, which he chooses to call mechanical memory, will somehow open up for the student "a brave new world—one in which he could learn to use his mind for creative thought and analysis instead of cramming it with masses of memorized information . . ." Actually, of course, whether information, ideas, or facts are placed before a student on a screen or in the more convenient codex book we now use, the problem of reading, absorb-

ing, and intellectually mastering it remains exactly the same, with the possible, but by no means certain, exception that the desired data may be found more readily by electronics. Also, according to Colonel Walker, "the customer of the automatic library of 1980 can not only have knowledge unlimited, but also books without cost." How this economic miracle can come about, in view of the intricate transmission, receiving, and reproducing machinery required, is not satisfactorily explained.

One point that this article misses entirely is that the automatic library envisioned, when and if it comes, will greatly complicate the problems of classifying and cataloging our written records. D. J. Haykin of the Library of Congress cataloging department, now deceased, pointed this out neatly as follows:

> Colonel Walker delves into the problem of classification without perhaps full awareness of its pitfalls. What is obvious and shocking about the various so-called automatic bibliographic controls of knowledge is that they overlook the very important fact that, before a bit of knowledge can be 'coded' it must be digested and understood and that, therefore, no substitute for the human mind is available for transmitting knowledge— not only facts, but what is more important, the numberless relationships between facts—in the form of visual verbal images in various languages and of arbitrary symbols and auditory expressions of language and music into 'code' symbols which 'J. D.'s' librarians can apply. Colonel Walker, . . . is unaware of the basic fact of the so-far inevitable intervention of the human mind

After all, 1980 is now just around the corner. Many, perhaps most, of the readers of these essays may still be around to observe the wonders of the automatic library and to enjoy books without cost.

Intellectual Implications

NEW JOURNAL after new journal is appearing on the scene, each devoted either to an increasingly narrow specialty or to a new field of knowledge unknown, possibly undreamed of, just a few short years ago. A whole host of concomitant new guide tools, abstracts, indexes, proceedings, surveys, reports of progress, is springing into being to keep some semblance of order and discipline in it all.

Hardly a day passes that there does not come to the academic and/or research library announcements of new and invariably costly publications of many types. This flood does not consist of only journal and other serial literature. Individual monographic books, in simpler times the solid base of every library, these too are flowing from the presses and to the libraries in a rising crescendo.

When the intellectual history of this century is written, thereby producing still further books, the efforts to control and channel the rising information flood by machine will have a prominent place. This history will show, as stressed above, the first efforts toward machine controls to have been fumbling albeit confident attempts by people little aware of the magnitude of the task or of the complexities and the infinite variety and range of Man's knowledge and of the ways in which it has been expressed.

Also, this history will show that librarians, whose control methods had been surprisingly effective, although laboring heavily, in keeping abreast of the rising tide were often criticized for not rushing to welcome machine controls with open arms. This, it will be found, was not because librarians resisted the machine or were jealous of their carefully developed and well-proven procedures and methodology, but because the earliest machine control efforts, whether by librarians or others, were so obviously too often poorly conceived and brashly undertaken.

It will be noted by the future historian of intellectual progress that machine organization and management of the trillions upon trillions of bits of knowledge appearing in a wide range of languages turned out to be less amenable to machine management and a far more formidable problem than even the most balanced and knowledgeable machine researchers and enthusiasts had ever supposed. It will be recorded that it was only when the complexities and needs and the sheer quantative mass of the problem was, after some decades, fully realized that progress toward effective machine controls began to be achieved. It may also be shown, although it is too early now to make confident predictions, that knowledge never did lend itself to machine management to the extent envisioned by the early enthusiasts.

One thing which the historian of things intellectual in the twentieth century will note and reflect upon, as perhaps evidence of the naivete of the times, is the assumption of all the custodians and managers of knowledge with their many-splendored names— librarians, documentalists, information specialists, systems analysts, data engineers, or whatever — that the problem was simply one of control. If only some system or plan or machine could be devised to yield up on call, quickly and economically, every bit of information, every thought, every concept, every theory, every historical fact, every ideology, every figure or statistic, every truth, every lie, every hope, ever recorded anywhere any time, all would be well. Management of knowledge would then be complete and absolute and intellectual progress assured.

Completely lost sight of, it will be noted, in the earnest striving to capture, record, and deliver, as required, the total record was the increasingly evident fact that the totality of knowledge was becoming so massive in the strictly intellectual sense, entirely aside from physical mastery and control, as to be completely overwhelming. Early alarmist predictions of Man's suffocation in his own intellectual excreta, which had been written off as a fanciful shrinking from the realities, turned out, it will be found, not to be so alarmist after all.

It will also be noted, perhaps wryly and with some amusement, that in the increasing leisure time and ever shortening work week of the twentieth century it was only the scholars, of all who labored, who found no leisure. These poor folk, reading furiously, day and night, the things delivered instantaneously to them in quantity by the keepers, controllers, and managers of knowledge, could not begin to keep up with everything there was to read and know. Some scholars were even, it will be discovered, known to sigh for the good old days when libraries could not instantaneously produce everything ever written on any subject whatsoever anywhere.

The real pioneers and heroes of the twentieth century managers of knowledge, it will be found, making their first timid and heretical stirrings at mid-century, were not the machine control enthusiasts but the proponents of "selective retirement," a movement that was eventually to attain massive proportions, with the euphemistic "retirement" changed to an absolute: "discarding." It was these realists, it will be gratefully noted, and not the machine enthusiasts, who pointed the way for Man to fruitfully and happily live with his accumulated knowledge.

Books in Chains

Evolving technology may chain the scholar once again to his books.

EVER SINCE books have been written, whether on clay tablets or papyrus, or waxed boards or on skins or on paper at first meticulously and painstakingly by hand and later as produced in quantity through the printing arts, they have been treasured and carefully guarded. This caretaking went to the extent, in some places, of physically chaining volumes to reading desks. These extreme precautions were taken because a book, particularly in the manuscript days, was a rare and precious thing into which was often poured the best years of author and scribe.

Further evidence of love and veneration for the physical book has been the artistic adornment and ornamentation which has been so often lovingly lavished on individual copies. Surviving books of this kind, and the great majority have happily survived, are the pride and joy of collectors and of rare book rooms in libraries everywhere.

Now, paradoxically, in a book-glutted world in which an individual book is a common thing produced in thousands of identical copies, and sometimes in hundreds of thousands, and in which new titles are appearing on the scene by the millions, books seem to be again headed for chains not because of their preciousness but because of their proliferation and tremendous quantity. Not literal chains, really, but rigid confinement, nevertheless, in a variety of machines and gadgets.

The efforts to organize the multi-millioned books with which the world is becoming so surfeited are now taking the direction of reducing them in micro image on cellulose and then incarcerating them on a variety of tapes and spools and whirling wheels designed to produce a desired volume on command. No great success, to be sure, has so far attended these control efforts, but the quest continues with mounting intensity year upon year. And year after year, the book, which has known some centuries of freedom and fruitfulness as it has multiplied and which has, through its very abundance, nourished and expanded and pleasured the intellect of Man has valiantly resisted machine confinement.

If Man's efforts to control the book by machine, and he came early to these attempts, are crowned finally with success, he will have placed it once again in chains, for some decades at least, just as surely as he once did when he literally chained ponderous tomes in medieval library and monastery. Even in those earlier days, aid from the machine was conjured up.

Annual reports and other publications of the Council on Library Resources illustrate this. The Council, more than any other agency of our times, is advancing the quest for machine control of our ever proliferating writings through judicious dispensation of Ford Foundation dollars. On its publications appears, appropriately, an illustration of the scholar at a ponderous book wheel which holds books ferris-wheel style and through which the scholar can roll a desired book into reading position without moving from his chair.

This apt illustration is taken not from some latter day publication but from an engraving in Agostino Ramelli's: *Le Diverse et Artifiose Machine*, published in Paris in 1588 when the printed book was still in its infancy. It was a pretty ponderous thing, and primitive, this medieval scholar's wheel. Perhaps this is why nothing much came of it, but the principles of modern mechanization are all there, the wheel, the sprockets and gears, and the printed page coming into view on command. The current efforts to expand, streamline, and sophisticate Ramelli's wheel of 1588 may well be as primitive to future eyes as his wheel seems to us now. It is not yet clear that present efforts will be any more successful than were those of Ramelli but the signs are good. If success does come, one thing seems sure: The future scholar who will sit tied to his console will be captive blood brother to Ramelli's hatted and gowned scholar of 1588.

The Quiet Giant

Xerography, like the genie of Arabian mythology, stands ready to serve in countless new ways.

MUCH OF THE TALK and to-do about automating the recording, storage, and organization of knowledge has been in terms of punched cards, magnetic tapes, and giant brains which will think. Much of this searching and dreaming has proceeded in a strange and new semantic miasma and fog, some of it pretty murky. The Utopian library which will produce instantaneously, on call, whatever portion of the total recorded store is necessary has not yet emerged from wordy probabilities as a practical and realizable entity. There are perhaps some signs that the fog is lifting and that the undiscovered land of automated knowledge may yet be revealed, if only in part.

While and as the glamorous turmoil of the automation search has been proceeding in a swirling sea of new words and terminology, there has come onto the scene, quietly and unobstrusively, an automation device so simple, in terms of use and operation, that most people have not even thought of it as automation.

This is the Xerox dry copier which is now busily and economically at work in every library of consequence.

From the time Man first invented the making of intelligible marks, by far the greatest of all his achievements, it has been highly desirable to reproduce in quantity what was written. For long centuries this could be done only by painstaking transcribing by hand. Throughout it all though, Man being Man, kept exercising his God-given gift of thinking there must be an easier, faster, better way.

Various impressing devices were developed until there came, finally, the invention of printing from movable metal type. This was the great breakthrough, greater than anything else that can possibly happen in the recording and storage of knowledge. It opened the floodgates for the torrents of words and other symbols which now stand, carefully and systematically ordered, on library shelves the world around. Through and because of this great heritage, Man has made his great advances.

Printing, however, even though it drastically reduced the cost of books in terms of time and effort, which in our modern world equates out to money, was still costly. Ever present was the need to reproduce a book or parts of it. Various photographic devices were successful but they were costly wet processes requiring chemicals and laboratories. Small wet copiers, a host of them, were developed with moderate success. But they were still messy, temperamental, requiring skilled operators and chemically treated papers subject to quick deterioration. The need, however, was great so they were used widely. With nothing better available they were, in fact, wonderful.

Then came Xerox. This electrostatic device fuses carbon dust on dry, ordinary paper, in exact image of whatever is desired to be copied. While the machine which does this is somewhat complicated and requires expert maintenance, as indeed does all our modern gadgetry, it does not demand an expert operator or laboratory equipment. It will work anywhere that sufficient electric current is available. It is no good for reproducing photographs, but all sharply contrasting lines and letters are reproduced beautifully, often so faithfully that it is difficult to distinguish copy from original.

This machine was a natural for library work. Indication of this is that it moved into the libraries, and into many other endeavors too, as quickly as the producing company could supply the machines. Through it interlibrary practices of libraries have been revolutionized with more and more requested materials now supplied in Xerox copy. No longer do library books needed elsewhere go buffeting through the mails to the extent formerly true. More and more things are being copied for transmission. While the glamorous computerizing of knowledge still remains somewhere in limbo, the quiet giant of Xerox, here and present, is rapidly, economically, and undramatically increasing the range and ease with which Man uses and produces his knowledge.

The Xerox machine consists of a scanner and a copying drum. It is quite possible to have the scanner in one place and the copier in another. The practicality of this has been demonstrated. It is highly likely, therefore, that in the emerging research library complexes scanners will transmit knowledge from one library to another to be there recorded by the copying drum or drums. Knowledge can then quickly flow from library to library. Inevitably the quiet giant of Xerox will continue to grow in stature and usefulness. There is, though, no dollar relief in prospect in all this, only quicker and better service.

Picasso and Mr. Otis

*Librarianship too needs
its Mr. Otis.*

In 1959 we had hanging in the Oregon State Library staff room a series of Pablo Picasso reproductions. These made good conversation pieces. One afternoon while at tea I remarked harmlessly, as I supposed, that the best thing about surrealist art is that it can mean to the viewer whatever he chooses to have it mean and that this will very likely be poles apart from what the artist had in mind, and from what other viewers will see. On the opposite wall from where I sat hung a print depicting a series of markings, angular lines, and assorted colors, among which three squarish mechanical robot faces were somewhat discernible. This Picasso had chosen to call "Three Musicians."

From the depths of my artistic illiteracy I asserted that these three so-called figures could, in these days of impending machine organization and control of knowledge, more aptly be dubbed "Three Librarians." This I thought would be appropriate since the robotic librarians of the future, if they cannot dispense service with a smile could easily do so to music. I also thought that Mr. Otis, the noted artist whom I had just met a day or two before, could have handled this theme and created these three figures even more brilliantly than Picasso has done. Mr. Otis, for those who do not know him, is the subject of a book done, tongue in cheek, by the noted late Portland, Oregon, author, Stewart Holbrook. In it he reproduced, with selected artistic comment, a goodly number of the more famous Otis canvases.

Little did I think that these passing remarks would send subconscious brain cells spinning. But they did, for that night I had a dream. A strange looking mechanical man with squarish robotic face was rescuing an equally strange mechanical woman from a castle moat. I was relieved, but not for long, when the woman, in squarish mechanistic swim trunks, was safely on the castle bank. No sooner was she rescued than the man, his square face sardonic and his eyes blazing, strangled her and flung her back into the moat.

I was so startled by this unexpected denouement that I came wide awake, thereby rescuing this fantasy from that strange limbo of the unconscious from whence it came and to which it would surely have hazily returned, little noted, or not at all, had I not awakened. What, I mused, as I became aware of the similarity of these vanished and so recently vivid faces to Picasso's musicians, what would Mr. Freud make of all this? Or Mr. Otis? Being as ignorant of psychiatry as I am of art, I concluded that a psychiatrist, if a librarian came to him with such a story of nocturnal subconscious caperings would, after lengthy probings of backgrounds and attitudes, come up with a diagnosis something like this.

My dear fellow, he would say, it is clear that you are in a subconscious anxiety state about control, confinement, and utilization of the rising sea of print. While you consciously welcome the prospect of machine push-button controls, subconsciously you resist this. It is obvious that the castle is the citadel of traditional librarianship with all its drafty corridors and its numerous dark, musty, only partially controlled, poorly lighted, and illy ventilated rooms of knowledge all bearing a mixture of room numbers compounded of the Library of Congress, the Dewey, the Expansive, the Bliss, the Ranganathan Colon, and many lesser classification schemes. From what you have told me, the corridors and the rooms of this castle are replete with numerous directional signs in all kinds of languages. Go here; go there; look some place else; keep looking; be sure not to miss the tenth and latest annex.

You, my friend, the psychiatrist would say, are the man on the bank. You know the castle is not the best possible castle but it is the only abode you know. It does serve after a fashion, so you defend it. The damsel you rescue is Miss Electronic Controls, an exotic, temperamental, complex, confused, adolescent personality. She is full of promise and allure, but also of contradictions, and she speaks a weird gibberish which you, the defender of the citadel, do not understand and which she does not understand either. You welcomed her eagerly, hoping she would make your castle more livable. Then not understanding her and enraged by her gibberish, you spurn her, hurling her back into the morass. This then leaves you free to turn to your castle to supervise the building of the eleventh annex, to check the architects plans for the twelfth, and to begin preliminary planning for the thirteenth. Oh yes, and also to order up a few million more signs. Simple, dear chap, when one understands the subconscious.

Surrealism, I now know, is potent stuff. And like surrealism, librarianship too needs its Mr. Otis.

The King of India's Library

Struggling with voluminous writings is no new thing under the sun.

IN ECCLESIASTES 12:12 it is stated "of the making of many books there is no end; and much study is a weariness of the flesh." Another early expression of the problem of the wearisome burden of accumulated writings, as well as a drastic solution of it, seems a fitting conclusion to this series of essays. It appears in the book, *The Queer, the Quaint, and the Quizzical,* authored by Frank H. Stauffer and published in Philadelphia in 1882. Mr. Stauffer points to the quintessence of all writing by presenting, as follows, an ancient abstract to end all abstracts:

> "Dabshelim, King of India, had so numerous a library that a hundred brachmans were scarcely sufficient to keep it in order, and it required a thousand dromedaries to transport it from one place to another. As he was not able to read all these books, he proposed to the brachmans to make extracts from them of the best and most useful of their contents.
>
> These learned personages went so heartily to work that in less than twenty years they had compiled of all these extracts a little encyclopedia of twelve thousand volumes, which thirty camels could carry with ease. They presented them to the king, but what was their amazement to hear him say that it was impossible for him to read thirty camel-loads of books. They therefore reduced their extracts to fifteen, afterwards to ten, then to four, then to two dromedaries, and at last there remained only enough to load a mule of ordinary size.
>
> Unfortunately, Dabshelim, during this process of melting down his library, grew old, and saw no probability of living long enough to exhaust its quintessence to the last volume. 'Illustrious Sultan', said his vizier, 'though I have but a very imperfect knowledge of your royal library, yet I will undertake to deliver you a brief and satisfactory abstract of it. You shall read it through in one minute, and yet you will find matter in it to reflect upon throughout the rest of your life.' Having said this, Pilpay took a palm leaf, and wrote upon it with a golden style the four following paragraphs:
>
> 1. The greater part of the sciences comprise but one single word—Perhaps, and the whole history of Mankind contains no more than three—they are born, suffer, die.
> 2. Love nothing but what is good, and do all that thou lovest to do; think nothing but what is true, and speak not all that thou thinkest.
> 3. O kings! Tame your passions, govern yourselves, and it will be only child's play to govern the world.
> 4. O kings! O people! It can never be often enough repeated to you, what the half-witted venture to doubt, that there is no happiness without virtue, and no virtue without God."

Part VII
BOOKS AND LIBRARIES IN
THE NEW EARTH AND
THE NEW HEAVEN

The essays grouped in this series are concerned, in one way or another, with Man's conquering of distance, his ability to hurl himself or objects made by him around his planet and even into the far reaches of the universe at speeds which would, as recently as when I entered the library profession, have been unbelievable and unbelieved. These advances have made the Moon and now even Mars reachable by Man more quickly and certainly more precisely than was Cathay by Marco Polo.

It is this mobility of Man and of objects made by him which has, more than any other one thing, changed the nature of our twentieth-century civilization, changed it at a rate for which Homo Sapiens has been entirely unprepared. Accustomed as he has been for centuries to a world of far and distant lands populated by interesting and different tribes and peoples whose mode of life, customs, traditions, and religions were of no direct or immediate concern to him, he has been propelled, all too quickly, to rubbing shoulders, literally, with alien beliefs and peoples. How different, how very different, and how much more complex, and simultaneously how much more difficult and also how much simpler, safer and more comfortable and, paradoxically, how much more dangerous Man has made his world through his amazing discoveries of ways to annihilate its distances.

In a world where one can breakfast in London, lunch in Moscow, and have dinner in Cairo the problems of and the necessity for understanding and getting along with individuals and peoples of differing languages, folkways, and ideologies, assume an immediacy and an urgency never before found on this globe. Somehow or other the citizens of Moose Jaw and Smith's Corner must, as the world grows smaller and ever smaller quite literally rub shoulders with the citizens of Bangkok and Smarakand. And they must do this within a framework of ideologies, philosophies, religions, customs, traditions, and above all languages, all slowly wrought out, in less mobile and literate times, in the crucible of the centuries, eons upon eons. This being so, as it incontrovertibly is, it is a wonder that the shoulder rubbing is not placing the times more out of joint than they are.

There is one bond, one vehicle, through which, more than any other, Man can and does meet his fellow man of differing background and beliefs on the common ground of respect and understanding. This is in the areas of the sciences and technologies and to a lesser extent of culture generally, as distinguished from political ideologies. And in these areas it is the book, the written word, that, properly used, is both the creator and the transmittor of understanding.

The essays which follow consider these and related things on the very broad front of how the world got this way and the place of the written word in it all. It seems appropriate to begin this section with some thoughts and facts on the picking up of the pieces which follows every war.

Hands Across the Oceans

ONE OF THE unhappy aspects of World War II was the unprecedented destruction and dispersal of the cultural resources of the countries most directly involved. In the first World War only one great library, that of the University of Louvain, was destroyed. In contrast, it is estimated that in World War II approximately 200 libraries of some consequence were either damaged, dispersed, or completely destroyed in Europe alone. Suffering heavy losses were England, France, Norway, Poland, Finland, Yugoslavia, Greece, Italy, Germany, and Russia.

To these losses we must also add extensive losses in China and the Philippines. Contrary to World War I, when the loss of one library was more or less accidental, the late war was marked, shamefully so, by looting, confiscation, and destruction of library and other cultural materials under official direction. A large part of Poland's loss of some 60 or 70 percent of all its library resources was the result of such "official" action. Italy, France, and Russia lost heavily from the same ruthless and conscienceless pillaging.

Long before the smoke of battle had cleared, or there was any certainty when it would clear, men of good will were beginning to give thought to the damaged or destroyed libraries. As early as 1943, the International Relations Board of the American Library Association and the Council of National Library Associations were laying plans to promote the rehabilitation of the libraries of the devastated countries. As a result of this forethought and planning, the *American Book Center for War Devastated Libraries* was incorporated in June of 1945 in New York state. It began its activities with more than $100,000 contributed by relief organizations, American commercial firms, labor unions, and foundations. During a period of about two and one-half years, this agency gathered from and through the libraries of America more than one million volumes and distributed them to libraries in thirty-four different countries. It is a pleasure for all who responded to reflect that the books they contributed so generously have been and are in service, in widely scattered areas of the world, in the rehabilitation of scholarship.

The happy sequel to this action is that the American Book Center was so successful that it grew into a permanent agency, the United States Book Exchange, Inc. In its permanent capacity, it has promoted an extensive two-way flow of duplicate materials among the libraries of the world. It would very probably never have come into existence had it not been for the war. Like many agencies created to bind up the wounds of war, it is now a continuing cultural resource in maintaining the world's bonds of cultural and scientific brotherhood.

"Hong Samud Kluan Thi, Sa-Aw, Sa-Aw"

"On a hot afternoon of June the village of Ban-Pang in northeast Thailand appeared much the same as always. The road was shady though the sun beat mercilessly. From the school came the steady chant of children repeating their lessons in the age-old fashion."

All was not, however, the same on that June afternoon of 1957. Something exciting and different was about to happen. People at all age levels stood about, expectant and curious, obviously waiting for something. At last a shout went up: "It's coming!" And so it was.

THROUGH THE FIELDS and under the arch of trees trotted a tired little brown horse. Behind him followed a sturdy two-wheeled cart bearing a contraption that looked like a little white house. On its sides were the words in the above title. Literally translated they say "The library that goes places." Yes a mobile library had come to Ban-Pang. When shyness and reserve before the new had worn away, the people eagerly clustered around, the literate helping the illiterate, showing and explaining the books to them. New worlds, new concepts, expanding horizons were entering Ban-Pang.

This was by no means an isolated incident. All over the world in the newly developing countries the magic of print as set down in books is, in many different ways, reaching the people. From 75,000 library service points in these countries, so little known in the West, books are going to users by every possible means, by bookmobile, traveling library, train, bus, mammy wagon, aeroplane, canoe, river steamer, bibliocart, bicycle, by camel, and on porters' heads. Many of the facts of this rapid cultural development have been set down in the October 1959 issue of *Library Trends* published by the University of Illinois Library School. This issue presents facts which make it clear that those of us who have been want to think of our highly technical civilization solely in western terms and, moreover, in western languages, need sharp re-orientation.

Everywhere in these rising countries there is increasing awareness, in governmental circles and in the culture generally, of the urgent need for educated citizens. One of the *Library Trends* authors, writing from the University of Malaya at Kuala Lumpur says it this way:

Only education can provide the newly developing countries in Asia with all the knowledge and all the technology that has so far been achieved in the more advanced countries of the world. Thus libraries in Asia, together with schools, universities and other educational institutions, start off with the advantage of popular and enthusiastic support from the people they serve.

This remarkably informative issue of *Library Trends* tells of schools of librarianship, established and in operation at Ankara, Kharkov, Jerusalem, Cairo, Ibadan, Port-of-Spain, Djarkarta, and Manila. For some western librarians at least it has been a revelation to learn that some of the finest major library buildings erected in the world in recent years are in places like Algiers, Dakar, Accra, Ibadan, Enugu, Kampala, Salisbury, Pretoria, Rehovoth, Kingston, Medellín, Bello, São Paulo, and Caracas.

There is the matter of languages too. These are formidable enough even in western scholarship and in the western libraries which are chiefly oriented around the European tongues. The newly developing countries, however, are producing writings in Arabic, Housa, Swahili, Hyanja, Chinese, Hindi, Hindustani, Urdu, Gyerati, Cinhalese, Tamil, Indonesian, Malay, and Thai. These native languages are essential if illiteracy is to be overcome. Obviously the translating machines, if indeed they reach a workable reality, will be none too soon.

From Thailand to Africa, in ten thousand Ban-Pangs, libraries are aggressively on the move, planting the seeds and laying the foundations for a culture and ways of life which may one day match and overmatch the complacent West. If this assertion seems far-fetched, think of the semi-illiterate Russia of post World War I in comparison with the Russia of today, full of books and libraries and blossoming with educational institutions. It is through these that she has hung new moons in the sky and is now hopefully reaching for world ascendancy.

Always a Young Heart

One of God's courageous men makes a moving and effective appeal.

THE SOME thousands of books that went out from the Oregon State University Library in the intelligently conceived and well-administered program of the American Book Center commented on above, went into use around the world without either users or owning libraries being aware, other than through possible occasional marks or writings in them, that they once were at and had been donated by Oregon State University.

In addition to participating in this nationally organized and administered program, the OSU Library also responded, from time to time, as many libraries were doing in those days, to appeals for books from individual institutions. These transactions, because they brought the library closer to the immediacy of the needs and the personalities involved were more exciting and possibly, in their modest way, more effective than our larger effort in the national program.

One institution assisted by OSU in the early postwar period was the Catholic Mission at Bayombong, N. V., Luzon, Philippine Islands. In 1953 came a second appeal from Father Lambrecht of that Mission. Father Lambrecht's letter, reflecting as it does, indomitable courage and steadfastness of purpose in the face of tremendous difficulties is a moving and very human document.

It is a welcome antidote indeed to the greedy and grasping motives, maneuverings, and passions of Man so much in the public prints. It is also dramatic evidence of both the awfulness and the grandness of these days. I am happy to be able to include it in these essays.

Wrote Father Lambrecht in his own typescript:

Some six years ago, I had the pleasure to make an appeal to you and your College, in order to reconstitute my library which was entirely devastated by the war. At that time a bamboo and grass building could do, and I could resume the work in this far away mountain region. But in December 1948, I got a nervous breakdown, my left eye was closed, and after lingering around for more than a year, I was sent home for recovery.

This was all evidently an immediate result of the Japanese occupation and brutality. You remember that I wrote then that four of our fathers were massacred, and that in Bayombong, I got three sisters burned alive at the time of the bombings. Everything went up in flames and the work of 25 years of toiling was destroyed in a few days. When home in Belgium I recovered very slowly, and it remained a question mark if I could come back to the Mission field, with my now sixty years.

Thanks the Lord I was back last year, in May, although about 30 years of missionary work on my shoulders. Although I have not any more the strength of my young days, I always kept a young heart, and I am back on the job. Things have improved, as I was able to erect already new buildings but my greatest worry remains my library. It is pleasant to mention that I have a very great and substantial increase of students, and more especially that many of my boys and girls are doing school duty in the mountain.

Sixteen new high schools have been created, and we can state that this destituted region is coming fast under the wholesome influence of intellectual and moral education, which had been upheld for long through the circumstances. May I ask you for some more books? What I need most of all are books of Education. Next come the cultural books History, Economics, Sociology and Philosophy, but any book you can send me is welcome.

I hope dear sir, that you will not rebuke an old missionary who feels that his years are counted after all the adversities he encounterd during his 30 years of missionary life."

Who, I ask, could "rebuke" the writer of a letter such as this? Father Lambrecht did indeed receive, and quickly, numerous additional books from Oregon State University.

A Valiant Warrior for Good

A missionary of thirty years, buffeted by evil times, "never forgot to request for books."

ALL MAJOR EDUCATIONAL libraries nowadays have world-wide contacts in exchanging publications, and sometimes services too, as well as in the inter-lending of books. These meetings, across the miles by mail, are often routine. More often than one would suppose, however, they are direct, unusual, and warmly personal. Such were our contacts with Father Godfrey Lambrecht of the Catholic Mission of Bayombong, N. V., Luzon, Philippine Islands.

The foregoing essay, written in 1953, was based on a personal letter from Father Godfrey Lambrecht, a valiant old warrior for good. In 1958 came a picture of Father Godfrey from Bayombong, a picture bordered in black, accompanied by a letter from Rev. Fr. Paul Zwaenepoel, Dean of St. Mary's College there, telling of Father Godfrey's death and the efforts to carry on the work he began, which he saw wantonly destroyed and which he reconstituted once again.

The face that gazed out from this picture looked just like it ought to look, strong, kindly, good, a face that had met the buffets of fortune, as well as accepted rewards and honors, with a deep understanding and sometimes perhaps with quizzical humor. One had a feeling that here indeed was a man un-dismayed by adversity. We at Oregon State University received this picture, and the letter telling of the continuing work, because we were on "a list of names and addresses written in Fr. Godfrey's own hand."

This letter could have only one result. More library books were soon on their way to Bayombong to support the work begun by this old friend, one of God's good men. Even in far off Corvallis, we somehow missed him and mourned his passing. How different and how much happier our world would be were more of us like Father Lambrecht.

> We speak to you from the faraway place called Bayombong where your friend Fr. Godfrey Lambrecht once worked. Fr. Godfrey is now dead. He has gone to his final reward; and his work of over thirty years has been passed on to us. The work never ends. We are only beginning, for this mountain region of Nueva Vizcaya has yet to equal the advance of civilization in the other provinces of the Philippines. But we try to do what we can.
>
> As you probably know, Fr. Godfrey began a college here in 1949 to take care of the education of the boys and girls of Neuva Vizcaya. He began with nothing but the name—St. Mary's College; and his own boundless enthusiasm and deep love for his people . . . St. Mary's College now maintains, besides the Liberal Arts, a school for education, commerce, and engineering. We are quite happy to say that the school has branched out further than Fr. Godfrey ever expected.
>
> Were he alive today, we are sure that Fr. Godfrey would be working, writing to his friends as he used to do, appealing for help. It is indeed a pity that Fr. Godfrey cannot be around to reap the little fruit that St. Mary's has begun to bear . . . We believe that in his appeals he never forgot to request for books to build up a library for he recognized its absolute necessity. The college library has become quite inadequate. It cannot meet the demands of the growing college . . .
>
> Fr. Godfrey has left a gap in the lives of the people of his mission . . . a gap which we doubt can ever be filled by us. We can only try. May we offer a prayer for you? You have been so generous and we are aware that God will not forget you.

On the Same Rope Together

East is East and West is West and now the twain must meet.

IN LATE MAY OF 1953 two men, one a farmer and beekeeper from New Zealand, the other an unlettered mountain man from Nepal, were slowly taking the last few weary steps to the highest spot on this earth, Mt. Everest. Hundreds, perhaps thousands before them had dreamed of this conquest. At least sixteen men had given their lives in the effort. Now these two had the supreme and hitherto unattainable conquest within their grasp. They were not thinking, as they toiled upward, about glory and prestige and rewards. They were driven forward and upward only by a fierce determination to do this thing which no one had ever before done.

At last they were there, on the very summit, rejoicing in the achievement, thumping each other on the back, happy and close in the camaraderie and friendship of men who have worked, struggled, faced death, and achieved together. The beekeeper, Edmund Hillary, readied his camera. The mountain man, Tenzing Norkey, unfurled a tightly rolled group of small flags, attached them to the handle of his ice pick, held it aloft and a picture was taken, the small flags snapping in the breeze, the United Nations flag appropriately above the other three, in order the British, the Nepalese, and the Indian.

This was not a studied arrangement of the flags which Tenzing had made. There was no thought of politics or nationalities or prestige in that happy moment of supreme achievement. That, and controversy and bickering about who was first on the mountain was to come later, and soon, from lesser men.

Halfway round the world, as Hillary and Tenzing stood atop Everest, a gracious and beautiful young Queen was about to be crowned. The electrifying news, that these men had indeed stood on the highest mountain, that Everest had been conquered, was saved for a day as an epic coronation gift to this new young Queen of Britain, and to her people. All the world rejoiced with her, when the news came, and with the valiant British who had launched assault after assault on Everest, only to go down in defeat and sometimes death, until this glittering and most appropriate of all moments.

For the British it was perfect, but not so for India or for the King of Nepal, who humiliatingly received from the other side of the globe, and late, the news that his mountain, the greatest of them all, had been climbed. This news spread like wildfire through Nepal, through India, and out over Asia. Tenzing was at once a national and Asiatic hero, revered, honored, and the object of adulation even greater than that showered on Lindbergh by the western world when he flew the Atlantic. In all this sudden fame and in the bickering and controversy about which of these two men was first on the mountain, this simple untutored man conducted himself with a dignity and a fairness worthy of his great achievement.

Who was first on the mountain? Who got there first? Who? Who? This question came at Tenzing from every direction, he relates with simplicity and candor in his book, *Tenzing of Everest, Tiger of the Snows* as told to the American novelist James Ramsey Ullman. Tenzing was under great pressure to confirm widespread rumors that it had really been he who first stepped onto the mountain, that he had in fact dragged Hillary to the top, or that Hillary had never gotten there at all. To quiet the rumors and the controversy he and Hillary signed a joint statement saying they had reached the top "almost together." But "almost" was not enough. It did not satisfy the eastern world which, no less than the western world, wanted the prestige and glory of their man being first.

So Tenzing answered the burning questions, directly and with dignity, not for his sake, he said, nor Hillary's, but for the sake and prestige of Everest, his beloved mountain. Mountaineers, he said, understand that there is no sense in the question of "first" and "second" that when "two men are on the same rope they are together. The rope that joined us was thirty feet long but I held most of it in loops in my hand. I was not thinking of 'first' and 'second.' I did not say to myself, 'There is a golden apple up there. I will push Hillary aside and run for it.' We went on slowly, steadily. And then we were there. Hillary stepped on top first. And I stepped up after him."

Thus, with simplicity and a

complete honesty which does more credit to this eastern man than would have the physical act of being first to set foot on the mountain top, it was told.

It is symptomatic of our times, and the rising place of the East in the world, this controversy and this eagerness to be first. We have it more dangerously on scientific frontiers, in the splitting of the atom, the detonation of H bombs, the perfecting of guided missiles, the hurling of new moons into the skies. Throughout it all, the conquest of the "Mountain of the Unknown," and the organization and utilization of the literature of the conquest, East and West are inextricably and inescapably partners, however unwillingly. We have now attained such Everest-like peaks of discovery, so fraught with promise of both success and complete disaster, that neither side can push the other aside and run for the golden apple of supreme and final achievement. From here on out the East and West of our present civilization are, for better or for worse "on the same rope together."

The Eel of Science

A poet centuries ago perceived the fundamental importance of the unsung Index Learners.

AT THE IMPRESSIVE ceremonies marking the inauguration in 1954 of President Meredith Wilson as the ninth president of the University of Oregon, Julian Huxley drew this analogy: If the entire period of life on the earth before the advent of Man should be represented by the height of the Empire State Building and the period after the emergence of Man should be added to the building this would increase its height by no more than the thickness of a postage stamp. This striking illustration of the recency of Man on earth should give pause to all who would achieve the Nirvana of complete world peace, social equality, and a mastering of all brutish instincts and urges, all within a single generation. The amazing thing is that Man, who took so long to emerge from the multitude of life on this teeming earth to become the dominant and controlling species should, once he had crossed the vague shadow line between the brute and the human, have advanced with such rapidity.

In all this long evolution, that dim and distant pre-history period when Man first laboriously began to consciously think and to take steps to master and improve his harsh environment is most important. Those long ago nameless men or near-men, who first had the courage and wit to tame and control fire, to create it at will, and to adapt it to their comfort and use must, in human history, rank in importance with their descendants of our time who, probing deep into the nature of matter, have come upon and partially understood the nature and the climactic forces of the atom.

Perhaps it is characteristic that culmination of the atomic probings of our time and the first unloosing of the terrible power thereby discovered should have been in war. It is quite likely that our primitive forbears too first used their great discovery of fire as a weapon. Having learned that a burning brand, hurled or in hand, would repel an enemy, the long step to discovering that it could also be used to warm a cave, fashion a tool, or make food more palatable was a step without which all the wondrous and complex progress that has followed could not have occurred.

None of the developments, or at least certainly very few, which stem from the first wondering gropings of the primitive mind could have taken place if Man had not learned to transmit his experiences and thoughts to his descendants. This was and is his prime and essential intellectual achievement. It undoubtedly first took the form of transmitting only meaningful sounds from father to son, from mother to daughter, generation after generation, in a complexity and richness attained by no other species.

There came eventually, in this transmission, the making of marks and the drawing of pictures. They too became, as the mind of Man flowered and developed, more profuse, more complicated, more complex, further removed from the immediate event which first called them into being. So far removed that they have now become abstract symbols which only the expert can trace to their origins, and then only imperfectly. Writing and the ability to quickly decipher it is the keystone without which the mind of Man could not have attained its present richness and quickness. Through it each generation has received from its predecessors, immediate and remote, a rich and marvelous heritage of the practical discoveries, the spiritual thoughts and ideals, the stimulating and entertaining adventures and experiences of those who have gone before.

Thomas Edison once said, "I begin where the last man left off." This is what has, through the mastery of writing, been going on down through all the ages of recorded human history. It is only in the last few centuries, and markedly so only in the last hundred years, that a whole profession has grown up dedicated to assembling the written and otherwise graphically recorded human heritage and standing ready, in effect, to tell each searcher and each new inquiring mind where the last man left off. This has become a costly business, tremendously complex and complicated. Without assigning some of his fellows this essential task, Man could not have tracked and plotted the limitless universe, ferreted out the prime secrets of the minute universe of the atom, hurled himself through the barriers of sound, or reached countless other attainments.

In all of this fantastic growth and progress, the librarians, whose task it is to keep the records of mankind organized and intelligible, are largely unsung. Alexander Pope however, perceptive as all poets must be, and writing in a time when the complexities were far less apparent than now, recognized the importance of those who keep the written record findable in these lines from the Dunciad:

"Index learning turns no student pale
Yet holds the eel of science by the tail."

New Moon in the Sky

The contrail of envy, consternation, fear in the wake of Sputnik I involved libraries and librarians too.

It was 6:30 p.m. on October 4, in the milestone year of 1957, that the portentous news of the successful launching of an earth satellite by the Russians came crackling over the telegraph wires. Contrary to the atomic bomb, which caught nearly all but those most directly concerned unawares, the world was not totally unprepared for the fantasy of space ships and exploration of the universe beginning to assume reality.

Comic books, monographs, and articles in magazines had for many years, and with increasing confidence, been predicting such scientific success and explaining, or attempting to explain, how it would come about. The geophysical year had given impetus and emphasis to such information. Just a few days before the world-shaking news, the OSU Library had without any prescient instincts, arranged, from its considerable holdings, an exhibit on satellites. Even so, at least for oldsters like myself, who began life in the primitive days when Man was still earthbound, the realization and the achievement, when it came, was a shock.

The first reactions of our side to what the Russians had achieved were not promising. They were compounded of envy, consternation, perhaps a little grudging admiration. Of fear there was, in high places and low, more than a little. Once again it had been demonstrated that men are but children grown big. All the emotions which were aroused among us by the fact that it was the Russians who took the first step into outer space can be observed in groups of children at play. Sure, say those accustomed to being in the vanguard and who have been vanquished, or overshadowed by the glory of some imaginative and spectacular rival achievement, we could have done that if we had wanted to, only we think other things more exciting or more important.

In spite of efforts to ignore or laugh off the achievements of the rivals, there arose disappointment, chagrin, and recriminations of the kind so often found among the alumni supporters of college and university athletic teams. We have been the champs, why can't we do as well as they have? Who is at fault? How come we are not as strong as they are, or as smart, or tricky, or aggressive? Let's get a new coach, or coaches, or buy more competent athletes, or give them better equipment, or break up the conference. All of these reactions, it seemed to me, were observable in the finger pointing which so quickly began after the Russians, in an autumnal season of upsets, scored the greatest and most brilliant upset, between major opponents, of all time.

It was perhaps natural for the world at large to think and to feel that it was the Russians, all by themselves, who had hurled this new moon into the sky. Actually it was not the Russians alone any more than it was the United States, all alone, which created the atomic bomb. It was Man the scientist who had achieved these fantastic goals, and the true scientist is neither Russian nor American, neither English nor Scandinavian nor German, but only a human being probing endlessly, curiously, and with increasing success into the mysteries of nature.

To the Russians went the prestige and the glory which their little moon carried in its whizzing orbit, but their success was possible, just as was the success of the United States with the atom bomb, only because they were standing on the broad shoulders of men of widely varying race and circumstance who had, over the centuries, pondered and thought, hypothesized, and experimented about these things. The first man, in the dim, distant, and unrecorded past, who made marks which were intelligible to himself and his fellow man and to those who came after him had a hand in the sending of this little moon beeping around the world. So was he who hurled the first sling shot, shot the first arrow, or first used gun powder to project a missile from a tube.

In the train of these innovators, and as their natural descendants, came the intellectual giants, Galileo for one, who in the law of inertia proclaimed that a moving object will continue in its course until something stops it. Generations followed Galileo, pondering, experimenting, devising better machines, and writing down thoughts and findings from which those who came after

them could begin. The writings grew so voluminous that they were assembled in great collections and persons were assigned to their care, organization, and interpretation.

Without these writings, organized, findable, quickly available, there would have been no combustion or steam motors, no rockets, no airplanes, no atomic bomb, no Sputnik. So the librarians too have had a hand in the first new moon which the modern world, in 1957, through

the Russians, hung in the sky. And once again it has become increasingly and more urgently clear that whether this and other scientific conquests mean catastrophe or new eons of achievement toward a God-like status will depend on whether Man the philosopher and creature of good will can match the seven league strides of Man the scientist. Supporting these efforts too, the best writings, noble, exalted, and quite as wonderful as Sputnik, are in the libraries of the world.

The Quickening Pace

The generations waiting in the wings to be born will write more and more books requiring more and more librarians.

THE PREVIOUS ESSAY, written in 1957 was concerned with the Soviet breakthrough in the launching of space satellites. One sure and quick result of this sensational achievement was to propel the United States into tremendous and hurried endeavor to match and to surpass the Russians. In this frenetic effort, there was little or no thought of monetary costs. Within a year, four United States satellites were whizzing about the earth in company of one lone survivor of the Soviet Sputniks. One U. S. satellite had joined two from the Soviet Union in the fiery death that seems to be the fate, sooner or later, of these little man-made moons. Dramatically, and astoundingly, the latest and largest of our satellites of 1958 presented to the world the phenomenon of the human voice coming back to

earth, upon request, from outer space. Included in the 1958 legacy, however, was also an extensive and at the time depressing record of satellite failures, no less than nine of them, along with four attempts to shoot the moon, only one of which could be classed as an experimental success.

The thing that impressed me most in all this satellite shooting, successful and unsuccessful, was the speed with which it came about. In this it was symptomatic of the quickening rate of scientific and technological advance which has continued unabated from the time of the Renaissance on. At first these advances were so few and so widely spaced as to make little impact on nations and governments. Some of them went so directly against prevailing concepts and ideologies that the men who conceived them were often persecuted, sometimes martyred. More often than not, those who fathomed the laws of nature, thereby achieving dramatic and unbelievable results, as do our scientists of today, were thought to be in league with the Devil rather than God.

Nevertheless, because Man is the curious, obstinate, and inventive creature he is, progress went on. This it could do in large part because each generation began, as has been so often emphasized in these essays, with the findings and beliefs of its predecessors. This permitted development and progress at an increasing tempo, a tempo so rapid that within the mere space of a half century, only an instant comparatively in the history of Man on this planet, we have come from the first feeble and faltering flights to beautiful and efficient corsairs of the skies and now to projected missiles and anti-missiles and flights into outer space. This locomotion of the heavens is, of course, only one aspect of the dramatic breakthroughs and advances in all areas of science and technology now being rapidly piled one on the other in a veritable crescendo of achievement.

One striking result of Man's understanding and mastery of the laws of nature is the rapid increase of his own species. No longer is he the prey he once was of hunger, of disease, of the elements, or even of himself, although some may rise to dispute this. As a result there are approximately 375,000,000 more of us on the planet now in 1966 than there were when young 1958 so apprehensively took the stage of our western world. Among the millions of new souls not here in 1958 are embryo doctors, lawyers, chemists, physicists, teachers, philosophers, poets, artists, farmers, engineers, and space scientists who will be

in full flower before this century is out. Let us hope that there are among them diplomats and leaders who will know how to manage the prejudices and passions, the greeds and the lusts of themselves and the ever more numerous succeeding generations as they come pushing out of the womb of the future and onto this steadily shrinking little clod which is already, in some areas, growing so uncomfortably crowded.

The generations waiting in the wings to be born and to take the stage of this incredible century will quite certainly be articulate. They will write books and more books in far greater numbers, both quantitatively and proportionately than do even the fecund writers of this mid-century. We can be sure of this because it is clearly evident that people who add to the store of the printed word are increasing at a far more rapid rate than the

population generally. The more people read, history has demonstrated, the more they write, and new readers, the United Nations tells us, are appearing on the scene at the rate of 25,000,000 per year.

There is no promise now or in the foreseeable future of bibliographical surcease or birth control. May an all-wise Providence then also provide librarians among the future generations, lots and lots of them, all gifted with greater wisdom and more ingenuity than those of today. May theirs be the wisdom to organize and codify, to miniaturize and house, and to trieve and retrieve through mechanical marvels yet undreamed of the prodigious recorded memory of the race. Above all may they know what and how to discard. Without this, the quickening pace of discovery and of thought, as put to print, will surely and inevitably bring suffocation.

Only Angels Can Fly

Bishops often do not know what their sons are up to.

ONE OF THE important functions of every library is to make the books and other materials it owns yield up whatever fact, series of facts, or information users may require at any given time. Occasionally libraries receive questions which cannot be answered fully from books. They must then move into the area of primary research by establishing facts and verifying data through letters, manuscripts, or in obscure and little-known publications.

Sometimes too they must rely, in return to the primitive processes, on word-of-mouth information for things that have never been set down in print or even in manuscript form.

A very interesting question of this kind was received at Oregon State University some years ago from Dean Samuel Prince of the University of South Carolina Law School. Dean Prince was interested in verifying a story about Bishop Milton Wright of the United Brethren Church and Professor John B. Horner, one of the early professors at Oregon

State. A careful search of newspapers and books revealed no mention of this story. It became necessary therefore to resort to word-of-mouth information. This was in itself an interesting revelation of how verbal narration of events can vary.

The final story turned out to be not quite so romantic as the first versions. From Dean F. A. Gilfillan of the Oregon State University School of Science and the late Professor Edward B. Beaty, long time professor of mathematics at Oregon State, both as young men contemporaries of Professor Horner, we pieced together, with the help of Professor Horner's daughter, Miss Vera Horner, the following story.

John B. Horner, who died in 1933, was an ordained minister of the United Brethren Church. In the late 1880's he was superintendent of schools in Roseburg, Oregon. One day he learned that Bishop Wright was going to visit his school. Being a conscientious young man, and wishing to make a good impression, he spent several weeks working on a speech for this visit. The time arrived and so did Bishop Wright. Mr. Horner met the Bishop and took him to his home as a guest. Next morning, young Horner delivered his carefully prepared speech, dealing with the miracles of the Lord, as revealed in recent scientific advances of mankind. It went something like this:

It took Columbus two months to come from Spain in 1492 on a sailing vessel; our forefathers on the Mayflower required about the same time in 1620, but today, steamships make this voyage in seven or eight days.

Our fathers spent many weary weeks coming by covered wagon from Independence, Missouri, to the state of Oregon, a trip which now can be made in less than three days by train.

The Pony Express riders needed many days to carry the news from St. Louis to San Francisco, news which now can be flashed over telegraph wires in the twinkling of an eye. But Brother, this is not the end of things.

There are other miracles still to be performed by science. I expect to live to see the day when we may look up and see men flying overhead in machines yet to be invented . . .

During the drive back to the Horner home, the Bishop was silent. When they were in the house, he took a chair close to the young superintendent and in a low voice said:

Mr. Horner, you are a young man and I am getting along in years. I hope you will not take it amiss if I, as your Bishop, attempt to correct your thinking.

I greatly appreciate all the effort which you must have put forth on the speech which you delivered this morning. It showed a great deal of scholastic ability on your part in getting the information and in organizing it as effectively as you did, but there is one point, Brother Horner, on which I must admonish you.

You spoke of expecting to see men flying overhead in machines yet to be invented. That, Brother Horner, is sacrilegious error. Only angels fly. Men will never fly. God has so ordained it.

Little did Bishop Wright realize that two sons he had fathered, Orville and Wilbur, would, in a relatively few years, disprove his admonition. At the time of his Roseburg visit, these young men were just coming into their majority. Even then they were busy tinkering with bicycles and other mechanical contrivances. Perhaps their active and fertile young minds were already grappling, sacrilege or no, with ways and means of flying. In 1903 a craft of their making did fly for a few seconds. A world was thereby revolutionized and Mankind had assumed still another divine prerogative. But as usual Satan was lurking around to make it certain that many of the uses of this new magic would be far from divine.

A Far-Away Strike Reaches OSU

Labor controversies shrink an index and complicate life for scholars present and future.

WHEN THE PHOTOENGRAVERS of the *New York Times,* a mere handful of the employees of that great newspaper, went out on strike in 1953, their action reached into libraries all over the world. This was so because the *New York Times Index,* published since 1913, has become an indispensable reference tool in nearly all libraries. All major libraries must have this *Index* because it is much more than just an index of a single newspaper. It is a complete, carefully prepared alphabetical and chronological classification of the news of the day. As such it constitutes a condensed record of the times and serves as a key to newspapers everywhere.

When the *Times,* for the dates November 29-December 8, 1953, suddenly shrank, through strike action, from its proud estate to a little two-page sheet, the *Index* naturally shrank with it, thereby creating a gap in the systematic classification of the news of our times, a gap which, though of only ten days duration, leaves the events of those few days less accessible to student and researcher. Ten days, more or less, in a forty-year continuity, should not, one would think, be much missed. We can be certain, however, that persons ferreting out the facts and happenings of those few days, or some chain of continuity including them, will again and again come upon the shrunken indexing of those days and be sent scurrying to make up the deficiencies in more troublesome and difficult ways. In so doing they may, and rightly so, call down maledictions on the strikers who caused it all.

The *Times Index* is one of the best bargains that comes into libraries. Running about one month behind events, it appears in twice-monthly summaries which are cumulated at the end of each calendar year into one alphabet supplied in clearly printed, compact, and sturdily bound volumes. So useful are these monthly issues and annual volumes that if libraries had to choose between them and the *Times* itself, many would choose the *Index*. They would do this in part because the *Times* itself would, without its *Index*, lose much of its reference value.

Another and very important reason why many libraries would rather own the *Index* than the *Times* itself is that it is a relative guide and index to all newspapers. As an illustration, if we in Oregon should wish to ascertain the facts of the loss of the leading state officials of Oregon, in two separate airplane crashes within a year, or of an approved pension referendum which, until declared unconstitutional, threatened to make our state insolvent, we can readily date these things through the *Times Index* and then turn to our local papers for a fuller account.

Had the *Times* been on strike when these things were in the news, the *Index* would be useless in finding this information and worse than useless to those not conversant with the strike since they would still expect to find their way through it to what they were looking for. Within the *Times* itself, university students can and do, of course, locate information through the *Index* on a wide variety of assignments and interests, such as, for instance, plotting the course of the stock markets. Faculty members with money to invest, if there be any such, can also, with the help of the *Index*, study the ups and downs of the financial world. But not for the November 29-December 8, 1953, period.

A comparison of the 1913 first volume of the *Index* with the latest bound volumes is revealing. How little we were aware, in that calm prewar year, of the bitter brew of strife and killing, and the ensuing years of suspicion, distrust, of misled peoples, and the major second war which was even then simmering in the cauldron of the future. No one whose memory does not go back to that earthbound and relatively primitive technological era can really understand with what awe and admiration we stood before those commonplace and essential components of our present day life, the automobile and the airplane, both then in their infancy.

The *Times Index* of 1913 outlines in a few brief columns, under Aeronautics, such things as the invention of the stabilizer by the Wrights, the first cabin planes, plans even then for transatlantic and world-circling flights, the German Zeppelins and the progress of Lincoln Beachey from one loop-the-loop to two, three, four and on up to a dizzy eight loops. How vividly I remember seeing Beachey execute such maneuvers at the Nebraska State Fair and my grave deliberation about whether I should spend my quarter (heavy money) to see him in person, and his plane, or the Wild Man from Borneo and similar wonders. The plane won, which as much as anything, illustrates what a wonderful thing flight was to the youngsters of the early days of our century.

By contrast, the *Times Index* of 1952, under headings ranging from Air Force to Air Ships and Balloons, has a solid 23 pages relating to air flight of which five, to point the unhappy times, are devoted to Airplanes—U. S.—Military. But for ten days in the Autumn of 1953, and all because of a strike, aeronautic and other news, in all of its fantastic ramifications, is not recorded in this classified record of the doings of Homo Sapiens.

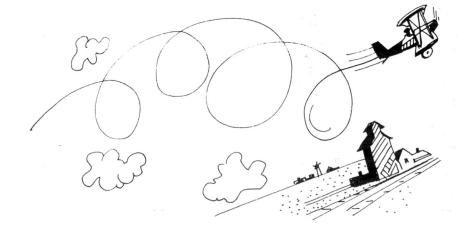

The Inhumanity of Man

Included in the awfulness of our century are piles of dentures and worn shoes that starving and dying men do not need.

WHEN STATEMENTS are made about libraries in their generality, or about books, these are if not universally, then certainly nearly always in idealistic terms. Men are wont to stand in tribute, in admiration, in wonder, and in gratitude too before the wisdom, the perceptiveness, and the noble idealism of great minds, past and present, and the clarity and beauty with which their thoughts have often been put to paper. Quotable statements of such admiration and gratitude are legion. I have sometimes thought of assembling and commenting on these, and on the bitter statements too if such can be found, as a pleasant occupation, God willing, of my retirement years.

Man, of course, is evil as well as good and noble, so there is, and has to be, another side to this coin. Since books and other graphic records and their assemblage into libraries encompass in these latter years, if not the whole of the human record, then most of it, they must necessarily record the evil along with the good. And evil there is, recorded on the shelves and in the vaults in generous, ever so generous quantity. Who, among those who will come after us will be able to read and ponder the writings and records of this troubled, warring, and ill-fated century without becoming appalled by the positive genius of Man, in his twentieth century manifestation, for being mean, selfish, cruel, heartless in ways beyond belief and which can only classify as inhuman.

I was set thinking on these things a few years ago when I went through the ordeal of watching the film, "Hitler's Mein Kampf." These thoughts were but reinforced when, just recently, I visited the Ann Frank house in Amsterdam and saw there the complete documentation of the shameful Nazi persecution of the Hebrew peoples.

The evil and the maniacal folly of the Hitler regime is of course recorded in libraries, volume upon volume, from the book *Mein Kampf* on, including particularly the records of the Nuremberg trials, but none of these, no matter how skillfully and eloquently written, has or can have the stark and awful reality of seeing people violated in their homes, robbed, pillaged, herded by the thousands into concentration camps, or of seeing them emaciated, starving, marched naked to the gas chambers, or, reduced to mere skeletons, lying dead or dying in the streets. Or the final indignity, their shrunken and mistreated bodies flung callously into the hopper to go sliding down to the lime pits or the soap factories. Or the mute and awful evidence left behind, worn shoes and piles of dentures that starving and dying men do not need.

I could not escape, somehow, a sense of personal shame and guilt as I watched the pompous strutting and listened to the eloquently demoniacal screaming of this picture, as I saw hundreds of thousands of people being captivated, swayed, and misled and as I witnessed the ensuing awful debacle and horror.

In safe and pleasant America, I had lived through all of this time in the prime of my years. Even at that distance, I had been troubled and uneasy. I had read *Mein Kampf*, been repelled by it, and argued violently about it with friends of German extraction, men of education and culture, who found in it the promise of a Messiah for the German peoples. Even they though, and all the multitudes of Germany, would have quailed and drawn back in horror if they could have foreseen the satanic lengths to which this arrogant leadership would go, once it had driven its roots deep into the economy and the souls of a great and enlightened nation, to there draw sustenance for tentacles spreading greedily over an entire continent and reaching finally for a world designed to be dominated by a super race.

It is to the credit of the responsible leadership of the world, a leadership busy with and beset by economic troubles and depression, that the realization finally came that it must once again gird itself, however wearily, to dispose of a grasping and heartless monster, if possible, finally and completely. So amidst rivers of blood and the offering up of millions upon millions of lives, this horrid orgy of evil did finally cease. As I walked away from watching the end, as depicted in one phase of its actuality in this picture, my chief thought was, would that it were possible to resign from the human race.

Since Man must however live with himself, the bad along with the good, I found myself hoping fervently that somehow, some way, we had learned from this awful blood bath how the troubles and strife and the clash of ideologies now taking place on this steadily shrinking planet could be brought to more intelligent and human solutions. Devoutly I wished that our libraries, as the custodians of the record, would one day record a happier outcome for our present difficulties, more fraught with dangers than even the Hitler years. I found myself thinking too, with keener appreciation, of these perceptive words about Man by Alexander Pope:

A being darkly wise and rudely great . . .
Created half to rise and half to fall;
Great Lord of all things, yet prey to all;
Sole judge of truth, in endless error hurled:
The glory, jest, and riddle of the world."

Wise Men Reading Good Books

Books and reading enter directly into a presidential election.

IN THE 1960 pre-election period, the *Saturday Review* directed a questionnaire to the candidates, Vice President Nixon and Senator Kennedy, seeking to ascertain their views on the arts and what actions they would take to support and develop the culture of our country. The ten questions asked ranged over the possible creation of a Secretary of Culture, the Cultural Exchange Program, the Voice of America, and pay TV. The answers of the two candidates, constituting something of a journalistic scoop for the *Saturday Review*, were published in adjoining columns in the SR issue of October 29, 1960.

It was clear from the two responses that whichever of these candidates our people would honor with the greatest office at their bestowal we would have in the White House a man deeply aware of the cultural status of our country and the need to create a climate and environment in which the arts would flourish. Since Senator Kennedy was elected, his response takes on sharp significance, constituting in a sense a kind of a supplement to or expansion of the plank in the Democratic Party platform, which, emphasized the Senator, proposed a Federal Advisory Agency "to assist in the evaluation, development and expansion of the cultural resources of the United States. We shall support legislation needed to provide incentive for those endowed with extraordinary talent as a worthy supplement to existing scholarship programs."

The unequivocal replies of President-elect Kennedy to the ten questions showed clearly that for him this plank was no empty gesture. The Democratic Party, he said, had accepted the responsibility of participating in the advancement of culture. It would fight for a renaissance of purpose in America and an end to apathy. It intended that our children would be prepared, in education, health, and vision to challenge a world of exploding technology, a world of great present danger but also of unlimited hope. The encouragement of the arts, in the broadest sense, has always been a function of government from the time of the most glorious days of Greece to the present, said the President-elect. The Advisory Agency "which will be appointed," he said, would decide in what manner our culture could be and should be strengthened.

The President-elect went on to say that the problem is not simply one of money. Quoting from some unidentified source, he said that in these days of crises "Wisdom is better than strength . . . a wise man better than a strong one." He recognized the importance and place of libraries in the achievement of wisdom in these words:

If this nation is to be wise as well as strong, if we are to achieve our destiny, then we need more new ideas for more wise men reading more good books in more public libraries. These libraries should be open to all except the censor.

We must know all the facts and hear all the criticisms. Let us welcome controversial books and controversial authors. For the Bill of Rights is the guardian of our security as well as our liberty.

WILLIAM HUGH CARLSON 119

"More good books in *more public libraries*," this is a highly significant phrase for all concerned with the writing and use of books. I have done no exhaustive research, but it is highly probable that never before has a presidential candidate made such specific reference to libraries as agencies to foster wisdom throughout our land. It is now a matter of record that the young President, so soon to be taken from us by an assassin's bullet, moved as rapidly as time and circumstance would permit to amplify and more generously fund the "Library Services Act" and to other actions in support of libraries and culture generally. We do now, as a nation, provide "more good books in more public libraries." Whether the reading of them, to the extent they are being and will be read, will provide the wise men and women our civilization so desperately needs, this it remains for the future to reveal. We may hope, prayerfully, that it will.

A New Ocean and a New Heaven

"We are as near to Heaven by sea as by land."

WITH THESE, the last known words of Sir Humfrey Gilbert, the first Englishman to conceive a settlement of English people on the North American continent, Felix Gilbert begins his book, *To the Farewell Address*, published in 1962.

Author Gilbert addresses himself to an examination of the efforts of the English colonists, once they had driven roots into the new continent, to keep free of the diplomatic and military entanglements of Europe, and indeed of the world. This practical or realistic or wishful objective, still flourishing among us, was by the sheer logic of events destined to failure. Tragic evidence of this is the involvement of the descendants of the colonists in two bloody world wars, a police action which was a war in all but name, and a current military action among a far distant and alien people that is rapidly moving toward war status. In addition the "Cold War" ebbs and flows, but flows more than it ebbs.

Gilbert takes his quotation from Richard Hakluyt's *The Principal Voyages of the English Nation*. Sir Humfrey had taken possession of Newfoundland in the name of his Great Queen say the *Voyages*. He hoped to establish there a settlement which would provide riches for himself, his family, his friends, and his country. But he sought more than this. He looked forward also to creating an ideal life and society. The first objective required close ties with Europe— the second separation from its intrigues, wars, alliances, and involvements. Both, as events have proven, could not be had simultaneously.

On the return voyage to England, a storm swept away part of Sir Humfrey's fleet, leaving only the Golden Hind and his tiny flagship, the Squirrel. This too soon foundered, taking Sir Humfrey and all aboard to a watery grave. As his flagship was going down, Sir Humfrey was seen seated on the quarter-deck reading. The book he held in his hands, and which moved him to his last words, says Felix Gilbert, must have been Thomas More's *Utopia* for it contains the words "the way to Heaven out of all places is of like length and distance."

There is food for reflection, in many directions, about these unusual events. What manner of man could sit calmly reading when all he had worked for and hoped for was meeting with catastrophe? Almost he would satisfy those librarians for whom reading is the be all and end all of existence and who chide and castigate their fellow practitioners for not reading enough. One thing seems clear: Obviously Sir Humfrey was not a sailor. Had he been, he might have been better occupied in trying to keep the Squirrel afloat so that he might live to read another day—and to found his Utopia.

Although Sir Humfrey probably did not realize it, his voyage and his aspirations were but one in a long series of human adventures and efforts through which men have marched, willynilly, toward a steadily shrinking planet where no continent and no peoples can be free from entanglements with the other inhabitants. This steady progression has reached dramatic and exciting climax in the voyages, or orbits, of a growing number of astronauts around the world, reporting all the while for all to hear on all parts of earth's surface, what they are experiencing and what they see. As these men have journeyed through the airless outer reaches, called by

President Kennedy the New Ocean, there has, happily, been no occasion for last words. Had there been, they would have been heard by tensely listening millions around the globe. Very likely they would not have been concerned with heavens and utopias. Rather, in all probability, they would have told, or tried to tell, realistically and factually, why there was failure, so that the next intrepid voyagers of the New Ocean would not similarly fail.

The current voyaging in the airless oceans of the universe, as well as the spectacularly successful close-up photography of the moon and of Mars, these have indeed put an exclamation point and final period to the inescapable fact that all humans everywhere, for better or for worse, are inescapably bound together in the great human drama. When Man can view all the continents and all the oceans of our little planet in a bit more than an hour, there can be no isolation, either political or economic, no matter how wishfully or stridently some may seek it.

And what about the Heaven that Sir Humfrey felt was reached as easily by sea as by land? Well, we have to revise our ideas about it, do we not? It has been made clear by the orbiting astronauts that wherever heaven may lie it is not in the skies of Earth where our mythology, our literature, and the scriptures of many faiths have placed it. The Utopia Sir Humfrey sought seems more identifiable and possibly, simultaneously, in greater danger. Through the current climax of marvels and achievements of which explorations of the new airless ocean are but one, it may, with great wisdom and some luck, yet be found.

Part VIII
ESSAYS DEALING WITH
SELECTED LIBRARIES

*E*veryone who has been engaged in the intellectual disciplines has, I suppose, worked in, or visited, or otherwise had experiences in or contacts with libraries which he or she has found unusually impressive. Certainly for professional librarians, who know many libraries, some stand out as exceptional. This may be for richness of resources, excellence of administration, efficiency of housing, or possibly just sheer size, although this, of and by itself, is not significant.

The following essays deal with libraries which in one way or another have impressed me. Curiously, one of them I have never been in and yet I feel, through the excellence of its annual reports, that I know it.

Almost a Book

I RANGE MYSELF, completely and without any equivocation, among the admirers of the Library of Congress. While this great library is far, very far from gathering and organizing in usable form all Man's recorded knowledge, it probably comes closer to doing this than any other library in the world. In 1964 it had 13,000,000 books on its more than 300 miles of shelves. In addition it had over 1,800,000 photographic prints and negatives, well over 3,000,-000 pieces of music, and about 3,000,000 maps. The collection and control of the recorded products of the human mind, in quantity, as carried on by the Library of Congress requires a staff of between two and three thousand people and a budget surpassing that of many entire universities. Managing all this is an administrative and intellectual problem complex in the extreme.

How and why has this library grown great beyond other national libraries and how has it been able to achieve, largely within the present century, substantial stature beyond and above the sum of all its parts? There is the Congress of the United States, of course, which has made the necessary dollars available, adequately but never generously. Money has been an absolute essential. The Library of Congress, however, has not grown great merely by spending money and accumulating more and more books. Over and above this, as is always true of superior enterprises, have been the intelligence, gifts, insights, and devotion of those at the controls and among the troops. We, as a nation, have been blessed and doubly blessed in the persons who have directed this great and growing enterprise down through the years.

It is significant that most people joining the staff of this library in key positions, those who have built the woof and warp, and coloration too, of its being, have remained in service on a lifelong career basis. In the earlier years this was at salaries which were woefully low, below even the low going-rates of those years in the major university and public libraries of the land. Why did so many of these able people, best typified by Herbert Putnam, long-time Librarian, remain with this library when they could easily have moved out at much greater salaries? Prestige perhaps was a factor, but if so it was a thing which they themselves were creating and of which they were the embodiment. Mostly, I would think, it must have been, and continues to be a sense of being constructively and fruitfully creative in the evolution of our modern voluminously articulate culture. Obviously, with less imaginative and dedicated leadership the Library of Congress could never have attained its present high eminence, no matter how generous its budget. It could, indeed, under less able leaderhip, have become a chaotic intellectual jungleland.

Among the many wise and constructive things which the library has done is to appoint, as honorary consultants, persons who have attained outstanding eminence in varied fields of culture. One such person was the poet Robert Frost. It was with obvious pride and pleasure that Librarian Quincy Mumford in May of 1962 set aside a Robert Frost Week in the Library during which he announced that Mr. Frost had accepted his invitation to serve a second three-year term as Honorary Consultant in the Humanities. More than 600 people, overflowing the available seats in Coolidge Auditorium, came, as the highlight of the week, to sit, quite literally, at the feet of the poet.

Mr. Frost responded to this occasion with sincerity and characteristic charm. His consultantship, he said, had been "one of the great things in my life." Through it he had become a friend of President John F. Kennedy. Replying to the audience applause which greeted the announcement of his reappointment, Mr. Frost said:

This all started between Mr. Mumford and me as a sort of joke. I came down (as Consultant in Poetry) expecting to have nothing to do with the city—I came down to be one of the poets who tell other poets how not to write poetry . . . but I rebelled—I said I had come under a misunderstanding: I'd thought I was to be a poetry consultant in *everything.* But I got all mixed up in the Government, so somebody called me, the other day, a statesman . . .

I've become a part of the Library, haven't I? Almost a book. If I act a little foolish tonight, pay no attention . . . It's just statesmanship.

Mr. Frost received a standing ovation when he entered and again when he had concluded reading from his poetry. Here with books all about in the wings, millions upon millions, this man, creator of some of the best ones, who felt himself to be a part of it all and "almost a book" was bringing dignity and the warm human touch to an enterprise which might well grow cold, possibly even surfeited and cynical, in the logistics of never-ceasing annual consumption of square footage by mile after mile of books; of classification schemes, ever more complicated; of growing millions of catalog cards; indexes upon indexes. How fortunate that those who manage this, the greatest library of them all, continue to invite gifted and learned men, Robert Frost and many others, to share their wisdom and contribute their insights not only to making the library great but to keeping it warmly human.

A Lover's Quarrel With the World

Robert Frost, who warmed the lives of many had something desperately needed in these uneasy, materialistic times.

THE CEREMONIES at the Library of Congress honoring poet Robert Frost and celebrating his acceptance of a second three-year term as Honorary Consultant in Humanities to that library, discussed in the previous essay, were among his last honors. Not long thereafter he was hospitalized with major surgery from which he was expected to recover. Fate, or Providence, or whatever it is that governs the lives and destinies of men decreed otherwise. So one of the wisest and most perceptive spirits of this mid-twentieth century, one who had enriched and warmed the lives of many and who had made an indelible mark on the culture and literature of our land, and of the world, left us.

For Robert Frost, life was long and rich. He was grounded in the physical verities, keenly aware of and attuned to the world about him. The New England countryside he knew and loved, he interpreted in disciplined poetry that for some of us at least requires reading and rereading for extraction of its best essence and flavor and meaning. Through all his years he continued to grow in wisdom, in stature, and in influence. It was his good fortune and ours that he retained to the very last his keen and sensitive perceptiveness and his great skill to express it in words.

Mr. Frost had something desperately needed in these uneasy and materialistic times of clashing ideologies and nationalistic ambitions, of missiles and antimissiles, of the strange delusion that somehow it is of vital importance, a matter of survival almost, for one nation or another to be the first to set foot on the moon. His was the ability to perceive, to analyze, to interpret, with wry humor sometimes, with understanding always, the minds and motives of men, ordinary, homely, everyday men and women for the most part, but men motivated by attitudes and emotions, by fears and joys, by love and hate not different from those of people who are front and center on the global stage, those on whose minds, convictions, passions, and whims so much, so very much depends. It was a good omen that the life and philosophy of Robert Frost touched, directly, in his last years, the supremest leader among us.

It was good, too, and an indication of the bedrock of his wisdom as well as his intellectual discipline, that Mr. Frost understood how basic the human record, as preserved in words, is to all we are and do. Speaking at Amherst in September of 1962 about a library and a new library building that is to bear his name, Mr. Frost said:

The difference between a college man and a man lacking college is that he has the resource of books, that he knows there's a book side to everything. He may use it or not, but he knows that he has the resource—a book side to everything . . . That makes the Library the heart of the whole thing.

It was at Amherst that the final rites marking the ending of life for Robert Frost took place. Among his friends who had come from the Library of Congress to do him honor at this final time was David Mearns of the reference department. His always gifted pen caught the flavor of this moment of parting in a line, which in its sensitive awareness of circumstance and scene is appropriately reminiscent of Frost. "When the services were concluded and the congregation walked down the long hillside, wind-caught snow wrought silhouettes of broad shoulders and white manes."

Frost, the poet, loved the world he found and lived in and marked with his presence, but he did not find it perfect. So among the many things he wrote were the lines quoted below, so directly appropriate at the time of parting:

> *I hold the doctrine of Memento Mori*
> *And were an epitaph to be my story*
> *I'd have a short one ready for my own.*
> *I would have written of me on my stone:*
> *I had a lover's quarrel with the world.*

Fifty Years at Fifth Avenue

Secure and solid behind its famous lions, a great library pauses to review its record of the past half century.

On May 23, 1961, an anniversary observance of great cultural and scholarly import was held in New York City. This was the fiftieth anniversary of the opening of the main building of the New York Public Library. It was on May 23, 1911, that this library, created by the gift of the great private libraries of John Jacob Astor and James Lenox and a $4 million trust fund bequeathed by Samuel J. Tilden, opened its doors for service, secure and solid behind its famous lions. Ahead of it lay opportunity, challenge, and a multitude of problems of which only those at the controls over the years can be fully aware. In responding to these challenges, the library grew rapidly in reputation, in stature, and in resources, attaining in the ensuing fifty years the proud status of a cultural and research agency which

draws into its halls and reading rooms scholars of many nations.

The *Library of Congress Information Bulletin,* to which I am indebted for the news of this celebration, reported that President William Howard Taft dedicated the building in 1911. Now, fifty years later, with a record of growth and of service surpassing, very likely, the fondest hopes of those participating in the 1911 dedication, the Library, said the *Bulletin,* was being rededicated both in recognition of its fruitful past and in expectation of continued growth and "the furtherance of public knowledge and enlightenment in service to the city, the Nation, and the world."

Dignified and colorful were the ceremonies of celebration. Two hundred scholars, heads of United Nations delegations, public officials, and librarians, marched, garbed in academic robes, from the grand foyer of the library to a platform in nearby Bryant Park. There, before an audience of about 3,000,

Mayor Robert Wagner and Governor Nelson Rockefeller "paid tribute to the services of this great Library and emphasized the unique partnership of public and private funds which made its possible."

At a following luncheon in the canopied courtyard of the library, the trustees presented four anniversary awards in recognition of distinguished service, three to other libraries and one to an individual. The libraries honored were three of the great national libraries of the western world, the Bibliothèque Nationale of Paris, the British Museum of London, and the Library of Congress—all for their contributions to the world of knowledge through the publication of their catalogs in book form.

It is significant that all three of these libraries have been created by professional librarians, as indeed has the New York Public Library too. Not in all instances by librarians who were or are graduates of schools of librarianship, of which there were none when the three honored libraries began, but by persons who have dedicated their lives to the assemblage, organization, and interpretation of the writings of their nations and of the world. In carrying out their important work these librarians have had to be conversant with the scholarship of the world and to be judges of the significant and the insignificant. They have had to plead for money and often to make-do with far less than enough.

These libraries have been required to devise schemes of classification encompassing Man's knowledge in all its widely ranging ramifications, to perfect catalogs, or try to perfect them, and to avidly search out and bring under shelter and control a literature more voluminous and more rapidly growing than those who made the first catalogs, planned the earliest classifications, devised the needed shelter, or ranged the first stacks could possibly have foreseen. Nor has the money required for all this, in ever increasing quantities, been easily found. Always there was the need to persuade those in charge of the purse strings, frequently persons who understood neither the intricacies of the problems nor the magnitude of the need. One index of that magnitude is that in 1959-60 it required $12,121,000 to operate the New York Public Library.

The individual honored by the library in 1961 was Keyes D. Metcalf, long time chief of the reference department of the New York Public and later director of libraries at Harvard. Now, in so-called retirement, he is active on a world-wide basis as a consultant extraordinary to librarians and to university presidents. Having contributed much to our time and culture, he richly deserved the honor bestowed upon him.

No one can assess or measure in tangible terms the true value of the New York Public Library to this nation and to the world. It has been and is a dynamic creative institution which has long since outgrown its immediate municipal responsibilities. Not that these have been neglected, far from it, but it has transcended them to become an institution of international importance and influence.

It is pleasant therefore, and appropriate too, that we, on the opposite side of the continent, should join in a salute to this great cultural institution, to its resources, to those who have administered it, and to those who presently hold the responsibility of continuing in the great tradition. The record is one in which all men of good will, and certainly all librarians, can take pride.

The Most Essential Single Facility

Cornell solves problems of finance, architecture, and sentiment to build one of the finest functional libraries in the United States.

IN THE SPRING OF 1961, three publications reached my desk from friends at Cornell University. At that critical moment in the planning of a new building for the Oregon State University Library, these publications had special relevance and interest for our entire campus. All of them celebrated the completion and occupancy of the magnificent new John M. Olin Library building. Most voluminous was the twenty-eight-page February 10 issue of the student newspaper, the *Cornell Daily Sun.* Supplementing it was the February 11th issue of the *Ithaca Journal* and an introductory guidebook to the new building.

All of these publications demonstrated the tremendous impact that a new and modern library building can have on any campus. This new building, it was clear, did not come easily to Cornell. In addition to working for and finding the 5.7 millions of dollars required to create it, the building, as has been true of so many library buildings, had had to struggle through and surmount the entanglements of architectural style, sentiment, love for one of the buildings it was to replace, variance of opinion as to where it should rise, and the well-established prerogatives of students, faculty, and alumni to be critical. There can be no doubt, however, that as it took shape, it emerged as one of the truly fine functional library buildings of the United States. Evidence of this in the *Daily Sun* was that several noted librarians have ranked it as "one of the three finest college library buildings in the United States."

Time was, and not long ago either, when the outcome would quite likely not have been so favorable. When I entered the professional library ranks in the late 1920's, the prevailing tradition and practice in erecting new university library buildings was that librarians should be seen but not heard. In those years some notable library buildings went up, notable that is as architectural show pieces, strong on ostentation, massiveness, adherence to some early architectural style, usually medieval, but giving little attention, and in some extreme cases almost none, to the functions they would be required to fulfill. This was the time when buildings such as the monumental and costly Sterling Memorial Library at Yale and the Henry Suzzallo Library of the University of Washington came onto the academic scene. It was hoped that they would be the supreme architectural and cultural adornment for their respective campuses. Whatever their successes in this direction, it has become crystal clear that as structures to house and service the massive literature of the modern world, and to make it easily and pleasantly available, these monumental earlier buildings and others like them have been failures.

The new Cornell building too has been required to struggle with architectural style and campus harmony, not too successfully some critics say. Within the exterior, which has made a bow to these traditions, the librarians have, nevertheless, as they did not in earlier days, had if not the first word, certainly the last. The result is an attractive, integrated, highly functional, and economically manageable library plant. And also one which is, happily, it is agreed by those who know, aesthetically harmonized and pleasant to be in and to use.

The *Daily Sun*, in celebrating and applauding this notable and long awaited achievement, featured articles of appreciation and hope by leading administrators and faculty members. These abounded in quotable phrases. The new building was spoken of as "one of the foundations for greatness," a "symbol of the spirit of learning," and as the "greatest single achievement during President Malott's tenure." No longer, it was said, would Cornell need to be "apologetic" about the housing of its library. John M. Olin, university trustee, and one of the principal, but by no means the only donor,

spoke of the Cornell Library as "the most essential single facility of any well-ordered and successful educational institution." In it are stored, he said, "the basic building blocks of progress."

President Malott said that the new building was "evidence of Cornell's enduring commitment to the scholar and to learning." The University he said, has built many buildings and will build many more, but "none is or will be so important to the University's capabilities or so descriptive of its character." There was, said the President, "no brighter omen" for Cornell's second century. Vice President Zwingle made administrative acknowledgment, not only of the great cost of erecting this building but of the increased amount of money which would be required to man it at the new tempo which would now be possible. This, he said, is "the price of ex-

cellence." He acknowledged, nevertheless, that fine facilities and numerous dollars are never enough to assure preeminence. Educational excellence, he said, is "essentially a matter of spirit."

Who can doubt that this splendid new educational resource and tool which Cornell has created will be a tremendous stimulus to its spirit, and through this to the excellence to which every university worthy of the name aspires. As we at Oregon State University, and this included especially the substantial number of Cornellians on our faculty, rejoiced with Cornell in its great achievement in spaciously and efficiently housing its library, in dignity and in beauty, we looked forward, expectantly and eagerly, and, as it happily turned out, with early realization, to a similar time of happy fruition and achievement for our own university.

Never Before Contemplated

The rising requirements of academic libraries in staff capabilities is an outstanding characteristic of the twentieth century.

IN HIS ANNUAL report for 1959-60 Stephen McCarthy, able director of libraries at Cornell, and highly instrumental in securing the fine building discussed in the previous essay, commented on the expanding program of his university and particularly on three programs financed by the National Defense Act of 1958 in Southeast Asia, China-Japan, and India. These programs, he

said, were placing demands on the university libraries for linguistic and bibliographical competence not now available. If these far flung programs were to be achieved in full potential, said Mr. McCarthy, "the library staff must be strengthened in a manner never before contemplated."

In a manner never before contemplated, here is a phrase which may well stand as weather vane for all librarianship, and particularly for university and research librarianship, during this latter half of the twentieth century. It presages that as our culture and the written record, which is both result and cause of its being, face into the years ahead, sharp gales of financial necessity will blow over the world of librarianship. Jet streams of fact and discovery arising from the low pressures and the high pressures of an increasingly articulate world in which the peoples of the planet have opportunity, as never before, to read and study, to think and write in all the varied languages of the world, these threaten to reach tornadic proportions in the years ahead. If they are to be harnessed and marshalled and organized for the benefit and cultural and scientific strength of the world, and this is the task librarians have, this will require heroic measures and financial support never yet approached in our society.

I comment frequently in these essays on the rising tide of publication. This tremendous growth is typified by the birth of new journals at the rate of 8,000 per year during the 1950-55 period and far more rapidly since then. Many of these journals are being translated into English at high cost and in quantity from the languages less well known in the West, chiefly Russian at the present time. Simultaneously, monographic volumes are pouring from the presses of the world by hundreds of thousands in an ever increasing range of languages. These things, far more than enrollments, are sending the library budgets of forward-looking universities zooming into the stratosphere. The extent to which many scholarly institutions of this century are facing up to the problem and the challenge, and the opportunity too, is shown by the increasing amounts of money which they are devoting to the maintenance of their libraries.

These are some of the facts of the rising financial requirements of university libraries in our time. In 1956-57 twenty-three university libraries of this country, not the giants of the academic scene, spent $4,872,000 for books and binding. Only two years later, 1958-59, these same universities spent $6,371,000. When we add to these book expenditures the money needed to employ the high-quality people required to organize and service these complicated materials and buying the space needed to house the increase, we reach money requirements which are becoming an important part of the world's expenditures for cultural purposes. Or for any purposes.

The significant thing in these rapidly rising library expenditures is that they are only in minor part affected by undergraduate enrollments and inflationary cost increases. Basically, they result from the tremendous explosion of knowledge and the necessity to keep up with it. All universities must, if they are to maintain academic vitality and strength, adopt budgeting for library purposes based not on enrollments and cost increases but upon the tremendous increase in publication of the literature essential in the modern university library. And they must do this "in a manner never before contemplated."

Commitment for Greatness

Greatness does not remain static. Every generation must achieve it.

IN A TALK before the Board of Overseers of Harvard University some years ago, Paul Buck, then director of the Harvard libraries, after reviewing the present status of the magnificent system of libraries he administered and the way they got that way said, "The Library's administration accepts wholeheartedly the broad commitment implicit in the possession of an outstanding Library for teaching and research—the commitment to keep it great."

A quantitative measure of the greatness of the Harvard libraries is, at the time of publication of these essays, a total collection approaching 7,000,000 books and pamphlets requiring upward of 200 miles of shelving. The greatness of this massive accumulation has come about through the dedicated generations of faculty members and librarians who have labored, over the years, with covetous zeal, conviction, and a catholic viewpoint to bring to the Harvard shelves the kinds of books the scholar needs, or may need some day, and to organize them for convenient and easy use.

In the earlier years, when the scholarly literature was less voluminous, the library sought practically everything. Librarian John Langdon Sibley voiced such a philosophy of acquisition somewhat over one hundred years ago when, in seeking alumni gifts, he said, "I think it would be well if it were generally known that there never was anything printed of which we would not be grateful for one copy." Under the onslaught of the bibliotecal deluge, this policy has necessarily had to give way to a more and more selective process. Growth has, nevertheless, proceeded on a very wide front.

Significant in the burgeoning Harvard libraries, now approaching some of the great national libraries in volume and richness, is that the tremendous increase has taken place without benefit of national treasuries. It has taken money, a great deal of it, as does the creation and maintenance of any great library, to bring the Harvard libraries to their present eminence. Nor has the money come easily. "There has been," said Mr. Buck, "a hundred years' war between librarians and presidents, resulting in unhealthy alternations of feast or famine." Obviously, the Harvard librarians have won the war more often than not, and the periods of feast have far exceeded the times of famine. Currently the librarians are winning the war, handsomely winning it. Evidence of this is a library budget for the 1963-64 year of $5,257,000. Of this, $1,061,000 were devoted to acquisitions and $2,808,000 to salaries.

The result of Harvard's hundred year intra-institutional war has been the creation of the world's greatest university library system quantitatively and qualitatively, libraries which have been and are a demonstration that the life blood of a university does circulate around and

through the library. The libraries which Harvard is maintaining at levels of highest excellence have clearly been fundamental in the greatness which the university has attained. It is a continuously demonstrated fact that the greatness of any university rests in the calibre and brilliance of the men and women it can attract to its faculty, at all levels. At Harvard the library has been a chief magnet which has drawn to the classrooms and laboratories the best minds and the most able scholars of this continent and of the world.

The development of the great Harvard libraries and of the numerous other great academic libraries of the world has relevance for all university libraries. Great and small, these libraries must wage the "war" for university dollars, valiantly and unremittingly wage it. This struggle may, in the evolving scene and with prospects for mechanization beginning to promise practicality and efficiency, take more and more cooperative forms. The prospect is, nevertheless, that providing high-calibre library service for students and faculty will cost the individual university more, far more, in comparative terms, than has ever before been true.

Early Day College Discipline

The western frontier absorbed the energies of restless, rebellious students of earlier generations.

SOME OF US, as we hear or read of particularly vicious or unruly conduct on the part of our teenagers, of which there seems to be an undue amount in these days, are inclined to feel that the world must be going to the dogs. To be sure the younger generation has been headed that way, in the eyes of oldsters, down through the ages. We can be certain that we do not, in our time, have any monopoly on troubles with our younger people. This was brought home to me by some notes I made many years ago during my brief service at Vanderbilt University, from a record book, for the years 1829-30, of Nashville University,

the predecessor of George Peabody College.

These notes seem to provide an appropriate change of pace for these essays. They make it clear that being a dean of men, or its equivalent, in a frontier educational institution was really a pretty rugged proposition. Certainly compared to this early university, modern student disciplinary problems are relatively mild. These are some of the things which the Nashville University faculty and trustees of 1829-30 had to contend with:

MAY 4, 1829. "Fielding G. Deaderick, ordered instantly to leave college for having fired a pistol at and wounded a fellow student in the arm, 5 o'clock p.m. It is vacation. Said Deaderick was expelled by a unanimous vote of the trustees May 16th. Joseph W. Perkins wounded by the above will be dealt with according to his deserts. He has been indefinitely suspended. Restored November 16, 1829."

MAY 11, 1829. "Isaac H. Hilliard (it is ascertained) brought into college last winter the pistol used by Deaderick and he is this day indefinitely suspended. Restored November 16, 1829."

JANUARY 7, 1830. "Joseph W. Perkins was this day indefinitely suspended for drunkenness, idleness, and general dissipation."

MARCH 4, 1830. "Constantine Perkins suspended for dissipation in house of ill fame."

MARCH 10, 1830. Seven students "were indefinitely suspended from the university. They having on the previous evening run away to avoid the civil authorities in consequence of dissipation, window-breaking, and a riotous attack on the city watch. The above (except Robertson) ran away without having been charged by the faculty with any offense on Tuesday evening, March 9th and were suspended by the faculty on Thursday the 11th because they went off without leave. Robertson was suspended because he went away on Wednesday, the 19th, not only without permission but in violation of the express command of the president. These youths had been engaged in a riotous attack on the town watchman on Saturday night (the 6th inst.) in company with and at the instance of Constantine Perkins, a suspended student, and it is understood that they ran away to escape prosecution. Wendell and Robertson were old offenders. The others had not been previously suspended nor were they obnoxious to suspicion."

AUGUST 13, 1830. Four students were dismissed for going away without leave, in the company of Wm. B. Robertson. "It is said they went down the river in a boat, going far into the West never to return."

Ah the West! There was the convenient and ever present escape valve of our earlier days for all the dissident and unhappy, for the economic and social failures and all who fell afoul the law. It beckoned too to all who loved adventure. Now gone forever, it exercised a harsh discipline of its own that either made or broke those who accepted its call. Those who survived did so through physical stamina, courage, ingenuity, and resourcefulness. It is in some considerable part, their progeny, not far removed, who come to our universities now for instruction and guidance, and they come, except for a very few, as well-mannered and reasonably well-behaved young people.

Part IX
THE OREGON STATE UNIVERSITY LIBRARY: EARLY DAYS—AND LATER

I hope readers will not think it inappropriate for me to include in these essays, which it has been my intent to present, for the most part, in generalized terms, a few commentaries dealing specifically with the Oregon State University Library. The following pieces, written at various times over the years, flowed naturally and easily from the ongoing work of the university and the library. Indeed, in a larger sense, this is true of all the essays.

A Century of Evolution

THE HALFWAY MARK of the century offered an appropriate time to reflect on Oregon State University library milestones past, present, and, by the grace of God, milestones yet to come. The milestone marking the beginning of the century was indeed modest. Then, according to the college catalog of 1899-1900, the library occupied a well-lighted room on the first floor of the administration building and contained "nearly" 3,000 volumes of standard works.

Presiding over this collection was handsome young Arthur J. Stimpson, graduate of the college with the class of '98 and late from the U. S. Army and the Spanish-American War. Mr. Stimpson, whose library training had consisted of "mostly trying to keep a bookstack between myself and the Librarian" was sought for and accepted the librarianship even before being mustered out of the service at the San Francisco Presidio. He came to his new responsibilities, as the first full-time Librarian, at the princely salary of $40 per month. He arrived to find books scattered "helter-skelter" all over the newly established library quarters, but he soon had things under control so that "the Librarian could find the books if no one else could."

Mr. Stimpson leaves a lively account of his brief stewardship of the library. One sentence I like says, "Something happened every day and the life of the Library was not a dull one."

Among these things, no doubt, was the day some pharmacy students released some H_2S in the library in a well-hidden spot. After that there was "quiet in the Library for the rest of the day."

So much for the library of 1900. What of the library of the year 2000? At the mid-century rate of growth, which is certain to be greatly exceeded in the remaining years of the century, the library will add perhaps 700,000 to 800,000 volumes in the second 50 years of the century, bringing its volume count to well over 1,000,000 volumes, and its linear shelf requirements, for our present kinds of books, to somewhere around 35 miles. It is more likely, unless the learned world masters the difficult problem of discarding books, that the OSU Library of 2000 will be well on its way to a second million volumes, for the housing of which the new building erected in 1963, with its proposed additions, may and probably will be inadequate. The library staff and library expenditures will also have increased correspondingly.

It is quite conceivable that the organization of knowledge will have been completely mechanized by the year 2000, as has been emphasized throughout these essays. I am among those conservatives who do not expect this to happen, at least not to the degree envisioned by the enthusiasts. If the brightest dreams are indeed realized, the Oregon State University Library and every academic library, will be an intricate push-button affair operated by functionaries who will push buttons to call up information and facts from the library's holdings or from regional and national reservoir libraries throughout the world. There may even be a control to reveal instantly how the library was organized back in those quaint mid-century days when the codex book was still in use and librarians worried about shelving for their space-devouring charges and about the cumbersome and costly cataloging of them.

And then again, by the year 2000, strife and bombs, atom and helium, and bacteriological warfare may have reduced all to chaos and ruin, bringing into fulfillment the prophecy of a statue which adorns one of the attractive rooms in the Love Memorial Library building of my alma mater, the University of Nebraska. This imaginative piece, which ante-dates the Bomb, shows an anthropoid in a debris-strewn area, seated on Darwin's *Origin of Species*, Adam Smith's *Wealth of Nations*, and a few similar books, scratching his head in wonderment as he contemplates a compass. I personally prefer to believe that things will not come to this and that university libraries will be flourishing institutions in the year 2000 in which the codex book will still have a primary and honored place. Perhaps someone may even be curious enough to push one of the buttons to see who the librarians of 1950 were, how wrong or how right they were in their predictions, and how they managed their affairs.

"Mother" Kidder

*A great librarian and
a choice spirit.*

WHEN I SAT DOWN at my desk at Oregon State for the first time, in March of 1945, I found the photograph of a middle aged lady, serene but determined, gazing out into the office from the top of a nearby book case. "With love, Ida A. Kidder," these were the words across the bottom of the photograph. To me this was then just a name of a former librarian and the photograph just a photograph which might well be retired to another location at some appropriate moment. But almost immediately there seemed to be something companionable, and commanding too, in this strong, uncompromising face which observed my daily doings.

More and more I found that I liked having it there. Increasingly I felt, from that implacable yet friendly gaze, that it was incumbent on all who occupied the librarian's chair to do well with this, her library. We became good friends, the photograph and I, and happily so, for it soon became apparent that the spirit of Ida Kidder was still, perhaps indirectly, but nevertheless definitely, present throughout the library. Gradually I came to understand and feel that she had built for herself, in this library, and throughout the campus and community, a place unique in the annals of American librarianship.

A graduate of the University of Illinois Library School with the class of 1906, when she had already passed the half century mark in years, Mrs. Kidder came west to serve briefly in the Washington State Library in Olympia. It was from the staff of the Oregon State Library that President Kerr brought her in 1908 to the college to be the first professional librarian. Immediately there was a new spirit and a new vitality in the little one-room library in Benton Hall.

Unfamiliar with the library problems and needs of technical institutions, Mrs. Kidder sent off a call for advice to Claribel Barnett, librarian of the United States Department of Agriculture. Back came a five-page, single-spaced letter which is a key document in the history of the OSU Library and which was also the beginning of a life-long friendship between these two outstanding women. On the foundations plotted for her, Mrs. Kidder built with sure instinct and complete devotion. Letters and budget requests at once began reaching the President in a never-ending refrain that still goes on—more staff, more book money, more space. And the requests were honored too, as time and circumstance permitted. In her twelve years, Mrs. Kidder brought the library from a small collection of 4,264 volumes in a single room with only herself as the staff, to a collection of 35,814 volumes housed in a new build-

ing, beautiful and well planned for its time, and to a staff of eight and one-half, of whom five were professional librarians. The weekly open schedule was quickly expanded to 71 hours.

While she was doing all this, Ida Kidder was also entering completely into the hearts and affections of faculty and students. She had a positive genius for reaching and understanding young people. But there was no pampering. She clearly held to a philosophy of spare the rod and spoil the child. This is clear in the instance of a young student, who came eventually to occupy a prominent and honored place on the campus, and who, under the compulsions of reserve reading, even as students occasionally do now, violated a fundamental rule. This matter went straight to President Kerr with recommendations for very drastic punishment. We have no record of how this case was settled, but the young man, fortunately for the university, survived.

It was during World War I that Mrs. Kidder particularly established enduring friendships and a voluminous correspondence, both with college students and young men from Camp Lewis, where she served as hospital librarian during the summer of 1918. "Dear Mother . . ." wrote one of these young men from France, "don't you dare call yourself 'old.' That applies only to people who have ceased to be interesting . . . not to such dynamos of kindness, sympathy and understanding as you. Mother, you will never get old for the companionship of your boys and girls and the immortals that live on your bookshelves has endowed you with a personality that defies the March of Time."

The place in public esteem which Mrs. Kidder reached is shown by one of her war letters from France, addressed only to "Mother Kidder, Oregon" which reached her promptly, without delay. When she passed away on February 29, 1920, after a brief illness, there was widespread mourning. On March 2, 1920, her body, and this is probably the only instance of its kind in American library history, lay in state in the library which was the crowning joy of her life. Guards were at the entrance and at the casket and all classes were dismissed from 10 to 2. This, and the naming of a building after her (transferred in these later years to the building she erected) was the way the then college chose to honor her and to show its realization that she was not only a great librarian but a choice spirit.

Romance in the Library

The first flutterings of the silken wings of love.

IN ONE of my early years at Oregon State, I was on my way east to a conference. The diner was crowded, as was customary in those immediate post-war days. As I stood waiting I was invited by an attractive young couple to share a table with them and their four-year-old son. In the usual exchange of questions, pleasantries and information, I learned that the young man was in business in Portland, and they learned that I was from Oregon State College. When I said further that I was the librarian, my friends exchanged significant glances and the young woman, smiling prettily, said, "You see, we first met in your Library."

We can be certain that these two were not the first to hear, in the precincts of the library, "the first flutterings of the silken wings of love," nor will they be the last. College and university librarians have long been aware that the reading rooms of libraries, and even more so the stacks, are a happy hunting ground for Danny Cupid and that the little fellow often finds, in these bookish and usually quiet surroundings, the propitious moment to send home a successful shaft and then to nurture it tenderly. These things happen, of course, wherever boy meets girl, and sometimes in the most unlikely of places, but long winter evenings in the library do offer unusually good and frequently recurring opportunities for the come-hither look and all the ensuing consequences. Librarians would be the first to agree, I think, with the Arab proverb, which has it that the whisper of a pretty girl can be heard further than the roar of a lion.

Even the scholarly atmosphere of Harvard University cannot exclude romance from the libraries. Marston Morse, in an article, "Science and the Library," commences by saying that when he began reflecting on the use of a library he thought first of a graduate student of his who had access to the stacks of Harvard's Widener Library. Among other students using these stacks was a particularly beautiful young Radcliffe graduate student. These two, the Harvard boy and the Radcliffe girl, made the stacks the scene of a successful courtship. They were married and appropriately called their first-born Widener. Here we certainly have a reversal of things—a person being named for a library, instead of a library for a person.

That true love does not always flow smoothly is something of which all librarians have frequent occasion to be aware. Long, serious, and hushed conversations in the halls, some pouting, a little sulking, and even occasionally tears, these all come under the observation of librarians, along with some of the more tender demonstrations of affection. It must all come out right in the end, because in the *OSC Barometer*, student daily paper, I noted, in 1951, a full page banner headline "Many OSC students to exchange summer wedding vows" and below this a good collegiate heading "New pinnings still popping."

How many of these culminating romances began in the library or were furthered there? We will never know, but we can be certain that one continuing extracurricular function of all academic libraries and not an unwholesome one, within reason, will be as a place where romances begin and flourish. It comes as no surprise to university librarians in the beautiful spring months and with June approaching, that pinnings continue popping.

Pappy Hayseed and the Boys of '97

*Green will be the memory
for many years to come.*

In the summer of 1950 we received at the Oregon State University Library, from Harvey L. (Pappy Hayseed) McAlister, OAC football star of the 1893-97 period, then living in a veterans' home at Napa, California, and now deceased, a box of early football pictures, clippings, and other college memorabilia of the time. Included in the box was the first football owned by the College, scarred, battered, and of course deflated, and giving evidence of frequent resewing. These pictures and early clippings offer rich materials for the historian of athletics at OSU and in the Northwest.

The first football game ever played in Corvallis, we learned from Pappy's scrapbook, took place on November 11, 1893, with Albany College. The Albany team, "all beef and no science," was no match for the OAC boys, who romped to thirteen touchdowns, no less. Enthusiasm, said the reporter, "ran high during the game, and amid the squeaking of horns and ringing of the college yell of 'Zip boom bee! Zip boom bee! OAC, OAC!' one could hardly think. The ladies got so excited they actually yelled . . ."

Things really happened. The band played, the ball (the same one that now reposes in an exhibit case in the Athletic Department) broke after a touchdown

goal kick, "which probably lost two points for the OAC," there were fumbles galore, mostly by Albany, and three Albany players were unable to resume the second half, so OAC loaned them three players. Final score OAC 64, Albany 0.

It was probably a couple of seasons later that an intercollegiate football association was

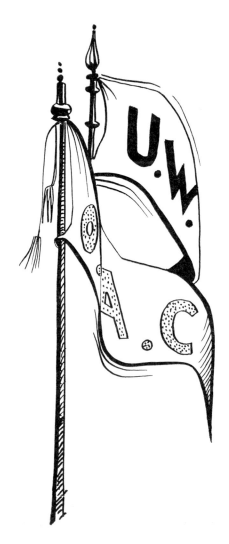

formed. The "Farmers" were defeated by the University of Oregon 16 to 0 that year. This game was notable for "the general good feeling that prevailed among the players and the absence of slugging on either side." This happy state of affairs did not long continue. It was probably the next year that the two rivals had themselves a game that must have been a dilly, and which ended 8 to 4 for the U of O. The account of it includes these paragraphs:

"Frick, Eugene's coach, U. of O., went on the field during the dispute and offered some advice. He was ordered off and, refusing to go, was carried off forcibly.

When referee Burckhardt gave Eugene the protested touchdown, Kelsay of the Farmers' team accused him of unfairness. Burckhardt told Kelsay he lied, and the latter knocked the referee down. Kelsay was then ruled off.

A spectator knocked down a college boy that attempted to keep him back of the lines."

The aftermath of this donnybrook was cancellation of a supposedly scheduled game between OAC and the Multnomah Athletic Club of Portland. In the piece reporting this action, it was stated that Kelsay, "who ran under Multnomah colors in the last championship games, is a horserubber in a livery stable there (Corvallis) and not a student at the College." But Pappy got into his scrapbook a sharp rebuttal for OAC which puts quite a different light on things and establishes Kelsay as the son of Judge Kelsay, Mayor of Corvallis, and that he had attended college for the past three years.

Ah me! Fortunately the long and colorful series of OSU-U of O athletic competitions has grown in sportsmanship, if not in zest. And the happy ending is that Pappy Hayseed and the boys went on to become the first great Oregon State team and to win the Northwest Championship in 1897 "without even an accusation of foul playing," beating the University of Oregon 24 to 8 and defeating the University of Washington in a challenge play-off at Corvallis 16 to 0. "Green will be the memory of the OAC football team of 1897 for years to come!" said the reporter of this one.

His Four-Year Plan

"I only know what I read in the papers."

THAT IS WHAT Will Rogers used to say and I subscribe fully to the same statement, for it was not until I read about it on the Portland *Oregonian's* editorial page of January 6, 1948, that I learned that one of our fall term graduating seniors had fulfilled a long-time urge to stand on his hands on one of the library reading room tables. The *Oregonian*, which I was then completely convinced, knows all, sees all, and hears all, said, and correctly, I discovered, that the young man picked a busy mid-afternoon, when the large second floor reading room was full to give vent to his urge to publicly reverse his perpendicular position.

Mounting one of the tables, said the *Oregonian*, he called for the attention of the variously startled and puzzled students. He had worked very hard since entering OSC he said, much of it in this very room, but he had always been determined that some day he would stand on his hands on one of the reading room tables. Now he was about to graduate and if those present would excuse him he would fulfill his long-nurtured ambition.

This he then proceeded to do, taking a few steps on his hands and coming down gracefully. Whereupon, according to the *Oregonian*, he departed from the "muted and sacred precincts" of the library with an expression of "beatific satisfaction on his face."

On this last point I am not so certain that the *Oregonian* was *correct*. The episode was something less than a world-shaking event in the library, as was indicated by the fact that it was not even reported to the librarian's office. For one thing the young man was not horse-collared by any horrified librarian, as he had perhaps expected to be, and was allowed to depart in peace, his beatific satisfaction undisturbed.

There was a member of the professional staff, probably not recognized as such by the young man, in the immediate vicinity. She was as much surprised and startled as the student users of the room but she had the good sense and the intuition to recognize a great moment of fulfillment and to leave it unmarred. A few titters, chuckles, and curious stares, and the room returned to the busy tenor of its ways, no more ruffled than a placid stream by a pebble cast upon its surface.

Library reading rooms, at OSU and elsewhere, are by no means always "muted and sacred." To be sure they must be kept quiet and orderly. If they are not, the librarian soon hears about it from unhappy users. Libraries though, deal with a pretty representative cross section of persons and personalities and those who work in them, and particularly those who work at the service desks and in the reading rooms, see a good bit of the human comedy, from the tragic to the funny and from the sublime to the ridiculous.

Anything can and often does happen in a library. So much so that I have had in mind to beguile myself, when I retire finally to the munificence that will await me, by writing a few essays on unusual library events in my experience, here and elsewhere. Perhaps I will call them "Reading Room Reminiscences." It will be a pretty varied lot of incidents that I can write about.

For instance, Ferdinand Hansen, the massive necked, gravel voiced Danish importer and ardent Nazi who had feathered his nest very softly indeed in America. There was the immediate pre-World War II day when Ferdinand pounded my desk in apoplectic rage and bellowed in tones that could be heard throughout the library. All because we would not accept and display in the library some propagandistic literature he wished to give us.

Then there are the two times, in my experience, and they would not be pleasant to write about, when persons in the reading room went off the deep end mentally. Also the calling of a young woman from among the readers with the knowledge that a message of her mother's sudden death awaited her. Somewhat similar to our own hand-walking senior, but less pleasant, is the incident of the V-12 trainee who had washed out and who, after having looked generously on the wine when it was red in the cup, entered the reading room, placed a chair on top of a table, seated himself, and proceeded in obscene and profane terms to unburden his soul of what he thought about the university, the library, and the United States Navy.

More pleasant to reflect on will be the joyous shriek, in a quiet reading room, of the homesick freshman whose mother arrived unannounced and unexpected from the distant home and walked into the room to find her daughter. Libraries muted and sacred? Well, sometimes. And then again sometimes not. It would be a bit awkward though, but interesting, if hand-walking on library tables should become a senior tradition.

Our Day

"The library as a hole is run very good."

THURSDAY, THE 18TH OF MAY, 1950, was planned from the beginning to be different, but not that different. This was the day we had chosen to hand out to every person entering the library a questionnaire designed to tell us who used the library, for what purposes, and with what success. We had also decided to run on that day a test on the efficiency of our service at the central circulation desk. We settled on this Thursday because we knew that it would be busy.

What we did not know and could not know was that the stars in their course, or whatever it is that guides human destines, would bring Ahmed Q. Din, all the way from Pakistan, to set up a great public lamentation in our lower foyer. This upset our questionnaire procedures no end. The dispensing of questionnaires came to a halt as students came flocking, from in the

library and out, to watch and listen (and who in the library could avoid it) as distraught librarians tried to calm and quiet the unhappy Mr. Din. That determined young man was bent, however, on bringing the inequities of his scholastic treatment and status to the attention of "the highest government officials." His lamentation and harangue continued, unabated, for some twenty minutes, ceasing only when the Law arrived in its uniformed majesty.

It took awhile, after that, for the library to resume the even tenor of its ways. And among the librarians they never did become quite as even as usual. We early found that we had underestimated the number of questionnaires that would be needed, even if there had been no Mr. Din, so an emergency mimeographing operation had to be undertaken. Also practically on the heels of Mr. Din an emissary of the physical plant arrived to announce that it would be neces-

sary to cut out the circulation department elevator for a half hour. This meant that the efficiency test of our circulation service went snafu and that the results for the day would be skewed.

Throughout the entire day (and week) it was obvious that students were finally aware that time is fleeting and that term papers were not yet written. Lines formed as harried librarians and student pages dashed back and forth and as returned books overflowed return shelves and book trucks and piled up on the floor. Of course, we could say it all began with the elevator, or even with Mr. Din, but the plain truth is that the machinery was overloaded, out of balance, and creaking at the joints.

As part of the total picture for the day, we had also decided to maintain a record of all questions asked, trivial as well as important, at our various information desks. These included such items as where to find four pages that had been neatly razor-bladed out of *Moody's Industrials*, also could Moody's be charged out over night and why not. One hopeful student wanted to know if we had a catalog of everything at the J. K. Gill Co. in Portland, Oregon. Another asked if I Corth V:15 did not mean First Corintheans, Chapter V, verse 15. And so it did, but the student was trying to find it in Chronicles. Another, obviously in the wrong place, wanted to see the file of old exams and was doubtful when told we did not have them. There were, of course, solid reference questions too, such as about Canadian export statistics, how many persons with college degrees have jobs and how many do not, and how did the custom of using sheep skins for diplomas originate.

As for the questionnaire itself, it could and did furnish materials for several cover essays. Over 1,100 students turned in filled out questionnaires which we were quite some time in analyzing. Through these answers we got a look at ourselves through student eyes, particularly as quite a few persons added comments. Some of these gave a sharp jolt to whatever tendency toward complacency we might have had. It was encouraging to find, however, that most statements were appreciative, friendly, and constructively helpful. We hardly knew, though, whether to be pleased or disturbed by one student comment that, "I think the Library as a hole is run very good."

Atmosphere, Tone, and the Library

To be great, a library must first be good.

THE "TONE" AND "ATMOSPHERE" of a university and the importance of these in the institutional life is a thing I have often reflected on and been impressed by on the basis of an intimate connection with nine universities. Four of these, including Oregon State, I have served as Chief Librarian. Each of my nine universities has been different, each has had elements of particular strength, effectiveness, and attractiveness. In some instances, at least from my point of view, there have been weaknesses.

Within each of my universities, the library has had an atmosphere or tone or personality separate and distinct from, although conditioned by, its parent institution. It has had a tone and personality, too, separate and distinct from all other university libraries.

No one of perception can be closely associated with an academic institution at its very heart, as librarians are, without sensing and learning much about the total institutional mores and personality, both in strength and in weakness. The depth and range and versatility of the faculty and equivalent lacks; the alertness, awareness, attitudes and outlook, and concern of the administration about the cultural heritage; the attitudes of faculty and administration toward each other and toward students, and of students toward the faculty; the place of athletic programs in the institutional life and being, and the degree to which these are kept properly in academic focus; the sense of purpose, goals, aims and objectives, academic ambitions and aspirations and rivalries; the status of the university in community, state, and region; these are the things librarians learn to know intimately as they serve in their many faceted capacities. They come to know also, and soon, their own place in the institutional hierarchy and scale of values. It is demonstrable fact that where the library and the librarians rank high in the scale, general institutional strength and excellence is also found.

No librarian, of course, can objectively assess and weigh his own library, any more than an individual can see himself as others see him. Within limits, though, universities, and within them their libraries, do have a sense, probably close to the actual, of their own importance, worth, contributions, and achievements. Like individuals, some universities are modest about themselves, while others give forth easily with peans of self praise and glory. To the extent that it can be done in a paragraph or two, I set forth here, rightly or wrongly, a partial and I hope not too inaccurate vignette of the Oregon State University Library as I have come to see and know it in my years of service.

First, contrary to things I have read once or twice in the local press, OSU does not have a "great" library. We are reasonably certain though that we are building sound foundations for greatness. While we do not and never have claimed greatness, we have and do maintain, stoutly, that we have a good library. This goodness, I believe comes in considerable part from the University having been fortunate in the early librarians who set the library on good paths. This they did with financial support so meagre that the resulting accomplishment must rank high, very high, in the annals of library management.

Although funds have been more generous in recent years,

they have not, in terms of buying power of the faculty, student body, and graduate program to be served and the burgeoning mass of print pertinent to the curricula and research, been any more adequate, possibly even less so, than in earlier days. This is one facet of the total OSU institutional tone which we have worked, early and late, to improve.

A part of the goodness of the OSU Library, to the extent that it is good, flows from sustained effort of all the administrations of the library to maintain public services at a high level. Ways to serve students and faculty best, these have, in the library range of values, ranked with, and possibly even ahead of building the collections. From the earliest days the prevailing philosophy has been that books exist to be used with a minimum of inconvenience. Even when the library seems to depart from this, as in the substantial restraints on the development of departmental li-

braries, the fundamental aim has been the greatest amount of book availability and use for the greatest number. As one example of placing use and users first, the new OSU building of 1963 does not, contrary to nearly all new university library buildings, place the technical processing staffs in prime first floor space adjacent to the main public card catalog. While we have stressed service, this does not mean that we have or will neglect the development of the collections. Efforts to increase our holdings in richness and in depth, these have been sustained and aggressive.

While users and their needs had a high place in the hierarchy of values during my administration at Oregon State University as well as earlier, the overall objective has been a balanced program, generously financed. To the extent that this is realized, the OSU Library may one day, God willing, rightfully be called great.

circulations as high as thirty per copy. Many had also become grizzled veterans of the railways, and sometimes the airways, through inter-library loan travels. Examination of one thesis showing the signs of its journeying to and fro, revealed it to have been out numerous times on inter-library loans in a single year. In order, it had made trips successively to the Board of Public Education, Philadelphia; State Teachers College, Buffalo, New York; Cornell University; Kent University; Santa Barbara College; Universities of Tennessee, Arizona, Arkansas, and Illinois.

One thing theses make clear in their introductions is that graduate students are grateful and appreciative people. Almost without fail, theses authors make polite, and, one supposes, sincere bows in the direction of their major professors and other advisers. One Oregon State thesis, the product of a foreign student, is dedicated as follows: "To the memory of my Mother, whose great motherly love inspired me to study . . ., this thesis is dedicated." One authoress shows wifely gratitude by saying "To her husband the writer acknowledges deep appreciation for his cooperation and constant encouragement making possible this study."

It is the wives though, who really come in for recognition. Of this the following from an OSU thesis is typical; "To my wife, I am most grateful for loyal support in this and all my endeavors." More explicitly another author says "The author wishes to express his appreciation for not only the encouragement but also the physical help given in the making of over 9,000 Rockwell hardness determina-

On Graduate Theses

Graduate students are grateful and appreciative people.

OF THE BOOKS owned by every university library, those which are peculiarly its own are the theses produced by graduate students. Even a casual examination of these varied studies in almost any university whatsoever will give the impression of very solid achievement. Certainly, an occasional one may seem pretty slight. Quite a few

may not be too well written; but by and large, these annual library increments are well done and a credit to the graduate work carried on in American universities.

That university theses are considerably more than a dust-gathering record of the work of graduate students is indicated by the fact that copies are withdrawn extensively. A random pulling down of recent volumes at Oregon State revealed annual

tions by his wife, as well as most of the editing and typing work. Without her help the work could never have been completed or have covered as great a scope as it has."

These statements bring to mind a verse appearing some years ago in *Pleasures of Publishing*, the sprightly, informative, and often entertaining house organ of the Columbia University Press. Ostensibly produced by a relieved and jubilant graduate student, as a Valentine, it goes, in part, like this:

At last, at last the book is done;
Lean close, sweetheart, and call me "Doc"—
No greener laurel can be won,
Though all we own is still in hock.
My Valentine, I give to thee
This bright and shining Ph.D.

The years of long research were rife
With Pedantry and pettifogging,
But you, sweetheart, my patient wife,
Have kept me free from doubt and grogging.
The flame, the plans, they all were mine;
The tears, the typing, they were thine.

Salute to the Courageous

Wives—especially student wives—have become a major factor in the functioning of the modern university library.

A CHARACTERISTIC of our twentieth century academic libraries is the extent to which young wives work in them. While there have during all my library years always been some young women of this kind in the employ of libraries and other university agencies, it has been only in the post World War II years that these employees have reached proportions making them a major factor in the functioning of the modern American university.

From the beginning of nearby World War II military Camp Adair and on up to the present time, the Oregon State University Library has had in its employ, in varying numbers, first the wives of soldiers stationed at the camp, then the wives of veteran students and more recently the wives of graduate students and also, and this is truly a phenomenon of the mid-twentieth century, the wives of undergraduate students. These young women have done much of the work of the library formerly carried by part-time student assistants. They have also increasingly done much of the work formerly done by professional librarians.

As army wives, as veterans' wives, and as student wives, these young women have, understandably, not been a stable group of employees because of the exigencies under which they have lived and do live. They have, nevertheless, been effective and highly valued employees. They have brought us skills, abilities, training, and a maturity of outlook and purpose not usually found in student assistants. We have found among them artists of professional ability, experienced typists and stenographers, accustomed sometimes to twice the salaries we have been able to pay, and yes, sometimes professional librarians too, all willing to work for whatever we could pay.

From the beginning of Camp Adair to the present, the library has employed, at various times, hundreds of these young wives, perhaps upward of a thousand. The high turn-over in their number has been due to many exigencies, change in family plans, graduations, sometimes more remunerative employment elsewhere, and of course, always pregnancies. To our considerable pleasure many of these young friends bring their babies back to see us, always with pride. The library now, indeed, has a large family of grandchildren.

I have been repeatedly impressed by the courage, spirit, and cheerfulness of these young wives. Living often under the most trying conditions, frequently on a very tight budget, cooking, washing, keeping house, helping out with studies and typing class papers and theses at home, they seem uniformly to take life in stride, babies and all, keeping up not only their own morale, but often, I suspect, that of their husbands too.

I take pleasure in here saluting these young Americans, whom I count it a privilege to have worked with. Sometimes, in those moments which must come to us all these days, when it seems as if the world is bent on going selfishly, greedily, and completely haywire I need only think of the selfless devotion of these fine young women. I like to think that it is they, rather than those achieving notoriety in unwholesome ways, who are typical of their generation. I like to believe too, and there is much substance for the belief, that in their hands and those of their children all will yet be well.

One of the wise and rewarding procedures of the academic world is to provide leaves periodically, on salary, during which faculty members are free to travel, to study elsewhere, to write, to consult with colleagues far and near in whatever ways and places professional interests may dictate. Or if they so choose, just to sit and think, free from the daily demands of classrooms, committee work, and conferences.

Most faculty members availing themselves of these opportunities find intellectual stimulus and renewal of spirit and interests in travels and pursuit of some orderly program of personal enrichment in their fields. It is a matter of record, which could be easily documented, that nearly every recipient of such leaves returns to his post with increased vigor, effectiveness, and enthusiasm. It is also a matter of record that the institution he or she serves is thereby enriched and strengthened.

It has been my privilege to enjoy, at Oregon State University, two such leave periods. They have been an integral part of my personal and professional growth and development. They have, and I state this categorically, made me a better librarian. Certainly they have helped me to understand what books and libraries are all about and the place they have taken and are taking in our culture and civilization. They have also helped me to better understand and more fully appreciate my fellow practitioners of the library arts.

The following essays are devoted, in some part, to the sabbatical leaves and experiences which have had such a constructive part in my professional career. I include with these accounts some other travels and experience which have brought me more than ordinary stimulus and growth. I sincerely hope that readers of these essays will find these lesser comments also of interest.

O Canada! Strong and Free!

IN JUNE OF 1955 it was my privilege, as well as my pleasant duty, to attend the tenth annual conference of the Canadian Library Association meeting in Saskatoon. This I did in the dual capacity of Chairman of the Liaison Committee of the American Library Association and the CLA and also as the official delegate of the ALA to the CLA. We journeyed by car entering Canada at Kingsgate, above Bonners Ferry, Idaho, for three unforgetable days in the magnificent Canadian Rockies. It was with some foreboding that we forsook these beautiful and awe-inspiring mountains for the serious business of getting to Saskatoon and for the long stretches of road construction which we knew awaited us. But the roads were passable, if at times challenging, and there was new and different beauty and interest.

After the watery greenness of muskeg country came rolling hills, agriculture with its accompanying towns and hamlets, and expansive prairie skies with grain elevators, nostalgic to one prairie bred and prairie nurtured, dominating the limitless landscape. It was here that we began to sense and feel the electric qualities of a country on the make.

Booming Edmonton, rapidly developing oil capitol and gateway to the far north country, stood for us as a symbol of a country which has been doubly blest in natural resources, as is being increasingly discovered as men probe the deep earth for the wealth of ages past to be added to the productiveness of fertile surface acres but recently, comparatively, put under the plow. Grain elevators, once and still dominant; oil derricks and refineries beginning, here and there, to stand against the sky; fabulous uranium deposits far to the north on the pre-cambrian shield left exposed by a retreating ice age—these too we found to be symbols of this dynamic, emerging country. But over and above these material goods was the greatest resource of all, the people.

Long before Moses led the children of Israel from the land of Egypt, men were on the hills and prairies of what is now Saskatchewan, following the retreating ice to live on the lush vegetation and animal life found there. Many centuries later the first waves of the white man, in the form of voyageur and trapper, faintly lapped this waiting land, to be followed slowly, then in rapidly increasing momentum, by men from many nations, the British of course, Germans, Scandinavians, Dutch, Ukrainians, and in lesser numbers, French, Poles, Russians, Czechs, Slovaks, men leaving national jealousies and rivalries behind and quickly learning, under the necessities of a land which can be bitter and harsh, to live in friendly intimacy, freely helping each other.

Among these amalgamating people, cooperative enterprises of many kinds successfully blending with private enterprise were to find their most fertile soil on the North American continent. These prairie settlers, of many origins, traditions, and faiths, free of the rivalries and jealousies of their native lands, learned, easily and naturally, to live in peace one with another. Even so, quarrels brewed, fomented, and bursting into flame from far distant chancellories have laid a heavy hand on them. Of this we were impressed at Ruddell.

At this little hamlet, of probably less than a hundred people, within the Saskatoon orbit, we stopped for lunch at what we took to be a small park. It turned out to be a war memorial, the gate carefully locked. We lunched, nevertheless, in the shade of its trees. From across the fence we could read, on a memorial shaft, these names: S. Davey, F. Salter, A. Miller, J. Beckette, S. Jackson, J. McMillan, J. Grandboys, G. Locker, C. Beechey, H. Mather, C. Pringle, H. Roberts, H. Campbell,—all lost in World War I, 1914-18. And for World War II, 1939-45, fortunately only one name, Sgt. W. H. Gillatt.

I was appalled that from this one small community of a new land where peoples of many origins dwelt so peacefully together, fourteen young men could have been swept up, in controversy and fighting not of their making, to find an early and bitter grave on foreign soil. It was sobering to lunch near this simple little community tribute to these long dead young patriots. As I reflected on the irony of these deaths, and the grief and suffering which must have accompanied them, it came to me that here was the key, really, to my presence at that moment on these prairies, on a mission of promoting, as best I could, better understanding and closer cooperation between two national organizations dedicated to the accumulation and the constructive use of the records of mankind.

Could men everywhere, in the towns and hamlets of the world, in the Ruddells of Thailand, China, Iran, South Africa, Argentina, Pakistan, the Ukraine, and a thousand other lands, no less than in Canada and the United States, could the people of all these places but understand and know, as they might through free access to and ability to read the human record, then there would need be no more making of wars and erecting of memorial tributes such as the one we had here chanced upon. With renewed purpose flowing from these thoughts, we resumed the road to Saskatoon and the stimulating and friendly meetings with Canadian librarians which there awaited us.

"We Stand on Guard"

Saskatoon, when we reached it, came as a surprise.

I WAS NOT prepared from my years at the University of North Dakota in the more plebian Red River Valley of the North, for the cosmopolitan flavor and atmosphere of the swank Bessborough Hotel, nor for the scenic and varied city that reposes so gracefully astride the south fork of the great Saskatchewan River. Fifty years ago this place of euphonic and appealing name was only a village. By the time of the fiftieth jubilee year of its province, 1955, it had grown to a thriving center of the industry and commerce of a thriving region.

But it does not live by bread and commerce alone. On the high banks of its crescent river is the University of Saskatchewan, an institution which will be increasingly heard from in academic circles. The hardy pioneers who peopled these prairies, no less than the pioneers of our own western states, believed in and took steps to provide advanced education. For their university they set aside a choice site overlooking the river and they had the vision to make it ample.

Here have been erected in architectural harmony, chiefly from native limestone, distinctive buildings designed to shelter and nurture the work of the university in dignity and beauty. Among those structures is a magnificent $10,000,000 hospital which will make this prairie and river city an important health center of its province and nation. It was fitting and in keeping with the times that, during this national conference of librarians the corner stone of a new and attractive university library building should be laid with appropriate ceremonies.

Going into Canada for a conference is no new thing for a librarian of the Pacific North-west. One year in five the Pacific Northwest Library Association meets somewhere in British Columbia and librarians on both sides of the boundary work so closely together that they often forget, on both sides, that the boundary exists. But this conference was different. I did have a feeling there of being not in a foreign environment exactly but in one distinctly different.

For one thing, I had brought home to me more strongly than ever before, that Canada is, in cultural matters certainly, and in many other ways, a bilingual country. Even in this western setting, this bilinguality was in evidence. It was present in publications, programs, and social events. It is embodied in the very name of the Association, one half of which is "Association Canadienne des Bibliothéques." It was a surprise too to find among those attending some, not many, but some, who spoke no English.

This official bilingual situation the United States, with its multi-languaged peoples fortunately escaped. But in Canada it is there, and there too often in the form of a fiercely proud heritage. This imposes on all who are concerned with the progress and development of the country the necessity for unusual tact and statesmanship. It would be, and undoubtedly on occasion has been, easy for one lingual group or the other to take offense and to withdraw more tightly within its own group, raising rather than lowering the thresholds of understanding. In a country as great as Canada, and with such great human and physical resources, there is no room for barriers to understanding.

I had the definite feeling, in

Saskatoon, that in library circles at least, bilingual barriers are being surmounted with skill and understanding. The librarians of Canada, I could clearly see and feel, are articulate, hard-working, forward looking, intelligent, and imaginative. By their deeds they are proving themselves equal to the challenge of a country with a great future. Plans have been evolved from the ground up and largely brought to fruition for a great National Library and Archives, including a magnificent new building to house them. Long strides are being made in numerous directions for the improvement of libraries and librarianship. More and more, the lesser language group is moving into concerns and activities at the national level where what is done is more important than the language in which it is carried forward. As I heard *O Canada* sung, and how well they sang it, I felt that these people do indeed stand on guard at the citadels of freedom of thought and spirit required in every true democracy.

Sabbatical in the Deep South

Service at Dillard University, adventures, some weariness, and a measure of satisfaction and understanding.

MY FIRST ELIGIBILITY for sabbatical leave at Oregon State University, falling in 1951, coincided with an invitation to assist Dillard University in New Orleans in the use of a substantial grant from the General Education Board for the upbuilding and strengthening of its library resources. The opportunity to be associated with this academic institution for colored people in a major and seminal project, I found both inviting and challenging.

We were not, through my having served for a year as visiting librarian of Vanderbilt University in Nashville, strangers to the South. As, traveling by car, we came out of the Ozarks south of Springfield, Missouri, evidences of the traditional South increased rapidly. Cotton fields were in process of harvesting, with here and there a mechanical picker, early harbingers of things to come, replacing the leisurely (or perhaps only seemingly leisurely) pace of the exclusively colored pickers. There were less tractors and more mules, or rather just mules since this has become an extinct species in the Midwest and Northwest. Grits, catfish, and hush puppies on the menus, these too brought us a distinct sense of differentness.

From Little Rock on we ran through the continuing cotton flatlands of the Mississippi Valley. The Mississippi itself, however, flowing high, serene, and mighty between its man-made levees, we never did see until we came up out of the flats opposite Vicksburg to see it in all its majesty and to cross it to roost for the night amid historic surroundings.

Natchez, famed in song and story and historically, and toward which we proceeded in the morning, was quite a revelation. After cruising through it carefully, the best we could do was to breakfast in a place that somehow kept us faintly apprehensive. Immediately south of Natchez we were lost (that feeling) on an endless detour, which really gave us a look at the hinterlands away from pulsing traffic arteries. When we finally did emerge from the woods, we were in Louisiana and by mid-afternoon we were in New Orleans where we were happily surprised to find the new and attractive Dillard campus in one of the nicer sections of the city.

Getting settled was somewhat of an ordeal. For one thing we arrived on October 1, which is traditional moving day in New Orleans. This meant that most landlords were fresh out of apartments. It became apparent finally that it would take a little something extra, over asking prices, to provide us acceptable shelter. By the afternoon of our first Saturday we were hot, frustrated, unhappy, and still unhoused. In this state I went to the Dillard-Morehouse football game, in part as an escape from the trials and tribulations of a nomad.

At this game, completely surrounded by colored people, I felt strange, alone and different. But not for long. The game grew in interest and Dillard, which usually gets beaten, and for which I found myself already developing some loyalties, was doing pretty good. So the sense of strangeness passed, never to return except momentarily. The thing that surprised and pleased me was how quickly I ceased to be aware of color differences. Almost at once we were simply people working together to get an important job done.

Dillard University was organized in 1935 by the merger of New Orleans College, operated by the Methodist Church, and the Straight College, operated by the Congregational Church. The merger and the opening of the University on a new and spacious sixty-two acres campus was made possible by liberal grants of money from the Julius Rosenwald Fund, the General Education Board, and other donors. Under the exceptionally able leadership of President A. W. Dent and a mixed Negro and white board, the university had steadily grown and prospered. Evidence of this was the most beautiful campus in the city, with fourteen buildings in use as of 1952 and a fifteenth, a half-million dollar Science Building, in the process of erection. Additional evidence was the operation of Flint-Goodridge Hospital and an outstanding Nursing School, erection and management of an attractive group of apartment buildings, good scholastic standards for a predominantly liberal arts curriculum, an able mixed faculty, and no subsidization of athletes. Dillard University was and is proud to be better known for its choirs and its nurses than for its athletic heroes.

The library, well housed in the first building to be erected, appropriately, on the campus, contained in 1951 some 21,000 volumes. It had lacked strong administration and its book collection badly needed infusion of the new blood and sinew which it would now receive through the book grant provided by the General Education Board and other donors. It would not be within the spirit and purpose of these essays to comment in detail on the library and my work

in it. During the brief months I was there, we introduced a completely new and streamlined system of book ordering, using multiple forms, thus eliminating several typing processes. We also established, with the cooperation of the business office, entirely new bookkeeping procedures.

Through a series of conferences the faculty was heavily involved in book selection. Books were quickly ordered, in the prevailing pattern, through a New Orleans bookstore. Many thousands of dollars were early committed, thereby flooding the catalogers with more work than they had seen in many a moon, or ever. Over and above these things a sustained effort was made to infuse the entire library program with a spirit of industry and application at all levels as well as eagerness for high excellence. It remained of course for the ensuing years to show how successful these efforts would be. From all reports progress has been excellent.

New Orleans itself, exotic, interesting, and different, has of course provided rich grist for many a writer. Certainly it is a city of contrasts. Churches and parochial schools there are in abundance, but in greater abundance, at least so it seemed to one not habituated to these things, are bars, hot spots, and dives. Thoroughfares are wide and handsome, but there are many streets so narrow they must be one-way. Fine homes, beautiful parks, and numerous playgrounds are offset by heart-sickening slums. A Kaiser aluminum plant, at that time the world's largest, had just been added to a substantial, creative, flourishing economy. Fattening on the wealth created by indus-

tries such as this are a generous quantity of parasitic enterprises which thrive on the deeply rooted instinct of the Louisianan to gamble. Even the climate is a thing of contrasts, with the thermometer bouncing up and down like a jack-in-the-box. But the terrifying rampages and extremes of the Father of Waters are gone forever. Shackled by the ingenuity of Man, he must here, whatever his excesses elsewhere, flow quietly to the sea.

It was shortly after Christmas that we pointed our car westward with a feeling, hopefully, that sound foundations had been laid. It was a thrill for uplanders like ourselves to come up out of the flatlands, marshes, and bayous to meet well beyond Baton Rouge, the pine-clad, rolling, and beautiful hills of northwestern Louisiana. Not far beyond Shreveport we were among the Texans. And, Texans in a hurry. At our sixty-five and seventy miles per hour they (millionaires no doubt) would glide by us as if we were standing still. I came to the conclusion that the next best thing to owning an oil well in those parts would be to have a Cadillac agency. In the quickening Texas tempo we were soon in Dallas. There we found that the pigeons, more bibliographically inclined even than the Corvallis variety, had appropriated the main library entrance of Southern Methodist University for their very own.

In Oklahoma we encountered, at both universities, that very special brand of hospitality for which that state and those two institutions are justly famous. The weather, however, was not as hospitable as the librarians. At Elk City, near the pan-handle, we were for two days iced-in in the heart of a new and expanding oil well field. During these two days they brought in two 1,000 gallon per day gushers.

The weather abating, I was soon, through the kindness and generosity of friends and colleagues, seated in my old office at the University of Arizona Library getting caught up on my home work, marveling all the while how that library had grown and expanded. During my years there, in the time when our nation was slowly emerging from deep depression, we had operated the library if not in adversity then in an austerity softened only by the substantial and gratefully received help of those depression spawned agencies, the WPA and the NYA, prototype of the present Economic Opportunity Act.

There were further library visits enroute northward. There were also further adventures with the weather, copious unremitting rain in supposedly dry southern California, flooding rivers, and ourselves having to be towed out of high water in Pasadena. With the weather everywhere contrariwise, we came up the beautiful Oregon coast in perfect weather and with a renewed sense of appreciation for the scenic beauty of the state in which we had now taken firm root both professionally and personally.

Soon we were home, sated with travel and content to sit for awhile by our own fireplace. There came then to mind the words of Mr. Booker, Director of the Dillard Choir, when he brought his young people home from an extensive tour of the northeastern states. He had said then, "We are far traveled and weary with the road." And so were we. It was for me a deeply satisfying weariness because of the sure knowledge that these few months had brought me new insights and new appreciations, that they had helped make me not only a better librarian but a better and more understanding citizen.

Välkommen till Sverige Clara

European libraries and ancestral lands are visited.

MY SECOND SABBATICAL leave, in 1957, was a visit to the libraries of northern Europe with emphasis on the Scandinavian countries and as a purely personal and long-hoped for mission, finding and absorbing as much as possible the flavor and tone of the small Swedish southeastern community, Rockneby, from which my parents emigrated to America in the great "utvandringen" of the last half of the 19th century. Thus it was that I found myself in late June of 1957 writing most of what appears in this essay in the beauty of a perfect summer evening and from atop a high rock in Renströms park in Göteborg, Sweden.

As I sat facing into a saffron western sky of this beautiful northern land where the twilight was now meeting the dawn, I knew that thousands of miles to the west, the affairs of my library were, under the direction of a good and strong staff, going forward with vigor. I reminded myself of this because I was deeply and gratefully aware that it was only because, far to the west, my colleagues were carrying on that I could be here on this bibliothecal mission of buying books, learning more of the libraries and librarians of other lands, and to enjoy this moment of beauty, which for me had more than ordinary significance. It was clear that the stars had been right the many months ago when this trip was planned because the thousands of miles between Corvallis and New York, by air, and the additional thousands, by sea, from New York to Göteborg, had been traveled in perfect weather with the ocean passage, in the log of M. S. Kungsholm, the smoothest in nine years.

The trip began in beauty even exceeding that golden moment in Göteborg. As I surveyed the green Willamette Valley from a West Coast Airlines plane, I felt that I would not, on my journeys, see any land more beautiful than that which I was leaving. As the United airplane, enroute to Seattle, climbed to 17,000 feet above the clouds, and as we looked down on the crystalline white peaks of Mt. St. Helens, Adams, and Rainier, alternately and variously visible below among white-plumed clouds and as we saw them increasingly assuming, in the waning light, deepening shades of pink, coral, and rose, the feeling about the beauty below became a certainty. I was unhappy then because, with eyes fixed on the far horizons of the land of my ancestors, my camera was riding uselessly in my checked suitcase. So I could not capture even a part of the spectacular and incredible beauty below. I consoled myself that no camera and no photographer could do justice to the God-given adornment of these mountains, at that moment. My sense of privilege and good fortune grew, but also the certainty that the picture-taking opportunity of a lifetime was being missed.

After confusions and delays in Seattle, our plane went winging into the night to meet the sun. There was no sense of sleep but surprisingly soon the sky was bright above massed white clouds, with huge atomic bomb-like plumes rising almost to our height. Very likely there was storm below but above it all we rode serene and in comfort. Soon we were in New York City, and the next morning I boarded the Kungsholm of the Scandiavian American lines. Since my only other experience with ocean travel was in the misery of Uncle Sam's troop ships of World War I, I was overwhelmed by this floating palace which was to be my home for the next eight days. I was not prepared either for the complexities and confusions of boarding 800 passengers.

I finally found my way to my cabin unaided and then went on deck to observe the commotion. After some hours of seeming confusion, and repeated exhortations, in Swedish and English, to visitors to go ashore, the boarding ramps were taken away, the Swedish flag went up, the ship moaned, and we moved majestically, but oh so slowly, out into the Hudson and came about to face the sea. Now, for a week, the 800 passengers aboard would live in a tight, pleasant, and well-managed little world of their own.

As the trip continued and we experienced the wonderful food, excellent service and the numerous recreational facilities, table tennis, trapshooting, shuffleboard, swimming, Finnish steam baths, the ship's library (located next to the bar), bingo games, dancing, movies, concerts, divine services, my admiration for both the ship and its management grew. I could not help but reflect, as we glided ever east by north, in comfort and luxury, on other journeys of long years ago westward over these same waters, in the squalor of the steerage, by ancestors of persons aboard who, like myself, were now on their way to visit the lands of their origins.

As the trip drew to conclusion, friends of a week were busy exchanging addresses and promises to write. Some of these friendships would undoubtedly quickly wither but others, like the seed which fell on good and waiting soil, would endure and flourish. On the afternoon of June 19, 1957, with the United States flag now flying, and under the tight guidance of four tugs, we came cautiously and slowly into Göteborg harbor. Finally, at six o'clock, after some weary hours of line waiting, I set foot for the first time on the soil of Sweden.

As the Kungsholm was slowly and gently brought to dock, a huge placard, perhaps a fifth the length of the ship, and blazoning the words, "Välkommen till Sverige, Clara!", was stretched high across the dock. From afar some fortunate Clara could see that she was indeed being given a royal welcome to Sweden. But she was by no means alone in her welcome. Hundreds of eager people lined the dock, bouquets of flowers were everywhere and

there were glad cries of recognition as the boat drew nearer and friends and relatives could recognize each other. Because of the complexities of a great ocean liner disgorging its human cargo on another shore, it was sometime before these waiting and impatient people could fall into each others arms, but some from the dock, more eager than the rest, or bolder, made their way up the landing ramps, regulations or no, leaping boat balustrades to find those they loved.

In the three weeks following that happy June arrival, I made a circuit of southern Sweden, living for varying periods in Göteborg, Lund, Kalmar, Gränna, Vadstena, and Stockholm. I traveled by train and bus, by taxi and train, and experienced eight hotels. In the many and varied adventures of the road I came to feel that the fortunate Clara's welcome was symbolic for me too, and for the many thousands of other visitors who were thronging this pleasant and progressive land. I did indeed feel welcome, in a special sense, as all the travelers from foreign lands, except those most churlish, must surely have felt. I learned much about the libraries and archives of Sweden in those weeks. Over and above this were the human contacts which are a rewarding part of any travel and which I found particularly so in this the land of my origins.

I recall with special pleasure the flaxen-haired, soft-voiced little twelve-year-old girl who, shortly out of Göteborg, boarded the train enroute to Lund and who stood shyly outside the first class compartment I had taken, how she gracefully and demurely seated herself when I invited her in and how the shyness began to disappear under my encouragement. She wondered, how could I learn to speak Swedish in the four days I told her I had been in Sweden. She herself had already studied English in school. To prove it she counted for me, with excellent enunciation. Had I ever seen an Indian? A Negro? Sweden, no doubt, would be too cold for them to live in. Did we, as she deftly speared a fly from her knee and took it to the window to throw it out, have flies in America? She, herself, hated them.

I showed her a Jefferson nickel, an Indian head nickel, a Lincoln penny, a Roosevelt dime, and told her something of the history they represent. When I gave her these coins she carefully arranged them in her purse in pleased surprise. My Swedish came in for correction. I had to say "Dom Kyrkan" at least a dozen times before she was satisfied. I was pleased when she finally was and I got an enthusiastic "alldeles rätt" (exactly right). When the conductor decided to see how the one passenger in first class was doing, he discovered that my little friend belonged in second class. He was persuaded, however, that there was an important language and history lesson going on, in which we were both teachers. Shaking his head wonderingly, he went his way.

I remember too, equally pleasantly, the young restaurant owner at Vadstena, who came out to sit with me while I ate, how he gave me his bicycle to ride around the town, how he let me in the back door for breakfast a half hour before opening time, so that I could eat before catching an early morning bus, and how he pinned a red carnation in my buttonhole as I left. I remember too his attractive young wife, who was the cook and how he said, and she demonstrated, that one need only mention America and her face would "stråla lik solen" (shine like the sun). This because she had two brothers in Minneapolis whom she would visit next year. A treasured part of my memories too would be finding, through great diligence and some luck, the house near Rockneby where my mother was born and in which she grew up.

The libraries I visited were, in order, the Göteborg Stadsbibliotek, Lunds Universitetsbibliotek, Biblioteket of Kalmar Län (county), and the regional archives in an ancient castle at Vadstena. In Stockholm I visited the Kunglige Skogshögskolan, where I was most graciously received by Rektor Streyffert who was with us at Oregon State University for the autumn quarter of 1956. The streamlined library of this school, in its new building, made me "avundsjuk" (envious). I also visited Kunglige Tekniska Högskolan Bilioteket, the Bibliotek of the Träforskningsinstitutet, the Bibliotek of the Kunglige Vetenskapsakadamien, and the greatest of all the Swedish libraries, Kunglige Biblioteket. With some of the librarians, I established lasting friendships.

All these libraries I found to be progressive and forward looking and in some instances, notably card mimeographing and compact shelving, in advance of anything I knew in America. Several new exchanges of our publications resulted from these visits. More important, I brought home a better understanding of European librarianship and, I believe, an increased two-way flow of good will.

"Farväl Elsa!"

The personal and professional rewards of a pleasant bibliothecal pilgrimage.

At 8:30 on the evening of August 26, 1957, I walked up the boarding ramps at the Copenhagen dock, in pouring rain, and into the Gripsholm, new ship of the Swedish American lines, lying so sleek, white, and inviting in those still waters. Behind me lay travels in five countries: Sweden, Norway, England, Holland, and Denmark, including stops in fourteen hotels and visits to twenty-two of the leading libraries of northern Europe and of England.

Many and rich were the experiences and the memories of this pleasant summer, outstanding in my life. They came thronging back, the adventures of the road, the people I met, the flavor and spirit of countries and the libraries I saw and learned about. As I recalled these things, the certainty grew that this bibliothecal pilgrimage had been not only a pleasant and rewarding professional experience for me but one which would be of profit to my library. Once again

I found myself grateful for the generous sabbatical policies which made this trip possible.

Aboard the Gripsholm, we were immediately given a full and excellent dinner. Well fed, I went immediately to the deck to observe the prolonged farewells which are a part of travel by ship and the to me always fascinating operations of readying a great ocean liner for voyage. Hundreds of people lined the dock rails to speed the departing and wish them well. Nothing deterred by the stormy night and copious rain, these people, under cover to be sure, stood waving, exchanging pleasantries, and shouting good-byes for the several hours it required to hoist an unbelievable amount of luggage and goods, including automobiles, skyward and drop them into the cavernous holds of the ship, both fore and aft. Those aboard too, many oblivious to the rain, participated from the deck rails in the protracted leave taking.

One of the most pleasant things was the good-byes to young students, of whom there were more than a hundred aboard, on their way to live and study for awhile in the United States. Among these was one Elsa, whose numerous friends on the dock were saying good-bye in varying themes and with all the exuberance and enthusiasm of teenagers. This went on amidst the laboring of the cranes which gradually reduced the mountainous luggage. It was eleven o'clock before the boarding ramps were, at long last, craned away, but there was still much preparatory bustle and commotion. Finally, at 1:30, the rain having now ceased, the Swedish flag went up, the ship

uttered its low-throated moan, and the crack of water between the starboard side and the dock began to imperceptibly widen, so gently that there was no sense of motion. Now flags and handkerchiefs waved with renewed enthusiasm.

Most exuberant and vociferous of all were the leather lunged young friends of Elsa. Not content to remain on the dock, as the Gripsholm glided majestically away, they walked to the quay's very end, shouting "Farväl Elsa! Farväl Elsa!" From the furthermost quay point we could see and hear them call, "Vi kan inte längre" (We can't come further). As the ship moved in earnest, beginning to widen that first small crack to miles, and when the quay could no longer be seen we could still hear, from the black of the night, faintly and ever more faintly, "Farväl Elsa! Farväl Elsa!"

After these farewell calls had dwindled to nothingness, I continued to stand at the deck rail, watching the lights of Copenhagen slowly dim and disappear and thinking of the many adventures and experiences of the summer. I thought too, in anticipation, of the home, and friends, and library, to which I was now eagerly returning and of the saying the Swedes have, and to which I fully subscribe, "Borta är bra men hemma är bäst" (To be away is good but home is best). Elsa's Farväl, I decided, would, in the opposite sense, be symbolic for my visit to these Scandinavian countries. I would probably never come again, I thought then; so, deeply content with a summer which had been rich and rewarding beyond expectation, I bade them a lingering Farewell, these beautiful and progressive far northern lands.

The Bird of Time

A jagged window and impaled thereon, in perfect symbol, a bird.

IN THE LATE SUMMER of 1963 it was our privilege to travel from Vancouver, British Columbia, east into rugged and spectacularly beautiful western Canada. Up the Frazer canyon over the old Cariboo trial, hacked and driven along the river by pioneer ingenuity, persistence, and no doubt suffering, we traveled in ease and comfort on what is now a modern highway. Leaving the Cariboo trail at the confluence of the Thompson and

Frazer, we rolled smoothly eastward.

We passed the Valley of the Ghost of Wallhachin, once a promising irrigated fruit and farming area, now largely unpeopled, eerie and living up to its name in the waning half light of a stormy afternoon. We passed the chain lakes of the upper Thompson to come to roost, in darkness, at Kamloops, since 1812 a crossroads of this Canadian hinterland. Here, the photographic Gods were kind. In the ancient and eternal battle between the darkness and the light, we were able to capture, on kodachrome, the eloquent color and beauty of a day dawning in glory over this historic and spectacularly situated community. Even in the rush and greed for furs and gold, men must surely have stood at times, humble and appreciative, in the beauty of dawnings such as this.

From Kamloops our route lay toward Revelstoke and the new Rogers Pass Road, the final completing link in the Trans-Canada Highway. Over its broad and smooth magnificence we rolled in and among abundant clouds and rain to come to Golden, and on toward the Kicking Horse River, over a highway in preparation on precipitous canyon cliffs and as yet without guard rails. This descent we managed in driving wind and rain with occasional cloud-obscured glimpses of the river far below.

The raging and turbulent Kicking Horse, when we crossed it, seemed most appropriately named. After customary tourist diversions in the Banff area, we turned southward toward the headwaters where the Kootenay brushes the Columbia only to turn away to wander for hundreds of miles through unmatched geographical and geological beauty before coming finally to lose itself in the Columbia it once had within sight and sound.

We too turned away from the Columbia headwaters, with the Kootenay, traveling eastward along this pioneer artery toward Waterton Park. On a sudden whim we left the highway, drawn by the magnet of a road sign pointing toward Ft. Steele of which we knew nothing. This fortunate decision brought us the highlight of these pleasant summer travels. We crossed the Kootenay at what had formerly been Galbraith's Ferry to climb quickly to a small tableland commanding the valley, the site of Ft. Steele. This was the first headquarters in this area of the Northwest Mounted Police, established there in 1887 to control the Indians and a brawling and boisterous frontier.

At Ft. Steele the term "ghost town," the Ghost of Wallhachin not excepted, took on a new poignancy and significance for me. There were a few people there to be sure, two or three occupied houses, a small general store, an apparently recently reconstituted but closed museum building, probably a functioning school in season, but for the most part buildings stood empty, widely spaced along generously conceived streets. A part of the haunting emptiness was two weatherbeaten churches, silhouetted against the mountains beyond.

These streets and houses, stores and churches, ferry and river, tablelands and mountains came easily alive for me with the people of a busy frontier crossroads. Gold-hungry men pouring in from the east, from the south, from the west, enroute to the rich Placer mines in Wild-

horse Creek, steamboat captains and crews, Indians, the teacher at the school, the clergy for the churches, and above all the red-tuniced and respected Mounted Police, these were all about. Drama, excitement, dyings and birthings, love and hate, greed and generosity were there—excitement, such as the successful saving of the water tower standing now charred, reinforced, and unused but still a monument to victory over disaster.

Peering through the dust covered windows of the churches we could see pews, still stocked with hymnals, organ, altar, chalices, all no doubt, along with the buildings that housed them brought together at great cost and sacrifice and by much loving labor. At what stage did these accoutrements of our western civilization finally fall into complete disuse? And with what regrets and grievings? Peering and prying we were startled to come upon a single jagged, broken window pane, impaled upon it a bird who had been surprised and speared by this lethal barrier to his untrammeled flight. Somehow this all belonged together, the forsaken buildings of a once bustling community, the charred but unused water tower, the empty churches still stocked with hymnals, the jagged window and impaled thereon, in perfect symbol, a bird.

As I thought of this symbology, the ending of vibrant pulsing life for community and for bird, there came to mind these lines from a quatrain of Omar Khayam's:

> The Bird of Time has but a little way
> to fly
> And Lo! the Bird is on the wing.

I belong, I emphasize, to the optimistic school which believes that our civilization will survive and flourish. Nevertheless, all of us may, in these times when the choice between disaster and holocaust and/or survival and progress toward a more understanding and harmonious civilization rests with a very few men in striped pants, be permitted moments of doubt. With many grave decisions behind us, and in front of us, it behooves us all to reflect that our entire civilization could indeed be a bird impaled through the blunderings of its own headlong and heedless flight. With one fundamental difference. If it is, there will be no tourists, for a long, long, long time peering and prying, wondering, and cogitating.

THIS BOOK was composed in 11- and 8-point Caledonia and printed by letterpress on Warren's Patina Offset Book Sub 70 by the Department of Printing, Oregon State University. Book design is by J. K. Munford and all illustrations are by Nelson Sandgren. Binding in Columbia Mills Bayside Chambray CYV-3711 is by Lincoln & Allen Bookbinders, Portland, Oregon